Evaluating Pharmaceuticals for Health Policy and Reimbursement

Edited by

Nick Freemantle
Department of Primary Care and General Practice, University of Birmingham, Birmingham, UK

and

Suzanne Hill
Faculty of Health, University of Newcastle, Newcastle, Australia

in collaboration with

World Health Organization

© 2004 by Blackwell Publishing Ltd
BMJ Books is an imprint of the BMJ Publishing Group Limited, used under licence

Blackwell Publishing, Inc., 350 Main Street, Malden, Massachusetts 02148-5020, USA
Blackwell Publishing Ltd, 9600 Garsington Road, Oxford OX4 2DQ, UK
Blackwell Publishing Asia Pty Ltd, 550 Swanston Street, Carlton, Victoria 3053, Australia

The right of the Author to be identified as the Author of this Work has been asserted in accordance with the Copyright, Designs and Patents Act 1988.

All rights reserved. No part of this publication may be reproduced, stored in a retrieval system, or transmitted, in any form or by any means, electronic, mechanical, photocopying, recording or otherwise, except as permitted by the UK Copyright, Designs and Patents Act 1988, without the prior permission of the publisher.

First published 2004

ISBN 0 7279 1784 6

Catalogue records for this title are available from the British Library and the Library of Congress

Set by SIVA Math Setters, Chennai, India
Printed and bound in Spain by GraphyCems, Navarra

Commissioning Editor: Mary Banks
Development Editor: Julie Elliott
Production Controller: Kate Charman

For further information on Blackwell Publishing, visit our website:
http://www.blackwellpublishing.com

The publisher's policy is to use permanent paper from mills that operate a sustainable forestry policy, and which has been manufactured from pulp processed using acid-free and elementary chlorine-free practices. Furthermore, the publisher ensures that the text paper and cover board used have met acceptable environmental accreditation standards.

Disclaimer: The authors have written this book in a personal capacity. Any veiws expressed in this book are those of the authors, and not necessarily those of the World Health Organization, their employers, or any other organization.

Evaluating Pharmaceuticals for Health Policy and Reimbursement

Dedication

Tragically our friend and colleague Bernie O'Brien died suddenly and unexpectedly between contributing to this book and its publication. He is very sadly missed.

An obituary to Bernie was publishing in BMJ: http://bmj.bmjjournals.com/cgi/content/full/328/7445/960-f/DC1.

Contents

Contributors   *vii*

1 Introduction   1
   Nick Freemantle, Suzanne Hill

2 Development of marketing authorisation
   procedures for pharmaceuticals   3
   Alar Irs, Truus Janse de Hoog, Lembit Rägo

3 Interpreting clinical evidence   24
   Nick Freemantle, Joanne Eastaugh,
   Melanie Calvert, Suzanne Hill, Jesse Berlin

4 International pharmaceutical policy:
   health creation or wealth creation?   46
   Karen Bloor, Alan Maynard

5 Development of fourth hurdle policies
   around the world   67
   Rod S Taylor, Mike F Drummond,
   Glenn Salkeld, Sean D Sullivan

6 Economic modelling in drug reimbursement   88
   Glenn Salkeld, Nick Freemantle, Bernie O'Brien

7 Priority setting in health care: matching
   decision criteria with policy objectives   105
   Gina Brinsmead, Alan Williams

8 Tensions in licensing and reimbursement
   decisions: the case of riluzole for
   amytrophic lateral sclerosis   121
   Stirling Bryan, Josie Sandercock, Pelham
   Barton, Amanda Burls

9 Relationships between stakeholders:
   managing the war of words   139
   Suzanne Hill, Kees de Joncheere

10 Medicine and the media: good information
    or misleading hype?   157
    Ray Moynihan, Lisa M Schwartz, Steven Woloshin

11 How to promote quality use of
    cost-effectivé medicines   174
    Hans Hogerzeil, Kathleen Holloway

12 Using economic evaluation to inform health
    policy and reimbursement: making it happen
    and making it sustainable   190
    Andrew Mitchell

13 Pricing of pharmaceuticals   208
    David Newby, Andrew Creese, Alan Stevens

14 Evaluating pharmaceuticals for health policy
    in low and middle income country settings   227
    *Andrew Creese, Anita Kotwani, Joseph
    Kutzin, Anban Pillay*

Glossary   244

Index   259

Contributors

Pelham Barton
Health Economics Facility, Health Services Management Centre, School of Public Policy, University of Birmingham, UK

Jesse Berlin
Center for Clinical Epidemiology and Biostatistics, University of Pennsylvania School of Medicine, Philadelphia, Pennsylvania, USA

Karen Bloor
Department of Health Sciences, University of York, York, UK

Gina Brinsmead
Health Economics, School of Public Health, The University of Sydney, Sydney, New South Wales, Australia

Stirling Bryan
Health Economics Facility, Health Services Management Centre, School of Public Policy, University of Birmingham, UK

Amanda Burls
Department of Public Health and Epidemiology, School of Medicine, University of Birmingham, UK

Melanie Calvert
Department of Primary Care and General Practice, University of Birmingham, Birmingham, UK

Andrew Creese
Department of Essential Drugs and Medicines Policy, World Health Organization, Geneva, Switzerland

Mike F Drummond
Centre for Health Economics, University of York, York, UK

Joanne Eastaugh
Department of Primary Care and General Practice, University of Birmingham, Birmingham, UK

Nick Freemantle
Department of Primary Care and General Practice, University of Birmingham, Birmingham, UK

Suzanne Hill
Discipline of Clinical Pharmacology, Faculty of Health, University of Newcastle, Newcastle, Australia

Hans Hogerzeil
Department of Essential Drugs and Medicines Policy, World Health Organization, Geneva, Switzerland

Kathleen Holloway
Department of Essential Drugs and Medicines Policy, World Health Organization, Geneva, Switzerland

Truus Janse de Hoog
MRFG and Medicines Evaluation Board, the Hague, the Netherlands

Alar Irs
State Agency of Medicines, Estonia

Kees de Joncheere
WHO Regional Office for Europe, Copenhagen, Denmark

Anita Kotwani
Department of Pharmocology, Maulana Azad Medical College, New Delhi, India

Joseph Kutzin
World Health Organization, Regional Office for Europe, Bishkek, Kyrgyztan

Alan Maynard
Department of Health Sciences, University of York, York, UK

Andrew Mitchell
Department of Health and Ageing, Canberra, Australia

Ray Moynihan
Journalist, Visiting Editor, *British Medical Journal*, London, UK

David Newby
Discipline of Clinical Pharmacology, Faculty of Health, University of Newcastle, Newcastle, Australia

Bernie O'Brien
Formerly Department of Clinical Epidemiology and Biostatistics, McMaster University, Hamilton, Ontario, Canada

Anban Pillay
Directorate, Pharmaceutical Economic Evaluations, National Department of Health, South Africa

Lembit Rägo
Department of Essential Drugs and Medicines Policy, World Health Organization, Geneva, Switzerland

Glenn Salkeld
School of Public Health, University of Sydney, Sydney, Australia

Josie Sandercock
Department of Public Health and Epidemiology, School of Medicine, University of Birmingham, UK

Lisa M Schwartz
Dartmouth Medical School, Hanover, New Hampshire, USA

Alan Stevens
Health Insurance Commission, Canberra, Australia

Sean D Sullivan
Pharmaceutical Outcomes Research and Policy Program, University of Washington, Seattle, USA

Rod S Taylor
Department of Epidemiology and Public Health, University of Birmingham, Birmingham, UK

Alan Williams
Centre for Health Economics, University of York, York, UK

Steven Woloshin
Dartmouth Medical School, Hanover, New Hampshire, USA

1: Introduction

NICK FREEMANTLE, SUZANNE HILL

Buy not what you want, but what you need; what you do not need is expensive at a penny.

Cato, 234–149 BC

History provides many different models of health policy in the modern world. In the UK the development of the National Health Service, intended to provide comprehensive health care free at the point of use, was just one solution to the fragmented evolution of modern health systems. Alternative systems based on national insurance schemes flourished in much of Western Europe. The USA, the richest country in the world, has limited state provision for the elderly and the very poor, although the health maintenance organisations provide health coverage to an increasing proportion of the US population.

Despite many differences in the style of health policy, a unifying challenge for all health systems is the provision of pharmaceuticals. No health system can reimburse every pharmaceutical that may potentially have an application in every circumstance, and so difficult decisions must be made. The challenge in all settings is how to make the difficult decisions in a way that is defensible, justifiable, ethical, and equitable. In the following chapters we attempt to describe how this decision making process may be formulated, and crucially how it may be informed.

This book was born from an informal programme of work that has been encouraged and supported by the World Health Organization (WHO), and to which almost all of the authors have contributed directly. Building from the experiences of the introduction of the evaluation of the cost-effectiveness of pharmaceuticals seeking reimbursement under the Australian Pharmaceutical Benefits Scheme, the WHO has supported a series of practical, problem based training courses for those engaged in evaluating the effectiveness and cost-effectiveness of pharmaceuticals. The courses have been international affairs, with 27 countries represented at the most recent event. They have been exciting, hard work, and intensely stimulating, not least for the faculty who have tried to meet the needs of participants. Although it is still early days, since the first programme was run in South Africa in 2000 it appears that some of the material is beginning to have a practical impact. South Africa is using the principles in establishing its pricing system for pharmaceuticals, and the Baltic States are developing a collaborative approach to making choices and evaluating the economic benefits of new pharmaceuticals for inclusion in their health insurance schemes.

In the following chapters we have attempted to address many of the issues that have been raised both through our work and directly from the WHO programme. For some of the topics, such as assessing the quality of clinical trials, there are well established methods and reviews, but for others, such as how exactly a decision making body should incorporate equity into choices about funding of pharmaceuticals, there is much less certainty. We expect that approaches to the use of clinical and economic evidence in decision making will continue to evolve over the next several years, and we hope that we will have a chance to contribute to their evolution.

2: Development of marketing authorisation procedures for pharmaceuticals

ALAR IRS, TRUUS JANSE DE HOOG,
LEMBIT RÄGO

Introduction

There are two aspects of the marketing authorisation system for pharmaceuticals that deserve discussion within the context of evaluating pharmaceuticals for health policy and reimbursement. First, there is a well established national and international scientific, legal, and institutional framework in place to study and assess pharmaceuticals before marketing authorisation is granted. The experience gained and the mistakes made in the development of this structure may prove useful today, when the rules and procedures are being considered to evaluate pharmaceuticals for wider health policy decisions. Second, a wealth of data about pharmaceuticals is generated to gain marketing authorisation. Availability and usefulness of this information for health policy decision making is worth critical review.

Development of the marketing authorisation system

Contemporary pharmaceutical control dates back to the early 20th century and is largely a result of a crisis led change to provide stronger safeguards for the public. Legislation developed in a piecemeal manner, each problem being dealt with as it arose.[1,2] The disaster of ethylene glycol containing sulphanilamide elixirs in 1937, the thalidomide tragedy in

1961, and the increasing number of potent substances used in medicine hastened the development of regulatory activities in many countries, and rules for providing evidence of quality, safety and, later, efficacy of new medicines were formulated.[3,4]

Today, proven quality, safety, and efficacy are defined as the criteria for granting a marketing authorisation. The marketing authorisation system should ensure the safe use of the medicinal products and provide reliable information about their efficacy. Although proving the quality of a product based on controls at different manufacturing steps and tests of the finished product is straightforward, safety and efficacy are evaluated in the relative context of the risk–benefit balance. Data from preclinical and clinical studies must demonstrate that potential risks are outweighed by the therapeutic efficacy of the pharmaceutical under investigation.

The drug regulatory system is forced to balance the protection of public health with the objectives of industrial policy. It must protect the health of people while ensuring that the measures taken to achieve this allow the pharmaceutical industry to operate. The latter has attracted increasing attention in the recent development of pharmaceutical policy of industrial countries, sometimes eclipsing the original purpose of the system.

This chapter focuses on the European drug regulatory system, with its scattered regulatory bodies and historically the most divergent views. The recent history of European drug regulation could be seen as a test ground for any international harmonisation of regulatory practices. At the same time, the chapter takes into account the fact that the global regulatory environment has been greatly influenced by the US Food and Drug Administration, the views of which determine to a large extent the technical requirements in current drug regulation, including clinical trial methodology.

Path to the current European Union marketing authorisation system

The foundation of the European Medicines Evaluation Agency (EMEA) in 1995 was the result of a long process of increasing harmonisation of scientific assessment of applications for new medicinal products and the creation of the single market in the European Union (EU).

The first European Pharmaceutical Directive (65/65/EEC) was issued in 1965, establishing quality, safety, and efficacy as the criteria for the assessment of medicinal products. Around that time, many national drug regulatory agencies were founded and the Directive was the basis for national legislation on the assessment of medicinal products. The first Directive was very general, and an amending Directive (75/318/EEC) was issued with more detailed guidance, because it had become clear that different national interpretations existed.

The second step in the harmonisation process was the acceptance of an assessment report made by one of the member states as the basis for national decision making in another country. The first European authorisation procedure, the multistate procedure, was based on this principle. After granting a marketing authorisation in one member state, the assessment report was sent to other member states if the same dossier had been submitted there. The applications were discussed at the Committee for Proprietary Medicinal Products (CPMP). At the end of the procedure member states could come to different decisions as to whether to accept the new medicinal product, and differences were allowed in the product information including the use of different clinical indications.

The increasing number of biotechnological products developed in the 1990s led to a need for closer cooperation between member states because of a relative lack of expertise in these novel techniques, and so for these products the concertation procedure was introduced. This was the first EU procedure in which no member state had issued a decision regarding the approval of the product before the procedure had started. The applications were discussed at the CPMP with the intention to achieve a common decision. For many of these products the member states agreed on identical product information documents.

The current European licensing procedures were built on experience gained from the first European procedures. The centralised procedure (CP) and the mutual recognition procedure (MRP) were introduced in 1995. With respect to harmonisation of the use of medicinal products in Europe, it became obligatory for all involved member states to have identical product information documents.

The EMEA was founded as a European Agency in London. It was never the intention that the scientific assessment should be performed in this central agency,[5] but the system was to be developed as a network in which the experts of the national agencies would perform the scientific assessment. With the introduction of two European licensing procedures (i.e. the CP and MRP), an element of competition was introduced. The responsibility for the duration and quality of the assessment in MRP is in the hands of the reference member state, and for the CP it is the responsibility of the European Commission. The industry is free to choose between these two different routes except in the case of certain biotechnological products that are included in what is known as part A products (see below).

Centralised procedure

Council Regulation 2309/93/EEC created a centralised EU procedure for which there is a single application, a single evaluation, and a single authorisation, allowing direct access to the single market of the EU. The Regulation responded to the need to protect public health within the EU while allowing rapid access to the single market for important new medicinal products. The Regulation was built upon the experience of the concertation procedure.

A marketing authorisation granted under the CP is valid for the entire EU market. However, a marketing authorisation holder has, under the current legislation, no obligation actually to market a product. This is particularly of concern for the so-called "orphan drugs" and smaller member states with less attractive pharmaceutical markets.

There are two types of products in the CP, commonly termed part A and part B products, according to the parts of the Annex to the Regulation 2309/93/EEC that describes them. Part A products are medicinal products developed by means of specific biotechnological processes referred to in part A of the Annex to the Regulation. For those products the CP is (and will be) obligatory. Applications for medicinal products that contain a new active substance and applications for innovative medicinal products with novel characteristics as defined in part B of the Annex may, at the request of the applicant, be accepted for consideration under the CP.

The CPMP appoints one of its members to act as a rapporteur and one as a ·co-rapporteur to coordinate evaluation of the application. The assessment procedure takes 210 days, and it is possible to freeze the evaluation at any point to await the answers of the applicant and resume it later. The members of the CPMP and the experts responsible for evaluating medicinal products rely on the scientific assessment resources available from the national competent authorities. Following the CPMP scientific opinion, a European Commission decision is needed before the product can be placed on the market. This requires an additional 90 days.

Mutual recognition procedure

The MPR requires that the member states rely on the assessment of the pharmaceutical product by a single member state and accept its evaluation as a basis for their own national decision. The legal texts setting out this procedure for human medicinal products have been codified from various earlier acts into Directive 2001/83/EC. With the exception of those products that are subject to the CP, a marketing authorisation in one member state should, in principle, be recognised by the competent authorities of the other member states, unless there are grounds for supposing that the product concerned may present a "risk to public health". The expression "risk to public health" refers to the quality, safety, and efficacy of the medicinal product for human use, but various interpretations are used by member states.

The mutual recognition can be achieved by asking the concerned member states to recognise mutually, within 90 days, the marketing authorisation granted by the reference member state. The reference member state is the member state where the dossier is first submitted and approved. The member states where the dossier is subsequently submitted are called the "concerned member states". In the event of a disagreement that has not been resolved by day 90 between the member states, a scientific evaluation of the matter should be undertaken by the CPMP, leading to a single decision that is binding on all the member states.

There was no special group established in legislation to coordinate the MRP. However, soon after the start of the procedure the member states recognised a need for a group that could coordinate and facilitate the operation of the MRP, and the Mutual Recognition Facilitation Group (MRFG) was established in March 1995. The MRFG, consisting of representatives from all of the EU member states, Norway and Iceland, meets monthly and provides a forum at which procedural issues can be discussed and problems resolved, but it does not give scientific opinions.

Collaboration beyond the scope of the European Union

Although different drug regulatory systems are based on the same fundamental obligations to evaluate the quality, safety, and efficacy of medicines, the detailed technical requirements differ. This leads to duplication of many time consuming and expensive test procedures to meet the various national regulatory requirements when the medicinal products are being marketed internationally.

Harmonisation of regulatory requirements was pioneered by the European Community, in the 1980s, as the Community (now the EU) moved toward the development of a single market for pharmaceuticals. The success achieved in Europe demonstrated that harmonisation was possible. Plans for broader cooperation were established at the World Health Organization (WHO) Conference of Drug Regulatory Authorities, held in Paris in 1989. A year later, representatives of the drug regulatory agencies and industry associations of Europe, Japan, and the USA met, and the International Conference on Harmonisation of Technical Requirements for the Registration of Pharmaceuticals for Human Use (ICH) was born.[6] ICH is a process by which the pharmaceutical industries and regulators of the EU, the USA, and Japan have tried to formulate consensus documents (guidelines) on the regulatory requirements for establishing quality, safety, and efficacy of medicines.

Although primarily aimed at the developed countries represented in its working groups, ICH has had consequences for the pharmaceutical sectors of the countries that were not involved in developing the consensus documents. This effect has been controversial, both from the point of view of public health and from the perspective of the local industry in developing or transitional countries with limited regulatory and economic capacity. The guidance developed by the ICH for new chemical entities may not be the most useful tool for controlling the properties of generic pharmaceuticals, and duplication of earlier WHO initiatives in pharmacovigilance imposes additional resource pressure on the agencies and enterprises involved.[7] Although having grown out of the WHO conference, the ICH currently lacks the global mandate, and even though the WHO has observer status at the ICH meetings this is not sufficient to represent the interests of its 166 member countries.

Failing trust, competition, and limited resources

The current marketing authorisation system can be proud of several of its achievements (Box 2.1), but there have also been disappointing developments. The solid legal basis of the system has been vital to its effective enforcement. The statutory nature of the procedures has provided a solid foundation on which regulatory agencies may base their activities. International collaboration has reduced the need for duplication of tests and trials by the industry, but it has also reduced the possibility of divergent views of different regulators when assessing the same data.

Box 2.1 Strengths of the current licensing system
- Statutory nature
- Good institutional network
- Agreed scientific standards
- Internationally accepted technical requirements
- Sufficient communication with pharmaceutical industry
- International pool of experts

One of the two European procedures – the CP – now runs smoothly after its slow start. The main aspect of this procedure that still needs improvement is the decision making process of the European Commission after the CPMP opinion has been determined. The early concerns about possible problems of enlargement of the EU in relation to the CP have not proven to be real, because the practical issues have been dealt with in a stepwise manner by phasing in the future member states as observers at all scientific working parties of the EMEA.

However, the MRP was not the success it was expected to be. It is more a "decentralised system" than a true mutual recognition one. The process has been hampered from the start by a lack of detail about the procedure in the legislation. It was left to the member states to agree between them on how to conduct it. In hindsight, one could conclude that the European Commission and the member states underestimated the existing national differences and probable difficulties associated with harmonising the assessment. Furthermore, many resources that were available to the CPMP for administrative and scientific support were not there for the MRP, which has been totally dependent on the resources of the national agencies (and these differed considerably). In this regard the impact of EU enlargement is harder to predict because the experience of most of the future member states with the procedure is limited. On the other hand, willingness to accept each other's assessment and avoid duplication of work may be greater, given the need to consider the resource issue even more carefully than is the case with the current member states.

The main reasons for the difficulties in the application of the MRP have been (and in some cases still are) as follows.

- Organisational and administrative difficulties. No details were given in the legislation regarding the different steps in the procedure. This was partly resolved by creation of best practices guides for the procedure by the MRFG and development of the European computerised tracking system.
- National differences in interpretation of European legislation. Although national legislations had been harmonised by European directives for a some time, there had been no previous need to ensure that there were common interpretations of key technical issues. For example, there were a number of different operational definitions of what constituted a new active substance or a specific dossier requirement.
- National assessment and lack of mutual recognition. The leading principle in the EU procedures is sharing the workload and harmonising the assessment. Despite this, many member states have difficulties in accepting

assessment carried out by another member state. Over 50% of the agencies still conduct a full assessment of the significant parts of the dossier.[8] Because of this, a different procedure (the decentralised procedure) is suggested in current legislation proposals in which all member states can participate in the first assessment phase.

- Different scientific views of assessors. Differences in scientific opinion between assessors and scientific discussions between assessors had not been foreseen in the MRP, and the current process does not allow for them in any significant way. Member states may conduct a so-called "break-out session" of the MRFG, but this is very limited in comparison with the possibility for scientific discussions at the CPMP. The normal debate and discussion of submitted data with the applicant are turned into an interagency or interassessor debate, in which the reference member state must defend "its product". When there are divergent views the recommendation is to refer the product to the CPMP. In practice, applicants prefer to withdraw their application from the objecting member state because a referral delays the introduction of the product to the market by 9–12 months and in most cases results in a restriction in the product information.

- Differences in national summaries of product characteristics (SPCs) for generic agents and brand-leaders. The product information for a generic product would normally be the same as for the original one (the brand-leader). The brand-leaders were approved in the member states following national procedures, and the product information for these products can vary considerably. It creates problems for generic products in the MRP, resulting in different product information given to health care professionals and patients for medicinal products containing the same active substance (vertical disharmony). After several years the member states decided to begin harmonising product information for brand-leaders in Europe. The marketing authorisation holders are not prepared to do this on a voluntary basis, and the only option is to make a referral to the CPMP based on Directive 2001/83/EC. However, some pharmaceutical companies have taken legal action against this initiative.

Why are there two European procedures?

From past experience it seemed logical to continue with the two existing licensing procedures. Industry has voiced a strong desire to retain but improve both of them in parallel,[8] but there are several other reasons.

First, the EMEA had no experience with an EU procedure, and only a small number of administrative staff members were available to begin with. Receipt of a large number of applications all at once would have created huge problems. These concerns should no longer be valid.

There are differences in the types of products dealt with by the procedures. Innovative products use the CP more, and generic companies can only use the MRP. The CP appears to be the first choice for companies for orphan drugs too. There is more flexibility for companies in the MRP. They can choose the number of countries, the reference member state, and the first market. They can use the procedure in repetition, and they can withdraw the application in countries that are against approval or that ask for restricted use. This, in fact, is against the spirit of European harmonisation, whereby a product should be available throughout the EU.

It is important that the European system is developed as a network in which scientific expertise is available at the national agencies. The EMEA is a body for administrative support of the system. For many national agencies it is important to maintain a large number of national licences (by the MRP) because they are dependent on fees for nationally approved products.

The conclusion of the legislators until now has been that the differences could make the MRP the best procedure for some products, from the perspective both of health care systems and of industry, whereas the CP is advantageous for others.[8,9] At the same time, there are product categories (generics, self-medication products) for which neither system works perfectly.

Major criticisms of the system: science or politics?

Major points of criticism of the current marketing authorisation system are, in one way or another, connected to

Box 2.2 Weaknesses of the current licensing system

- Agenda determined by industry; reactive approach
- Industrial rather than health perspective in legislation
- Secrecy surrounding data and decision making
- Inability to tackle therapeutic groups or active substance related matters (rather than product specific issues)
- Forced competition between the agencies and pressure to "fast-track"
- Inability to communicate important information to patients and professionals

the issues of subordination, accountability, and transparency (Box 2.2). The major question posed is whether the current absolute reliance on industry data, and thus the focus on commercially attractive products, is right.[10,11] It has certainly led to a situation in which there are very few drugs developed for rare diseases and diseases that are prevalent only or mostly in poor countries.[12] The questions of the integrity of scientific data are not so black and white. Where there is evidence of selective publication of research findings,[13] there is not so much concern about the availability of data to the regulatory agencies. Although concerns have been raised by agencies regarding the handling of specific problems,[10,14,15] deliberate misinformation from industry has mostly not been the case in developed countries.

Perspective of legislation and subordination of the European Medicines Evaluation Agency

The main purpose of any regulation on the production and distribution of medicinal products for human use should be to safeguard public health. In EU policy, careful consideration is also given to avoiding hindrance of development of the pharmaceutical industry or trade of medicinal products in the EU. In contrast to its member states, the EU sees pharmaceutical legislation as part of its industrial policy rather than public health. The product (rather than active substance) centred approach of the legislation is causing problems in harmonising product information for generics and in safety related actions in which a whole class of drugs is under scrutiny.

Concerns have been voiced that the interests of the pharmaceutical industry prevail over those of health care professionals and patients in developing the legislation as well as scientific guidelines.[10,16] Furthermore, the institutional location of the EMEA under the Directorate General Enterprise has been questioned,[11,17] and the Public Health Directorate has been proposed as its umbrella in the European Commission. Another aspect seen as a potential danger is the dependence of the EMEA on fees paid by the industry. As a minimum, a financing scheme in which fees are paid to the European Commission and the Agency receives public funding has been proposed.[17] Issues relating to European national regulatory agencies and the Food and Drug Administration in the USA are similar.

Secrecy and transparency

The word "transparency" has taken numerous meanings within the context of regulatory affairs. Almost certainly, patient groups and industry talk about different things when they refer to transparency. Generally the term means either giving detailed reasons for regulatory actions or gaining access to regulatory data. In the EU, public access to information about medicines is limited to the SPC and patient information leaflets. The data submitted to regulatory authorities by the industry (so-called "commercially valuable intellectual property") are kept secret, presuming that their publication will affect the rights and commercial interests of the manufacturers.[15] The USA, and until recently Japan,[18] have had a more open policy concerning these data. European pharmaceutical companies have been using the US Freedom of Information Act to gain access to the data,[19] and it is questionable whether having the same information provided directly by the EU regulators could have any detrimental effects. Not publishing the data, however, will almost certainly affect the quality of any independent attempt to evaluate the risk/benefit ratio or added value of a medicinal product, because selective reporting of study findings has been documented.[13]

From 2001, the EMEA has been publishing the CPMP summaries of opinion and European Public Assessment Reports, which reflect the scientific conclusion drawn by the CPMP at the end of the CP at its website. Together with the published SPC, they are the public outputs of the licensing system. The European Public Assessment Report is the most useful of these because it summarises the clinical data submitted to the EMEA and provides details regarding the individual studies. These documents also provide necessary transparency and the basis of the regulatory decisions for the industry. Unfortunately, similar data are not available for national applications or for MRP products.

The quality and usefulness of the public information produced by the regulatory system needs thorough evaluation. The readability of patient information has been criticised, and health care professionals have questioned the real value of SPCs in everyday use. The impact of these documents on the way in which drugs are actually being used may be substantially overestimated.[20,21]

Race for the title of fastest drug regulatory agency

There is recognised competition between the two European authorisation procedures, as well as between national regulatory agencies. There is also a less recognised competition globally to make sure that patients in a particular region get timely access to a new drug as compared with their counterparts elsewhere. In addition, there is political pressure[22] to "fast-track" products with specific characteristics, either for a life-threatening disease or because of "substantial benefit over currently available therapies". Does it affect the quality of assessment?

In the MRP and the CP, the scientific standard is quite well controlled by a peer review type process conducted either by concerned member states or by CPMP members, avoiding the possibility of substandard evaluation. On the other hand, the fast-track procedure, established formally in the USA and also proposed in the new legislation for the EU, has been seen as lowering the regulatory standards and has been criticised accordingly. The basic problem with the fast-track procedure is its conditional nature. The authorisation is given with the obligation for the manufacturer to conduct further studies. First, there is limited incentive for the manufacturer to complete these studies quickly, causing a feeling described as "reduced urgency" by a US Food and Drug Administration advisory committee member.[23] Second, even if the commitment from the sponsor's side is there, it may be difficult to enrol patients into these studies. There is confusion over the place of these products in relation to standard treatment among practitioners[24] as well as health policy decision making bodies, and the criteria for withdrawing the product if the results of confirmatory trials are found to be negative are not clear.

Is it getting better? Review 2001 and G10 Medicines Group

There is a legislative proposal known as "review"[25,26] at a late stage of the political process. There is "light and shade" in the proposal, as characterised by Garattini (a member of the CPMP)[17] and summarised in Box 2.3.

Box 2.3 Pros and cons of Review 2001[17]

On the "light" side are the following:

- The expanded scope of the CP: it should no longer be possible to opt for the MRP or decentralised procedure with respect to medicinal products containing new active substances and for which the therapeutic indication is the treatment of AIDS, cancer, neurodegenerative disorder, or diabetes
- Several transparency measures such as the publication of assessment reports for procedures other than the CP and the publication of withdrawals of applications
- Formalised coordination and stepwise explanation of the decentralised procedure and MRP
- Generic manufacturers may refer to data from an originator authorised in any member state while applying for marketing authorisation; this is important progress for the smaller current and future member states

The "shade" side includes the following:

- Expanded data exclusivity period
- Data protection for switching to over-the-counter status
- No consideration of the concept of "added therapeutic value" or relative effectiveness, other than mentioning that "the European Medicines Agency shall collect any available information on methods that member states' competent authorities use to determine the added therapeutic value that any new medicinal product provides"

The G10 Medicines Group was convened as a practical measure to bring together, under the European Commission umbrella, a variety of people from the governments, non-government organisations, and industry to identify potential solutions to problems that have proven difficult to resolve in the past. Its recommendations[27] were published in 2002 and have been echoed in a recent communication from the Commission.[28] Among many issues relating to the competitiveness of the EU pharmaceutical industry, topics of relative effectiveness and enhanced public availability of information were tackled.

In relation to providing information to interested parties, a shift in attitude can be seen, as the Commission states that:

> Competent authorities hold substantial information on medicines and much of this is of significant interest to health professionals and the general public. It is important that this is made widely available and the Commission, involving the EMEA, will be pro-active in encouraging the Member States to share this information with a wider group of stakeholders, including the general public.

The issue of relative effectiveness, on the other hand, has been cut short with:

> It is the Commission's view that the authorisation process for medicines must continue to focus on the key public health criteria of safety, quality and efficacy. The issue of relative effectiveness, while important, should be kept entirely separate from this process as it is most useful once the medicines are on the market and being used alongside existing therapeutic options.

This statement will leave us in the future with the regulatory data of current quality, and this is a disappointing development.

Limitations of the value of the clinical data used in licensing

Efficacy within the context of marketing authorisation is established by showing superiority over placebo in a placebo controlled trial or, more rarely, superiority over an active control treatment. As a rule, more than one confirmatory trial is required, although exceptions are possible.

Usually, the clinical decision of whether to use or not to use a specific intervention, or the health policy decision "to pay or not to pay" for a new technology, is not made in a therapeutic vacuum;[11] there are alternative possibilities. As postulated 40 years ago by Sir Austin Bradford Hill,[29] "the doctor will wish to know whether a new treatment is more, or less, effective than the old, not that it is more effective than nothing". For that purpose, studies comparing new drugs with standard treatments, if they exist, are needed (Box 2.4).

Box 2.4 Common limitations of the licensing data in real life decision making

- Placebo controlled (rather than active comparator) studies
- Short follow up periods
- Restricted patient population that does not represent future patients in the community
- Surrogate end-points that are not readily translatable into clinical outcome measures
- Missing information about resource use
- Data locked away (not at all or partially published)

Typically, for marketing authorisation purposes, placebo controlled studies have been and still are used. There are several good reasons for this approach.[30,31] One of the reasons is that these trials do not rely on external information to support a conclusion of effectiveness. "Equivalence" trials, which are designed to show that the new intervention is at least equal to a currently available treatment, are carried out with active controls and assume that the evidence of effectiveness of the control obtained from the previous studies holds true under the conditions of the present study.[32] For sponsors, placebo controlled studies also mean smaller sample size, and faster and less costly trials. Ethically, it could be argued that fewer subjects are exposed to risks of experimental therapy. The only "drawback" is that the data gathered can only be used for obtaining marketing authorisation. Their use in real life decisions is limited to the situations in which we have no therapy with established efficacy (which is not that rare a situation) or we evaluate an add-on drug.

To add to the scientific debate about the approach to the design of trials, the ethical issue must be addressed, as discussed in conjunction with the amendment to the World Medical Association's Declaration of Helsinki from 2000.[33] The amendment states that "the benefits, risks, burdens and effectiveness of a new method should be tested against those of the best current prophylactic, diagnostic, and therapeutic methods." However, "this does not exclude the use of placebo, or no treatment, in studies where no proven prophylactic, diagnostic or therapeutic method exists." The paragraph was commented upon by the organisation two years later, stating that "a placebo-controlled trial may be ethically acceptable, even if proven therapy is available, under the following circumstances: where for compelling and scientifically sound methodological reasons its use is necessary to determine the efficacy or safety of a prophylactic, diagnostic or therapeutic method, or where a prophylactic, diagnostic or therapeutic method is being investigated for a minor condition and the patients who receive placebo will not be subject to any additional risk of serious or irreversible harm." The regulators still require placebo controls for the medicines tested for several conditions,[34,35] although their greater interest in studies with active comparators has been noticed, at least by industry,[8] and is also expressed in ICH guidelines.

As for the trials with active controls, the regulators have their concerns: "Because of the interpretative difficulties of active control equivalence trials in many settings, trials of new products using active controls would not be able to provide persuasive evidence of efficacy unless the new treatment proved statistically superior to the active control".[31]

The methodology of equivalence trials is an issue and such trials often include too few patients or have intrinsic design biases that tend toward the conclusion of no difference.[36] The opponents of placebo control agree that, to estimate comparative efficacy or to show equivalence, there is no escape from designing studies that are much larger than the usual placebo controlled studies.[37]

The "gold standard" for clinical study data as a part of economic evaluation has been described as being based on a trial carried out in naturalistic settings, with adequate duration of follow up and being conducted within a time frame that allows the resulting information to inform important decisions.[38] In the current regulatory environment there is no need for sponsors to conduct such trials.

The comparative trials may eventually get done, but the problem is their timing in relation to, for example, reimbursement decisions. The comparative trials tend to be finished and reported much later, well after the launch of the product[38,39] and well after the product has gained an established but perhaps unjustified place in the therapeutic armamentarium.

The setting of regulatory trials is far from being naturalistic. The problem of comparator has been discussed. The study population tends to be highly selected to form a homogeneous group in which the effect of intervention can best be shown and maximum compliance ensured. The study subjects are rarely representative of normal clinical practice (being of different age, different sex distribution, having less comorbidity and co-treatment, etc.). The trial end-points may or may not be naturalistic. Too often the end-points are surrogate outcome measures rather than end-points with clear clinical importance or value to patients. Being of established value in certain steps of drug development,[40] the surrogate outcomes are hard to use in clinical or health policy comparisons. There are two main concerns; the surrogate outcome may not be a true predictor of the clinical outcome of interest and it may not yield a quantitative measure of clinical benefit that can be weighed against adverse effects. Finally, there is the question of the duration of follow up in regulatory trials. Therapies for chronic diseases may be authorised based on the results of a 4, 8, or 12 week study. It is uncertain whether the outcomes observed during the study period accurately describe the long-term results.

Conclusion

Even between the 15 member states of the European Union, differences in interpretation of the law based on the same EU directives and the guidance documents developed by the consensus process have hindered the mutual recognition of each other's decisions. Detailed and well negotiated interpretations of regulations, and strong technical and administrative support are needed in any attempt at international decision making. It may be easier for member states to agree the technical standards than to actually recognise each other's assessment and decisions. Scientific, organisational, and financial independence of the regulatory system (even from imaginary influences) is of crucial importance in preserving the credibility of its assessment.

The data used for marketing authorisation purposes are of modest value in health policy decision making, where comparative effectiveness or cost-effectiveness of interventions is under consideration. Unfortunately, they are often the only data available. Access to submitted study data should be free to anyone, whether they are interested in challenging the regulatory decisions, trying to establish the overall risk/benefit ratio, or evaluating the drug for reimbursement decisions. Access to the data can be achieved either by the requirement to publish all industry generated data or by lifting the confidentiality clause from the data that are in possession of the drug regulatory agencies.

The current regulatory approval system does not consider comparative efficacy as an authorisation criterion, and it appears to be under political pressure to continue in this regard. Nevertheless, ethical considerations force the use of more active comparator studies. The current regulatory system needs building upon to make decisions about the comparative effectiveness and cost-effectiveness of medicines. Experience gained by the drug regulatory agencies in capacity building, relations with involved parties, and international cooperation can serve as an example or as a warning.

Summary

- The strengths of the marketing authorisation system lie in its statutory nature and well defined technical standards.
- Access to data generated for marketing authorisation purposes should be open to everyone because they are often the only existing data about a new pharmaceutical.
- The basic weakness of the system lies in its inability to consider the existing treatments as comparators (instead of placebo) and provide reliable comparisons for real life clinical or health policy decisions.
- Experience gained over the years in developing the marketing authorisation system may prove useful in shaping the institutional, technical, and legal framework for evaluation of pharmaceuticals for health policy decision making.

References

1 Ratanawijitrasin S, Wondemagegnehu E. *Effective drug regulation: a multicountry study*. Geneva: World Health Organization, 2002.
2 Appelbe G, Wingfield J. Development of the law in relation to pharmacy, medicines and poisons. In: *Dale and Appelbe's pharmacy law and ethics*. London: Pharmaceutical Press, 2001.
3 Dumitriu H. Historical overview. In: *Good drug regulatory practice*. Buffalo Grove, IL: Interpharm Press, 1998.
4 Wax PM. Elixirs, diluents, and the passage of the 1938 Federal Food, Drug and Cosmetic Act. *Ann Intern Med* 1995;**122**:456–61.
5 Anonymous. European medicines in the 21st century. *Lancet* 1995;**345**:1–2.
6 Anonymous. A brief history of ICH. http://www.ich.org/ich8.html (accessed 12 July 2003).
7 Anonymous. Concerns about ICH. In: *The impact of implementation of ICH guidelines in non-ICH countries. Regulatory Support Series, No 9*. Geneva: World Health Organization, 2002.
8 Anonymous. Evaluation of the operation of Community procedures for the authorisation of medicinal products. CMS Cameron McKenna, Andersen Consulting, 2000. http://dg3.eudra.org/F2/pharmacos/docs/Doc2000/nov/reportmk.pdf (accessed 12 July 2003).
9 Salmonson T. Introduction to the mutual recognition procedure. In: *NLN regulatory seminar 1999: The mutual recognition procedure for the authorisation of new medicines*. Uppsala: Nordic Council on Medicines, 1999.
10 Abraham J. The science and politics of medicines control. *Drug Saf* 2003;**26**:135–43.
11 Garattini S, Bertele V. Adjusting Europe's drug regulation to public health needs. *Lancet* 2001;**358**:64–7.
12 Trouiller P, Olliaro P, Torreele E, *et al*. Drug development for neglected diseases: a deficient market and a public-health policy failure. *Lancet* 2002;**359**:2188–94.
13 Melander H, Ahlqvist-Rastad J, Meijer G, Beermann B. Evidence b(i)ased medicine: selective reporting from studies sponsored by pharmaceutical industry: review of studies in new drug applications. *BMJ* 2003; **326**:1171.
14 Horton R. Lotronex and the FDA: a fatal erosion of integrity. *Lancet* 2001;**357**:1544–5.
15 Roberts I, Li Wan Po A, Chalmers I. Intellectual property, drug licensing, freedom of information, and public health. *Lancet* 1998;**352**:726–9.
16 Abraham J. The pharmaceutical industry as a political player. *Lancet* 2002;**360**:1498–502.
17 Garattini S, Bertele V, Li Bassi L. Light and shade in proposed revision of EU drug-regulatory legislation. *Lancet* 2003;**361**:635–6.
18 Beppu H. Japan's loss of leadership role in access to drug data. *Lancet* 1999;**353**:1992.
19 Abraham J, Lewis G. Secrecy and transparency of medicines licensing in the EU. *Lancet* 1998;**352**:480–2.
20 Figueras A, Laporte JR. Failures of the therapeutic chain as a cause of drug ineffectiveness. *BMJ* 2003;**326**:895–6.
21 Wong I, Sweis D, Cope J, Florence A. Paedriatic medicines research in the UK. How to move forward? *Drug Saf* 2003;**26**:529–37.
22 Pripstein J. When science and passion meet: the impact of AIDS on research. *CMAJ* 1993;**148**:638–42.
23 Mitka M. Accelerated approval scrutinized. *JAMA* 2003;**289**:3227–9.

24 Koopmans PP. Registration of drugs for treating cancer and HIV infection: a plea to carry out phase 3 trials before admission to the market. *BMJ* 1995;**310**:1305–6.

25 Amended proposal for a regulation of the European Parliament and of the Council: laying down Community procedures for the authorisation and supervision of medicinal products for human and veterinary use and establishing a European Agency. http://dg3.eudra.org/F2/pharmacos/docs/Doc2003/June/council10449en03.pdf (accessed 12 July 2003).

26 Amended proposal for a Directive of the European Parliament and of the Council: amending Directive 2001/83/EC on the Community code relating to medicinal products for human use. http://dg3.eudra.org/F2/pharmacos/docs/Doc2003/June/council10450en03.pdf (accessed 12 July 2003).

27 High Level Group on innovation and provision of medicines: recommendations for action. http://dg3.eudra.org/F3/g10/docs/G10-Medicines.pdf (accessed 14 July 2003).

28 Communication from the Commission to the Council, the European Parliament, the Economic and Social Committee and the Committee of the Regions: a stronger European-based pharmaceutical industry for the benefit of the patient – a call for action. http://pharmacos.eudra.org/F3/g10/docs/G10_CommComm_EN.pdf (accessed 13 July 2003).

29 Hill AB. Medical ethics and controlled trials. *BMJ* 1963;**1**:1043–9.

30 Temple R, Ellenberg SS. Placebo-controlled trials and active-control trials in the evaluation of new treatments. Part 1: ethical and scientific issues. *Ann Intern Med* 2000;**133**:455–63.

31 Ellenberg SS, Temple R. Placebo-controlled trials and active-control trials in the evaluation of new treatments. Part 2: practical issues and specific cases. *Ann Intern Med* 2000;**133**:464–70.

32 Al-Khatib SM, Califf RM, Hasselblad V, Alexander JH, McCrory DC, Sugarman J. Placebo-controls in short-term clinical trials of hypertension. *Science* 2001;**292**:2013–15.

33 World Medical Association. World Medical Association Declaration Of Helsinki: ethical principles for medical research involving human subjects. http://www.wma.net/e/policy/b3.htm (accessed 13 July 2003).

34 CPMP. Note for guidance on the clinical investigation of medicinal products in the treatment of schizophrenia. CPMP, 1998. http://www.emea.eu.int/pdfs/human/ewp/055995en.pdf (accessed 13 July 2003).

35 CPMP. Note for guidance on clinical investigation of medicinal products in the treatment of depression. CPMP, 2002. http://www.emea.eu.int/pdfs/human/ewp/051897en.pdf (accessed 13 July 2003).

36 Jones B, Jarvis P, Lewis JA, Ebbutt AF. Trials to assess equivalence: the importance of rigorous methods. *BMJ* 1996;**313**:36–9.

37 Rothman KJ. Placebo mania: as medical knowledge accumulates, the number of placebo trials should fall. *BMJ* 1996;**313**:3–4.

38 Glick HA, Polsky DP, Schulman KA. Trial-based economic evaluations: an overview of design and analysis. In: Drummond M, McGuire A, eds. *Economic evaluation in health care: merging theory with practice*. Oxford: Oxford University Press/Office of Health Economics, 2001.

39 Henry D, Hill S. Comparing treatments. *BMJ* 1995;**310**:1279.

40 Biomarkers Definitions Working Group. Biomarkers and surrogate endpoints: preferred definitions and conceptual framework. *Clin Pharmacol Ther* 2001;**69**:89–95.

3: Interpreting clinical evidence

NICK FREEMANTLE, JOANNE EASTAUGH,
MELANIE CALVERT, SUZANNE HILL, JESSE
BERLIN

Introduction

Numerous problems may be encountered when evaluating
and interpreting estimates of comparative clinical efficacy as
highlighted by an evaluation of pharmacoeconomic analyses
assessed by the Australian Pharmaceutical Benefits Scheme.[1]
Such problems include the availability or quality of trials,
analysis or interpretation of results, use of appropriate
outcome measures, and determination of therapeutic dose
and equivalence. Aspects of the assessment of treatment
effectiveness were addressed in recent major work;[2] however, a
number of areas specific to pharmaceutical evaluation and
reimbursement were not addressed there. These include
equivalence, non-inferiority, and the use and interpretation of
surrogate and composite clinical outcomes. In this chapter we
first present general discussions of randomised trials,
systematic reviews, and meta-analysis of randomised trials.
We next consider special topics not previously addressed
elsewhere.

Randomised trials

For all sorts of reasons, but primarily because of the inherent
difficulty of the aim, most health care interventions have only
a modest impact on health outcomes. This means that
attempts to estimate the magnitude of effects of health care
interventions are subject to obfuscation by biases (confounding
factors), which can be considerably greater than the

underlying health benefit that we are attempting to estimate. The randomised trials has become viewed as the "gold standard" in pharmaceutical evaluation because this is the only design available that can adequately deal with both known and unknown sources of bias or confounding.

It might be argued that known biases can be dealt with through careful and appropriate use of statistical models. Although to some extent this is true, it is also clear that unknown biases cannot be dealt with in such a manner. So how is bias dealt with in randomised trials?

In a simple trial in which patients are allocated one of two treatment options (option A and option B) it is sometimes erroneously considered that randomisation makes the groups the same. A quick mental example will identify the error in this argument. Consider a class of 30 students, of different sexes, races, ages, blood groups, social class, and so on. Simply using a coin flip to allocate them between two groups will not make those groups the same; indeed, the modest numbers of students means that quite large differences between the randomised groups may exist. For example, although unlikely, it is not impossible that all of the females will be in one of the groups.

Although randomisation does not make the groups the same, it does ensure that they differ only with respect to the treatment allocation (membership of group A or group B, and thus the intended treatment) or (at enrolment) in particular characteristics only through the play of chance (the result of the coin flip). Thus, when we compare the two groups with respect to health outcomes, any differences between them should have only two explanations: either the effects of treatments A and B differ, or the play of chance has generated apparent differences that are not related to true underlying differences between the treatments. Statistics helps us to decide whether an observed difference may be attributable to the play of chance, and if this is considered implausible then we accept the alternative that a difference in the treatment strategies is the cause of the observed difference.

In any particular trial, "bad luck" in the randomisation process can produce differences between the treatment groups with respect to baseline prognostic factors. Such differences can lead to apparent effects of treatment that may be related, in the specific trial, to differences in the prognostic factors. Design features, such as blocking and stratification, can be used to ensure that the play of chance does not place all the more severe patients in one or other group (at least using markers of severity that are known in advance). Even when such predictors are not available, simple randomisation with adequate numbers of subjects will ensure that, on average, the comparisons between the groups will be unbiased.

The p value, which is useful for yes/no hypothesis tests, informs us of the probability that the observed difference, or a larger one, would have occurred by chance alone if there were in fact no effect of treatment. More helpfully in most contexts, confidence intervals provide the plausible range of the true estimate of effect, given the observed data. Unlike p values, confidence intervals provide us with both a best estimate of the treatment effect (the observed difference) and a plausible range in which the true effect may be considered to reside (the width of the confidence interval). Thus, estimation (rather than hypothesis testing) and confidence intervals (rather than p values) will typically be more helpful to our needs in pharmaceutical evaluation and reimbursement. Nevertheless p values do provide complementary information about the strength of an association that may not be obvious from a confidence interval alone.

Meta-analysis of multiple trials

Drug licensing authorities tend to require more than one randomised trial to support the licensing of a pharmaceutical. Meta-analysis is a statistical technique that allows data from several clinical trials to be combined.[3,4] Pooling results across trials provides a greater number of patients on which to base estimates of effect, leading to greater power and increased precision. When performing secondary analyses, the main aim (primary outcome) of an original study is not pertinent, provided the trial meets prespecified inclusion criteria for the review and provides data on the outcome that is the main focus for the review. For example, it is often not possible to examine mortality in individual trials because these may not have the necessary statistical power (i.e. there are too few participants). However, a meta-analysis of individual trials may have sufficient statistical power to examine mortality differences, as well as providing more precise estimates of the effects of treatment on the primary outcome parameter.

In order to assess fully the effect of a treatment, it is necessary to review all available data and to gather this information in a systematic manner. This has led to the increasing use of systematic reviews, many of which incorporate meta-analysis. For example, the Cochrane Collaboration[5] has undertaken a programme of systematic reviews that are produced in a standardised format and are available to anyone who wishes to see the results.

Although such approaches as those taken by the Cochrane Collaboration enhance the availability of evidence based information, the analyses are tailored to the specific requirements of those undertaking the review. The versatility of meta-analytic techniques means that results from a previous review may not be relevant to a different group of researchers if their perspective differs, but it also means that any new analyses can be tailored to requirements. Choices relate to comparator, patient population, outcomes, setting, statistical methodology,[6] scope of the review, associated economic analyses, and many other factors that make meta-analysis an important and flexible tool for aiding decision makers.[7-10] In particular, it allows consideration of outcomes of interest that may not have been addressed specifically in any individual clinical trial. Stratification can be performed at the trial level to describe, for example, possible differences between drugs in the same class, and the effects of covariates may be assessed using meta-regression.[11] Meta-regression, however, may fail to detect important subgroup differences, because of insufficient statistical power[12] or because of biases inherent to the use of group level data.[13] Meta-analytic techniques combine results from clinical trials that are randomised at the patient level (within each trial), but comparisons between groups or types of trials are not random.[2] This has implications when analyses are extended beyond a simple assessment of pooled treatment effect, which is done in a subgroup analysis. Caution is therefore necessary in the interpretation of results, and in particular it is important to avoid over-interpretation or assertions of associations that may not exist. Further subgroup analysis is possible through the use of individual patient data,[14] although data are often unavailable or insufficient for these types of analyses and they may not be appropriate.[3,15]

The complexity of performing a review means that critical appraisal is appropriate in the same way as for clinical trials.[16]

Analyses based mainly on smaller trials present particular problems because these trials are more likely to be heterogeneous and suffer disproportionately from publication bias.[17,18] Additionally, when a positive result is found the effect size is often overestimated.[19] Large, well designed trials are less susceptible to these biases, and consequently the results from a single study of this kind may actually provide a more accurate estimate of effect size than a meta-analysis of several small trials.[16] However, large sample size alone does not guarantee freedom from bias.[20]

Meta-analytic techniques provide great flexibility in the types of analyses that can be performed, and consequently they permit analyses that are appropriate to the research question under consideration. This means that funding agencies and policy makers may need to commission their own analyses in order to gain relevant information and fulfil their specific requirements. It is important to recognise the limitations of these techniques. The use of meta-analysis does not guarantee sufficient power to detect a difference in treatment effects. Pooled results represent the best available estimate of effect at the time the analysis is performed, but these estimates should be updated in the light of new information as it becomes available. Similarly, although systematic reviews or meta-analysis should be developed according to a strict protocol, using *a priori* identification of primary and secondary outcome measures,[21] there is the possibility that analyses may be made available (for example, by a sponsor presenting evidence on a product) that present a specific treatment in a particularly positive light, perhaps simply by putting greater emphasis on the positive and interesting results and less on the neutral or negative ones. This could be in the form of bias in the selection of studies, in the selection of topics, or in the selection of items to be mentioned. In fact, this criticism may be levelled at meta-analyses and other forms of secondary research more generally.

Indirect comparisons

Meta-analysis may also be used to evaluate indirectly the efficacy of competing interventions. Indirect comparisons, where interventions are compared through a common comparator, may be used to provide evidence on competing interventions, or on treatment versus placebo, when such an assessment has not been addressed directly in a randomised trial. When direct comparisons of treatment efficacy have been assessed, indirect comparisons may provide useful supplementary information, particularly when there are concerns over the methodological quality of a single trial.[22] Indirect comparisons may also be usefully combined with direct evidence (within-trial comparisons) in network meta-analysis to provide evidence on the relative safety and efficacy of multiple treatments.[23] Network meta-analysis has, for example, been used to establish the relative benefit or harm of existing anti-hypertensive agents.[24]

Interpretation of indirect comparisons should, however, be made with caution. The results of direct and indirect comparisons usually agree, but this is not always the case.[22,25] The validity of indirect adjusted comparisons depends on both the internal validity of the trials used in the comparison and on the assumption that the relative treatment efficacy is generalisable across the trial populations used for comparison.[25] Direct estimates of treatment efficacy from randomised trials remain the "gold standard", but the internal validity of both direct and indirect comparisons of treatment efficacy may suffer from biased trial design, implementation, or reporting.

Composite outcomes

One of the situations in which meta-analysis may be particularly useful is in the assessment of outcomes that are included as components of composite measures in individual clinical trials. Composite outcomes, in which multiple endpoints are combined, are frequently used as primary outcomes in randomised trials, and interpreting the results from such outcomes can prove challenging.[26] The use of a composite primary outcome may prove to be a useful strategy if a single primary variable cannot be selected from multiple measurements associated with the primary objective. As a result, trials examining treatments that are expected to have an impact on mortality and major morbidity often adopt a primary composite outcome measure that includes mortality along with other non-fatal end-points.[26,27] This approach "addresses the multiplicity problem without requiring adjustment to the type 1 error";[27] however, this is not the only motivation behind their use. Issues of statistical efficiency appear to be prominent, with composite outcomes leading to higher event rates, thus enabling smaller sample sizes or shorter durations of follow up (or indeed both).

A substantive risk associated with the reporting of composite outcomes is that the benefits described may be presumed to relate to all of the components. This is illustrated by press releases describing the results of the ASCOT-LLA (Anglo-Scandinavian Cardiac Outcomes Trial – Lipid Lowering Arm) study.[28] That trial was designed to assess the benefits of cholesterol lowering in the primary prevention of coronary heart disease (CHD) in hypertensive patients who had total cholesterol concentrations of 6·5 mmol/l or less and had a primary composite end-point of non-fatal myocardial infarction and fatal CHD. Two separate press releases describing the results of this study stated the following.

- "Study finds drug can cut chance of a heart attack by more than a third."[29]
- "Patients with normal or mildly elevated cholesterol levels, who took the cholesterol-lowering medicine Lipitor, had 36 percent fewer fatal coronary events and non-fatal heart attacks."[30]

These statements may be considered misleading because they imply that the treatment reduced the number of patients experiencing a non-fatal myocardial infarction and the number dying from CHD. However, because neither of the individual components was specified as a secondary outcome, the evidence for benefit relating to the constituents of the composite cannot be scrutinised.[28]

Additional problems associated with the use of composite outcomes and important considerations for appraising the evidence have been identified by a systematic review on the incidence and quality of reporting of composite outcomes.[26] Problems may arise when the constituents do not move in line with each other, particularly when there is a principal end-point (often all-cause mortality) "supported" by additional and more common end-point(s).

A further problem with interpreting composite outcomes is that, although the composite as a whole may appear to be affected by treatment, the evidence for benefit relating to its most important constituent may not exist or may lack persuasiveness within the trial, as observed in the ASCOT-LLA trial described above. Additional challenges to interpretation are introduced when clinician driven outcomes, such as revascularisation or hospitalisation, are included as part of the composite outcome. This is because such outcomes appear generally to be more amenable to change by the treating physician and could potentially bias results, particularly in a trial in which neither the patients nor the treating physicians are masked to the actual treatment assignment of the participant.

When evaluating the results of composite outcomes, it is important to consider whether CONSORT (Consolidated Standards of Reporting Trials) guidelines, a series of published recommendations on reporting clinical trials,[31] have been followed and whether the composite outcome has been prespecified as the primary outcome. In addition, components of primary outcomes that are composite outcomes should always be defined as secondary outcomes, and reported alongside the results of the primary analysis. Where trials report composite variables as primary outcomes, it is important to consider whether these have been interpreted together rather than erroneously regarded as demonstrating efficacy of individual components of the composite.

Equivalence and non-inferiority issues in clinical trials

Equivalence claims are frequently made in drug evaluation and reimbursement, and these claims bring specific considerations. To put it succinctly, no evidence of a difference is not evidence that there is no difference.

The randomised controlled trial traditionally examines superiority with the aim of demonstrating that a new therapy is of greater benefit than its comparator. Terminology has been developed because of the emergence of different types of clinical trials, two of which are discussed in this section.

Equivalence trials compare treatments with the aim of showing that their therapeutic effects are equivalent. Non-inferiority trials consider the one sided case in which a new drug is assessed for being "no worse" than the existing therapy. The first theories on this subject were published in the late 1970s[32] and methodology has since been adapted from that used in bioequivalence studies. Both equivalence and non-inferiority trials are becoming increasingly relevant in clinical research as more pharmaceutical therapies are developed and the numbers of patients needed to verify superiority against an established effective agent become prohibitive.[33]

Equivalence margins

The assertion of equivalence or non-inferiority depends on estimation rather than hypothesis testing. For licensing purposes, this requires definition of an equivalence margin within which the estimate (point estimate and confidence interval) of the difference in effect between the two treatments must fall entirely for equivalence to be claimed. Figure 3.1 shows how boundaries are used in establishing equivalence and non-inferiority. This practice ensures that inference is based on stochastic testing rather than on informed but subjective reasoning. Unfortunately, the definition of what constitutes equivalence or non-inferiority is not absolute. The International Conference on Harmonisation (ICH)[27] and the Committee for Proprietary Medicinal Products (CPMP)[34] have both issued documents stating or discussing guidance on equivalence margins and acknowledge that it may not be possible to provide definitive advice on this topic.[35] An example of the difficulties this can cause is given by Greene *et al.*,[36] who describe two prominent trials of thrombolytic therapy after myocardial infarction, namely the International Joint Efficacy Comparison of Thrombolysis (INJECT)[37] and the Continuous Infusion versus Double-Bolus Administration of Alteplase (COBALT)[38] studies. Equivalence was defined differently in each trial, but both definitions were based on legitimate scientific reasoning using different aspects of the results from an important earlier trial.[39] Conclusions from the two trials were subsequently at odds, although the results were numerically similar. The absolute difference in all-cause mortality was smaller in the COBALT

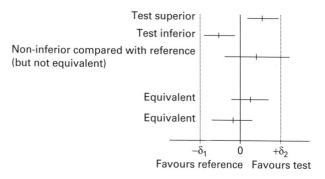

Figure 3.1 Estimation approach to equivalence testing showing point estimates and confidence intervals. Dotted lines represent upper (δ_2) and lower (δ_1) equivalence boundaries.

trial, in which equivalence was rejected (0·44% COBALT versus 0·51% INJECT), and the confidence interval around this point estimate also fell entirely within the equivalence margin specified in INJECT.

Much effort has been invested in developing appropriate methods for assessing equivalence and non-inferiority in clinical trials.[40–44] Although these rules are necessary for licensing and regulatory purposes, establishing equivalence in the context of secondary research does not have to be concerned with the original aim of the study. If the results of a trial are valid they can be used to judge equivalence against our own requirements. The studies outlined above illustrate this concept. The results of the COBALT study[38] can be judged as demonstrating equivalence, regardless of what the authors of the original study conclude, if the boundaries we choose to demonstrate equivalence include the point estimate and confidence intervals of the trial result. The fact that there are no fixed rules for assessing equivalence may seem confusing but can also be viewed as an advantage for decision makers. It ensures that priorities and perspectives of those concerned with funding pharmaceuticals dictate definitions of what constitutes equivalence and prevents data being presented in a way that "fits in" with what is required. This in turn gives funding agencies and policy makers greater leverage for negotiating listing and pricing. We note, though, the difficulty of defining equivalence in a truly *a priori* manner, when the results of previous trials are already likely to be known to the individuals generating the definition.

A review conducted by Greene et al.[36] aimed to assess claims of equivalence in clinical trials using relatively crude text searches of related words for equivalence. The authors found that 67% of reports used standard superiority methods on which to base claims of equivalence, erroneously implying that "no evidence of an effect" is the same as "evidence of no effect".[15,45] In total 10% of papers made claims of equivalence without specifying an equivalence margin or using statistical tests. The terminology and methodology associated with these trials appears to be poorly understood, but even if appropriate methods had been used for making claims of equivalence the issue of perspective remains. This is the key to equivalence and non-superiority and is demonstrated by the INJECT and COBALT studies outlined above. Both sets of results and conclusions were valid; the investigators for each trial simply had different perspectives.

Because the assessment of clinical trial data in relation to funding decisions based on equivalence or non-inferiority should not rely solely on analyses and conclusions presented in published study reports, secondary analyses are often necessary. This can be advantageous for policy makers and funding agencies because it ensures that information is presented appropriately, measured against relevant indicators, and ultimately appraised in the context of their own specific requirements and perspectives.

Surrogate outcomes

Surrogate end-points are extensively used in clinical studies, particularly those for regulatory purposes. A surrogate end-point is a physiological or biochemical marker (such as blood pressure or low-density lipoprotein cholesterol concentration) that is used as a substitute for a clinically important end-point, such as how a patient feels, functions, or survives.[46] The surrogate is expected to provide a reliable indirect measurement of treatment effect when the direct measurement of the clinical end-point is impractical or unfeasible.[27] Regulatory authorities have allowed and encouraged the use of surrogate markers over the past decade in an attempt to speed up the licensing process, particularly for drugs for life-threatening diseases. For example, the use of CD4$^+$ cell counts and plasma viral load as surrogates has allowed the rapid development of effective antiretroviral therapies for HIV/AIDS.[47]

Although the use of surrogate end-points has several potential advantages, including smaller sample sizes, shorter trial duration, and reduced cost, there are important concerns over their use. Critically, such end-points may not be able to assess the long-term benefits or adverse effects of treatment or be able to predict the full range of actions on the clinical outcome, and they may result in an inadequate or even misleading evaluation.[27,46,47] The widespread use of sodium fluoride to prevent fractures in postmenopausal women at risk of osteoporosis illustrates this point. Although sodium fluoride increased bone mass, a surrogate that is presumed to predict a reduction in fractures, evidence from a randomised trial indicated that despite this increase the newly formed bone had reduced strength, and in fact those women taking sodium fluoride were at increased risk of fracture.[46,48]

For it to be a useful substitute for a clinical outcome the surrogate must be in the causal pathway of the disease process and capture the entire effect of an intervention. Several levels of evidence demonstrating such a relationship should be provided.[46] The relationship should be biologically plausible, and the prognostic value of the surrogate for the clinical end-point should have been demonstrated.[27] Although epidemiological studies may provide valuable evidence of such a link, further evidence that the surrogate and clinical outcomes respond in the same way to treatment should also be provided from randomised trials. The problem with many surrogate markers has been establishing such relationships between the surrogate and clinical end-points of interest. Even when a trial provides evidence of such a relationship for a particular intervention, generalising such a result to other drug classes, or even within the same drug class, may be inappropriate.[47,49]

The challenge for reimbursement decisions arises when the relationship between surrogate and clinical outcomes has not been quantified, because it then becomes necessary to extrapolate under conditions of uncertainty and to estimate the possible benefits and value for money. For example, unsupported assumptions have been made regarding the use of endoscopically detected lesions as a surrogate for upper gastrointestinal complications to evaluate the safety of non-steroidal anti-inflammatory drugs.[50] Cost-effectiveness analyses of these drugs will only be reliable when the nature of the relationship has been established. Until the policy of regulatory authorities changes to require trials that evaluate both clinical and surrogate end-points, reimbursement decisions on the basis of surrogates will remain uncertain. Even when useful surrogates have been identified the long-term evaluation of treatment effects is still required.

Sponsorship of studies

Are industry funded trials biased?

In this instance, we are in fact asking whether there is a risk that somehow, whether explicitly or through ostensibly unintended consequences of choices in trial design, industry funded studies are conducted in a manner that favours the sponsor's product.

Over the past decade, the nature of clinical research funding has undergone a rather dramatic change, shifting away from public funding and resulting in the pharmaceutical industry being the single largest sponsor of medical research. Although this undoubtedly has beneficial effects, providing needed support for research and leading to medical advances, this has also caused concern over conflicts of interest.[51,52] Several studies and systematic reviews have shown an association between industry sponsorship and pro-industry conclusions.[53-55] What are the reasons for these pro-industry conclusions, and how do they affect our evaluation of industry sponsored research?

Several potential explanations for the favourable conclusions observed in industry sponsored research have been identified.[56] They could reflect the fact that therapies evaluated in industry sponsored trials may have undergone a greater degree of preselection, with only those therapies that are expected to perform well being allowed to proceed to advanced clinical testing. This selection has important ethical implications because it is inconsistent with the principle of equipoise (a trial should only be undertaken when the relative value of one treatment versus another is uncertain).[57] Pro-industry conclusions may reflect biased interpretation of the trial results, and thus conclusions should be evaluated to assess whether they reflect the quantitative results from the trial.[58] In any case, evidence from all trials should be carefully evaluated, whether industry sponsored or not.

Are industry funded trials of poorer quality?

It has also been suggested that pro-industry results may be the consequence of poor quality research; however, we can be reassured that generally this is unlikely to be the case. There is evidence that the research methods of trials sponsored by drug companies are at least as good as the methods employed by trials sponsored by public resources, and in many cases they are better,[56-59] possibly as a result of increased use of the ICH guidelines, which set a common quality standard.[60] Industry funded studies used in support of drug approval are subject to regulatory scrutiny, and so there is some incentive to perform high quality studies.

What features of trials may lead to positive results and pro-industry outcomes?

Trial features that may lead both to pro-industry outcomes and potentially biased results include inappropriate choice of comparator, study population, and outcome measures. Comparisons with placebo may be appropriate in some cases, but they are likely to favour the new therapy.[54] Unfortunately, a potential for bias also exists, even when active controls are used. Meta-regression analysis comparing conventional and atypical antipsychotics has shown that use of conventional drugs at excessive doses may have reduced their efficacy and increased adverse effects.[61] Evidence from randomised controlled trials of non-steroidal anti-inflammatory drugs and fluconazole has also shown that inappropriate dosing and administration decrease the effectiveness of active controls.[62,63]

Choice of the trial population can also lead to potential bias, particularly when results from narrow patient populations are inappropriately extrapolated and generalised to a wider population.[64] Conversely, results of subgroup analyses may attract particular attention when therapy appears to be particularly effective within a particular subset of patients. Whereas for individual patients subgroup analyses and secondary end-points can potentially provide the most closely tailored guide for clinical intervention, results in subgroup analyses and secondary outcomes (which may or may not have been prespecified) can be hard to interpret, particularly if the effect is not observed on the entire trial population.[21]

Publication bias, in the form of selective publication or selective reporting of results based on their statistical significance or, more generally, on the nature of the findings, may at least in part explain findings of bias in favour of pro-industry outcomes.[51,53,54,56,65] For example, selective reporting of per protocol results, which can overestimate treatment effects, and multiple publications of a single study have been observed.[65] Furthermore, researchers (in both industry and publicly funded trials) are more likely to submit trials reporting positive findings for publication, whereas unfavourable or insignificant findings may be associated with delayed publication.[54,66] Biased trial design and reporting is a serious problem and may result in potentially misleading evaluations of therapeutic efficacy and cost-effectiveness.

Trial reporting and metrics

Clinical trial results may be reported in a variety of ways, for example binary outcomes may be presented as relative risks, odds ratios, absolute risk reductions, or in terms of numbers needed to treat. Care must be taken in the interpretation of such data because results may be presented in a way that could favour the product under consideration. Some of the different ways in which the results from a trial may be presented are exemplified in Table 3.1. Here we show the results of a trial designed to "determine whether the dose of inhaled corticosteroids can be stepped down in patients with chronic stable asthma while maintaining control".[67]

Relative versus absolute differences

Many trials present the beneficial effects of treatment in terms of odds ratios, relative risks or relative risk reduction,

Table 3.1 Alternative ways of presenting trial results with dichotomous outcomes

		Step down group	Control group
Outcome (asthma exacerbations) present	Yes	40 (a)*	33 (b)*
	No	90 (c)	96 (d)
	Total	130 (a + c)*	129 (b + d)*
Risk of events		0·31 (a/[a + c])	0·26 (b/[b + d])
Odds		0·44 (a/c)	0·34 (b/d)
Odds ratio	(a/c)/(b/d)	1·29* (95% CI 0·75 to 2·23)*	
Relative risk	(a/[a + c])/(b/[b + d])	1·20 (e) (95% CI 0·82 to 1·78)	
Relative risk reduction	1 – e	–0·20 (95% CI –0·78 to 0.18)	
Absolute risk reduction	[b/(b + d)] – [a/(a + c)]	–0·052 (f) (95% CI –0·161 to 0.058)	
NNTH	1/f	20† (95% CI NNTH 7 to ∞ to NNTB 18)	

*Results from Hawkins et al.[67] Other estimates of treatment effect and their corresponding confidence intervals (CIs) were calculated in Stats Direct v2.29 (http://www.camcode.com). †Reporting of the number needed to treat and construction of CIs has been described by Altman.[68] NNTH, number needed to treat for one additional patient to be harmed; NNTB, number needed to treat for one additional patient to benefit.

but this information alone does not provide us with enough evidence for effective decision making.[69] Although these statistics provide us with evidence regarding whether a treatment is beneficial, they provide no information on the size of the treatment effect on an absolute scale. This information can be gained from calculation of the absolute risk reduction and its corresponding confidence interval. For example, Hawkins et al.[67] presented their results as an odds ratio and conclude that, "By adopting a stepdown approach to the use of inhaled steroids at high doses in asthma a reduction in the dose can be achieved without compromising asthma control" – a conclusion that is incorrectly based on the fact that the confidence interval for the odds ratio includes unity. Results in terms of absolute risk difference are more informative because they are in natural units. Although the odds ratio is 1·29 (95% confidence interval [CI] 0·75 to 2·23), when the results are reanalysed using this strategy the 95% confidence interval includes the possibility that the step down strategy leads to a 16% increase in exacerbation of asthma (95% CI −5·8% to 16% on the risk difference scale).[70] Setting an upper limit of an equivalence margin at 16% appears too high, and thus it seems implausible that the results of this trial demonstrate equivalence.

Although relative risk reduction gives a sense of the effect of intervention in proportional terms, it provides no information on the incidence of the event. For example, a 10% risk reduction may not be considered clinically relevant if the event rarely occurs; however, the same reduction in a common event may have an important impact on health.[71] With this in mind, let us consider what the 36% relative risk reduction for the composite primary end-point of non-fatal myocardial infarction and fatal CHD described in the ASCOT-LLA trial press releases[29,30] means in absolute terms. This relative risk reduction actually corresponds to an absolute risk reduction of a coronary event of 3·4 per 1000 patient-years in hypertensive patients on lipid-lowering therapy,[28] a result that has been described as "less impressive"[72] than the 36% relative risk reduction. The expression of results in terms of reduced relative risks can augment the perception of efficacy of an intervention and have considerable influence on doctors' and patients' preferences for treatment and on health policy decisions made by health authority members.[73–76] Thus, viewing trial results in more than one of these metrics is likely to be more informative in the decision making process. Because participants in a trial are "seldom representative of the general population", the generalisability of such estimates must also be considered.[77] An individual trial may not be the best place to obtain an estimate of baseline risk because the untreated control group may not be representative of the population that we wish to assess. In such cases, estimates of baseline risk from external data may provide a more realistic estimate of the effect of treatment in routine practice.

Conclusion

Most economic analyses have problems, and most of those problems relate to the estimate of comparative clinical effectiveness.[1] Clinical effectiveness drives cost-effectiveness, and if unduly favourable estimates of clinical effectiveness are input into cost-effectiveness analyses, then unduly optimistic results will be produced.

Those producing economic analyses to support applications for reimbursement are often making a commercial case, rather than necessarily a scientific one, and the situation is necessarily adversarial. Therefore, from the health policy perspective, we may be suspicious that the estimates of effectiveness included in an economic analysis may not always be the most objective estimates that are available. Reviewing clinical trials is not necessarily a game of fixed rules but more properly considered as a scientific inquisition based on basic principles.

Summary

- Critical evaluation of clinical effectiveness plays a key role in the generation of unbiased estimates of cost-effectiveness.
- Randomised trials provide the best estimates of treatment effect because they employ the only design that can most reliably avoid bias.
- Common issues that potentially lead to bias in randomised trials include the use of surrogate and composite outcome measures, claims of equivalence or non-inferiority, and trial sponsorship.

- There will often be more than one trial examining the effectiveness of pharmaceuticals, and results may often be helpfully summarised using meta-analysis.
- In order to assess the results of clinical trials it is important that outcomes are expressed on absolute rather than (or in addition to) ratio scales (thus making the absolute difference in survival preferable to the relative risk or hazard ratio).

References

1 Hill SR, Mitchell AS, Henry DA. Problems with the interpretation of pharmacoeconomic analyses: a review of submissions to the Australian Pharmaceutical Benefits Scheme. *JAMA* 2000;**283**:2116–21.
2 Egger M, Davey Smith G, Altman DG (eds). *Systematic reviews in health care: meta-analysis in context.* London: BMJ Publishing Group, 2001
3 Petitti DB. *Meta-analysis, decision analysis, and cost-effectiveness analysis. Methods for quantitative synthesis in medicine.* New York: Oxford University Press, 1994.
4 Hedges LV, Olkin I. *Statistical methods for meta-analysis.* London: Academic Press, 1985.
5 Bero L, Rennie D. The Cochrane Collaboration. Preparing, maintaining, and disseminating systematic reviews of the effects of health care. *JAMA* 1995;**274**:1935–8.
6 Berlin JA, Laird NM, Sacks HS, Chalmers TC. A comparison of statistical methods for combining event rates from clinical trials. *Stat Med* 1989;**8**:141–51.
7 Davey Smith G, Egger M, Phillips AN. Meta-analysis: beyond the grand mean? *BMJ* 1997;**315**:1610–14.
8 Davey Smith G, Egger M. Meta-analysis: unresolved issues and future developments. *BMJ* 1998;**316**:221–5.
9 Naylor CD. Meta-analysis and the meta-epidemiology of clinical research. *BMJ* 1997;**315**:617–19.
10 Bailar JC. The promise and problems of meta-analysis. *N Engl J Med* 1997;**337**:559–61.
11 Smith TC, Spiegelhalter DJ, Thomas A. Bayesian approaches to random-effects meta-analysis: a comparative study. *Stat Med* 1995;**14**:2685–99.
12 Lambert PC, Sutton AJ, Abrams KR, Jones DR. A comparison of summary patient-level covariates in meta-regression with individual patient data meta-analysis. *J Clin Epidemiol* 2002;**55**:86–94.
13 Berlin JA, Santanna J, Schmid CH, *et al.* Individual patient versus group-level data meta-regression for the investigation of treatment effect modifiers: ecological bias rears its ugly head. *Stats Med* 2002;**21**:371–87.
14 Higgins JP, Whitehead A, Turner RM, *et al.* Meta-analysis of continuous outcome data from individual patients. *Stats Med* 2001;**20**:2219–41.
15 Senn S. *Statistical issues in drug development.* Chichester: John Wiley & Sons, 1997.
16 Pogue J, Yusuf S. Overcoming the limitations of current meta-analysis of randomised controlled trials. *Lancet* 1998;**351**:47–52.
17 Egger M, Davey Smith G. Meta-analysis: bias in location and selection of studies. *BMJ* 1998;**316**:61–6.

18 Sterne JA, Egger M, Davey Smith G. Systematic reviews in health care: Investigating and dealing with publication and other biases in meta-analysis. *BMJ* 2001;**323**:101–5.
19 Begg CB, Berlin JA. Publication bias: a problem in interpreting medical data. *J R Statist Soc* 1988;**151**:419–63.
20 Ioannidis JP, Lau J. Pooling research results: benefits and limitations of meta-analysis. *Jt Comm J Qual Improv* 1999;**25**:462–9.
21 Freemantle N. Interpreting the results of secondary end points and subgroup analyses in clinical trials: should we lock the crazy aunt in the attic? *BMJ* 2001;**322**:989–91.
22 Song F, Glenny A-M, Altman DG. Indirect comparison in evaluating relative efficacy illustrated by antimicrobial prophylaxis in colorectal surgery. *Control Clin Trials* 2000;**21**:488–97.
23 Lumley T. Network meta-analysis for indirect treatment comparisons. *Stat Med* 2002;**21**:2313–24.
24 Psaty BM, Lumley T, Furberg CD, *et al.* Health outcomes associated with various antihypertensive therapies used as first-line agents. *JAMA* 2003;**289**:2534–44.
25 Song F, Altman DG, Glenny A-M, Deeks JJ. Validity of indirect comparison for estimating efficacy of competing interventions: empirical evidence from published meta-analyses. *BMJ* 2003;**326**:472–6.
26 Freemantle N, Calvert M, Wood J, *et al.* Composite outcomes in randomized trials: greater precision but with greater uncertainty? *JAMA* 2003;**289**:2554–59.
27 ICH. Statistical principles for clinical trials: topic E9 (CPMP/ICH/363/96); 5 February 1998. http://www.ich.org/pdfICH/e9.pdf (accessed 14 August 2003).
28 Sever PS, Dahlof B, Poulter NR, *et al.* Prevention of coronary and stroke events with atorvastatin in hypertensive patients who have average or lower-than-average cholesterol concentrations, in the Anglo-Scandinavian Cardiac Outcomes Trial-Lipid Lowering Arm (ASCOT-LLA): a multicentre randomised controlled trial. *Lancet* 2003;**361**:1149–58.
29 Imperial College London Press Release. Study finds drug can cut chance of a heart attack by more than a third. http://www.ascotstudy.org/ 02/04/2003 (accessed 14 August 2003).
30 News Release Pfizer. Reduction in heart attacks and strokes shown in hypertensive patients treated with Lipitor; 2 April 2003. http://www. pfizer.com/are/news_releases/mm_2003_0402.html (accessed 11 June 2003).
31 Moher D, Schulz KF, Altman D, for the CONSORT Group. The CONSORT Statement: revised recommendations for improving the quality of reports of parallel-group randomized trials. *JAMA* 2001;**285**:1987–91.
32 Dunnett CW, Gent M. Significance testing to establish equivalence between treatments, with special reference to data in the form of 2×2 tables. *Biometrics* 1977;**33**:593–602.
33 Djulbegovic B, Clarke M. Scientific and ethical issues in equivalence trials. *JAMA* 2001;**285**:1206–8.
34 CPMP. Points to consider on switching between superiority and non-inferiority. (CPMP/EWP/482/99); 27 July 2000. http://www.emea.eu.int/ pdfs/human/ewp/048299en.pdf (accessed 13 August 2003).
35 CPMP. Concept paper on the development of a committee for proprietary medicinal products (CPMP) points to consider on biostatistical/ methodological issues arising from recent CPMP discussions on licensing applications: choice of delta (CPMP/EWP/2158/99); 23 September 1999. http://www.emea.eu.int/pdfs/human/ewp/215899en.pdf (accessed 13 August 2003).

36 Greene WL, Concato J, Feinstein AR. Claims of equivalence in medical research: are they supported by the evidence? *Ann Intern Med* 2000;**132**:715–22.
37 International Joint Efficacy Comparison of Thrombolysis (INJECT). Randomised, double-blind comparison of reteplase double-bolus administration with streptokinase in acute myocardial infarction: trial to investigate equivalence. *Lancet* 1995;**346**:329–36.
38 The Continuous Infusion versus Double-Bolus Administration of Alteplase (COBALT) Investigators. A comparison of continuous infusion of alteplase with double-bolus adminstration for acute myocardial infarction. *N Engl J Med* 1997;**337**:1124–30.
39 The GUSTO investigators. An international randomised trial comparing four thrombolytic strategies for acute myocardial infarction. *N Engl J Med* 1993;**329**:673–82.
40 Snapinn SM. Noninferiority trials. *Curr Control Trials Cardiovasc Med* 2000;**1**:19–21.
41 Jones B, Jarvis P, Lewis JA, Ebbutt AF. Trials to assess equivalence: the importance of rigorous methods. *BMJ* 1996;**313**:36–9.
42 Ebbutt AF, Frith L. Practical issues in equivalence trials. *Stats Med* 1998;**17**:1691–701.
43 Wiens BL. Choosing an equivalence limit for noninferiority or equivalence studies. *Control Clin Trials* 2002;**23**:2–14.
44 Garrett AD. Therapeutic equivalence: fallacies and falsification. *Stats Med* 2003;**22**:741–62.
45 Altman DG, Bland JM. Absence of evidence is not evidence of absence. *BMJ* 1995;**311**:485.
46 Fleming TR, DeMets DL. Surrogate end points in clinical trials. *Ann Intern Med* 1996;**125**:605–13.
47 Bucher HC, Guyatt GH, Cook DJ, *et al.*, for the Evidence-Based Medicine Working Group. Users' guides to the medical literature: XIX. Applying clinical trial results; A. How to use an article measuring the effect of an intervention on surrogate end points. *JAMA* 1999;**282**:771–8.
48 Riggs BL, Hodgson SF, O'Fallon WM, *et al.* Effect of fluoride treatment on the fracture rate in postmenopausal women with osteoporosis. *N Engl J Med* 1990;**322**:802–9.
49 Furberg CD, Herrington DM, Psaty BM. Are drugs within the same class interchangeable? *Lancet* 1999;**354**:1202–4.
50 Freemantle N. Cost effectiveness of non steroidal anti inflammatory drugs (NSAIDs): what makes a NSAID good value for money? *Rheumatology* 2000;**39**:232–4.
51 Bodenheimer T. Uneasy alliance: clinical investigators and the pharmaceutical industry. *N Engl J Med* 2000;**342**:1539–44.
52 Stelfox HT, Chua G, O'Rourke K, Detsky AS. Conflict of interest in the debate over calcium-channel antagonists. *N Engl J Med* 1998;**338**:101–6.
53 Kjaergard LL, Als-Nielsen B. Association between competing interests and authors' conclusions: epidemiological study of randomised clinical trials published in the *BMJ*. *BMJ* 2002;**325**:249–52.
54 Bekelman JE, Li Y, Gross CP. Scope and impact of financial conflicts of interest in biomedical research: a systematic review. *JAMA* 2003;**289**:454–65.
55 Yaphe J, Edman R, Knishkowy B, Herman J. The association between funding by commercial interests and study outcome in randomized controlled drug trials. *Fam Pract* 2001;**18**:565–68.
56 Lexchin J, Bero LA, Djulbegovic B, Clark O. Pharmaceutical industry sponsorship and research outcome and quality: systematic review. *BMJ* 2003;**326**:1167.

57 Djulbegovic B, Lacevic M, Cantor A, *et al*. The uncertainty principle and industry-sponsored research. *Lancet* 2000;**356**:635–8.

58 Als-Nielsen B, Chen W, Gluud C, Kjaergard LL. Association of funding and conclusions in randomized drug trials. *JAMA* 2003;**290**:921–8.

59 MacLean CH, Morton SC, Ofman JJ, *et al*. How useful are unpublished data from the Food and Drug Administration in meta-analysis? *J Clin Epidemiol* 2003;**56**:44–51.

60 ICH. International Conference on Harmonisation Guidelines. http://www.ich.org/ (accessed 14 August 2003).

61 Geddes J, Freemantle N, Harrison P, Bebbington P. Atypical antipsychotics in the treatment of schizophrenia: systematic overview and meta-regression analysis. *BMJ* 2000;**321**:1371–6.

62 Rochon PA, Gurwitz JH, Simms RW, *et al*. A study of manufacturer-supported trials of nonsteroidal anti-inflammatory drugs in the treatment of arthritis. *Arch Intern Med* 1994;**154**:157–63.

63 Johansen HK, Gotzsche PC. Problems in the design and reporting of trials of antifungal agents encountered during meta-analysis. *JAMA* 1999;**282**:1752–59.

64 Montaner JSG, O'Shaughnessy MV, Schechter MT. Industry-sponsored clinical research: a double-edged sword. *Lancet* 2001;**358**:1893–5.

65 Melander H, Ahlqvist-Rastad J, Meijer G, Beermann B. Evidence b(i)ased medicine-selective reporting from studies sponsored by pharmaceutical industry: review of studies in new drug applications. *BMJ* 2003;**326**:1171–3.

66 Easterbrook PJ, Berlin JA, Gopalan R, Matthews DR. Publication bias in clinical research. *Lancet* 1991;**337**:867–72.

67 Hawkins, G, McMahon AD, Twaddle S, *et al*. Stepping down inhaled corticosteroids in asthma: randomised controlled trial. *BMJ* 2003;**326**:1115–21.

68 Altman DG. Confidence intervals for the number needed to treat. *BMJ* 1998;**317**:1309–12.

69 Nuovo J, Melnikow J, Chang D. Reporting number needed to treat and absolute risk reduction in randomized controlled trials. *JAMA* 2002;**287**:2813–14.

70 Freemantle N. Evidence of equivalence rather than difference; 18 June 2003. http://bmj.bmjjournals.com/cgi/eletters/326/7399/1115 (accessed 18 January 2004).

71 Sanchez RG. Do clinical trials tell us all the truth? Relative versus absolute risks and their influence on the therapeutic decisions of cardiologists. *Rev Esp Cardiol* 2002;**55**:1018–20.

72 Lindholm LH, Samuelsson O. What are the odds at ASCOT today? *Lancet* 2003;**361**:1144–5.

73 Malenka DJ, Baron JA, Johansen S, *et al*. The framing effect of relative and absolute risk. *J Gen Intern Med* 1993;**8**:543–8.

74 Fahey T, Griffiths S, Peters TJ. Evidence based purchasing: understanding results of clinical trials and systematic reviews. *BMJ* 1995;**311**:1056–9.

75 Bucher HC, Weinbacher M, Gyr K. Influence of method of reporting study results on decision of physicians to prescribe drugs to lower cholesterol concentration. *BMJ* 1994;**309**:761–4.

76 Lacy CR, Barone JA, Suh DC, *et al*. Impact of presentation of research results on likelihood of prescribing medications to patients with left ventricular dysfunction. *Am J Cardiol* 2001;**87**:203–7.

77 Mant D. Can randomised trials inform clinical decisions about individual patients? *Lancet* 1999;**353**:743–6.

4: International pharmaceutical policy: health creation or wealth creation?

KAREN BLOOR, ALAN MAYNARD

Introduction

Public and private expenditure on pharmaceuticals accounts for a significant and increasing proportion of health expenditure in all countries, making a substantial contribution to improvements in population health. At the same time, the pharmaceutical industry creates considerable wealth – it is currently the second largest global industrial sector by market value.[1] In many developed countries (particularly the USA, UK, France, Japan, Germany, and Switzerland) the industry is a substantial employer, investor, and exporter, generating extensive lobbying power which can influence the hearts and minds of politicians seeking to regulate health expenditure. Pfizer, the largest and most powerful pharmaceutical company, is the fifth biggest company in the world[1] and makes profits at the rate of £1 million per hour[2] from pharmaceutical products funded by tax finance, insurance revenues, and individual patients paying out of pocket.

What are the objectives of national health policies with regard to pharmaceuticals? How can policy makers efficiently regulate the trade-offs between health creation and wealth creation? In all countries, with varied systems of public and private funding and organisation of health care, there is some form of rationing of pharmaceuticals and other health interventions. Is there a "best" system for reimbursing pharmaceuticals? Are there lessons to learn from the varied mechanisms in place, or is the answer simply to spend more money with little critical appraisal of the cost-effectiveness of the expenditure? In this chapter we explore the objectives of pharmaceutical policy, outline some of the regulatory mechanisms aimed at achieving these objectives, and discuss (where the evidence is sufficient) the success or failure of the mechanisms and lessons that can be learnt from them.

Objectives of pharmaceutical policy

Controlling pharmaceutical expenditure

In developed countries, health care expenditure generally grows at a rate faster than that of the overall economy. The US health care system consumes 14% of the largest national income on earth, and in countries such as Switzerland and Germany expenditure exceeds 10% of the gross domestic product (GDP). Even in the UK it is planned that more than 9% of GDP will be spent on health care annually by 2008. Controlling overall health expenditure is a matter of concern to policy makers in tax financed health systems, as well as in private systems, because costs often fall on employers, influencing competitiveness, profits, and economic growth.

Market orientated health systems like the US system use competition to control costs and maximise efficiency through the price mechanism. In other health systems, such as that in the UK, global cash limited budgets, predominantly tax financed with substantial regulation, are thought necessary (but not sufficient) conditions for cost control.

The characteristics of expenditure growth in the pharmaceutical markets of selected OECD (Organisation for Economic Co-operation and Development) countries, over time, are shown in Table 4.1.[3] The USA is a very significant market (despite pharmaceuticals using a relatively low percentage of the health care budget), and markets in France and Japan are also large, with pharmaceutical bills approaching 20% of their health care budgets. The expenditure characteristics of the UK, Australia, and New Zealand are modest in comparison, but all are currently undergoing rapid growth.

Table 4.1 Expenditure on pharmaceuticals in selected countries

Country	1987			1992			1998		
	% total health expenditure	% GDP	$US per capita expenditure	% total health expenditure	% GDP	$US per capita expenditure	% total health expenditure	% GDP	$US per capita expenditure
Australia	8·1	0·6	90	9·9	0·8	143	11·6	1·0	239
Canada	10·6	0·9	141	12·3	1·2	233	15·0	1·4	344
France				20·5	1·5	300	18·5	1·7	391
Germany	14·1	1·3	191	14·2	1·4	260	12·7	1·3	312
Italy				20·4	0·7	294	21·8	1·7	388
Japan	20·3	1·3	185	22·0	1·4	281	17	1·2	295
New Zealand	14·7	0·9	104	14·2	1·1	152	14·4*	1·1*	196
Spain	18·7	1·0	98	18·3	1·3	181	19·0*	1·4*	246*
Sweden	7·5	0·6	95	9·7	0·7	146	12·8*	1·0*	227*
Switzerland	10·0	0·8	147	9·4	0·9	207	10·2	1·1	302
UK	13·6	0·8	107	14·2	1·0	167	15·9*	1·1*	236
USA	9·3	1·0	186	8·8	1·1	280	10·3	1·3	428

*1997.
Data from Organisation for Economic Co-operation and Development (OECD) 2002. GDP, gross domestic product.[3]

Efficient use of pharmaceuticals: quality, safety, efficacy, and cost-effectiveness

In all countries, resources available for health care (and all other goods and services) are limited. The demand for health (in terms of duration and quality of life) is effectively unlimited, and this highlights the inevitable problem of scarcity. Where resources are scarce, if improvement in population health is assumed to be the primary goal of a health care system, then patients' health status must be improved at least cost. Current regulation of the pharmaceutical industry worldwide requires companies to establish safety, efficacy, and quality (defined as sound manufacturing) of new products for licensing (Chapter 2). Regulators in Australia, Canada, and some countries in Europe increasingly require companies to provide evidence of relative effectiveness and efficiency, using broad measures of health outcomes, for products to be reimbursed by purchasing agencies. This supplements the three existing regulatory "hurdles" of safety, efficacy, and production quality with a "fourth hurdle", namely cost-effectiveness, which is explored in Chapter 5.

Equity and access to pharmaceuticals

Equitable access to pharmaceuticals is first determined by whether they are reimbursed by government or insurers at all, as illustrated by the recent US debate about including them in the Medicare benefits package.[4] Inclusion may be total or partial, and access may be limited by user charges (co-payments and deductibles). Equity criteria may influence the content of lists of reimbursed drugs, by the application of often ill-defined criteria (for example, high social values attached to the health of children) and by political choices.

International experience of pharmaceutical regulation

All health care systems face the same policy objectives relating to pharmaceuticals: expenditure control, efficient use of products, and equitable access to them. However, the weight attached to each objective and the mechanisms used to address them vary across a spectrum of approaches, largely relating to the public–private mix of health care funding and provision. In market orientated systems, national pharmaceutical policy is minimal but regulation emerges through contracting mechanisms such as managed care. In public orientated systems, regulation tends to be centralised at the system level and is more directly imposed on users, prescribers, and manufacturers. Across the spectrum of public–private mix for health, industrial policy aims – particularly that of maintaining a profitable industry – may not coincide with health policy goals of maximising health outcomes from scarce health care budgets and ensuring equitable access to health interventions. To achieve their objectives, policy makers regulate to varying degrees the three main groups of decision makers within the pharmaceutical market (Box 4.1): patients and doctors on the demand side of the market, and manufacturing industry on the supply side. In all pharmaceutical markets there are dual objectives of creating health and creating wealth.

Box 4.1 Policies to regulate pharmaceutical expenditure

Demand side

- Influencing patients: Access constraints – restricting coverage; co-payments and user charges; OTC switching; restrictions on DTC advertising
- Influencing doctors: information, feedback, and guidelines; limited lists and formularies; encouraging generic prescribing; budgetary controls and use of incentives

Supply side

- Regulating industry: direct price controls (for example, reference pricing); indirect price controls (for example, profit controls); "fourth hurdle" restrictions on reimbursement (cost-effectiveness regulation)

Influencing patients

To ensure national cost containment, it is necessary either to reduce patient demand for pharmaceuticals or to restrict access. However, policies that reduce patient demand (such as co-payments) tend to reduce utilisation of necessary, cost-effective products as well as unnecessary or inefficient ones.[5] Restricting access (for example, by capping reimbursement) and penalising use (for example, by co-payments) can also breach equity goals. Ideally, efficient systems should encourage patients to use products that are relatively cost-effective and have an established evidence base, and discourage use of products that are of unproven cost-effectiveness.

In market orientated systems such as that in the USA, access to pharmaceuticals and their cost to patients depend on the type of insurance package held. Like many other aspects of this fragmented health care market, there is no one system for reimbursing pharmaceuticals. Some insurance plans have limited or no coverage of pharmaceuticals, which leaves patients paying for many prescribed drugs out of pocket. Where there is insurance coverage, patients' use may be influenced by cost sharing options (co-payments) such as user charges and deductibles. The RAND Health Insurance Experiment[6] is the most rigorous experimental study of cost sharing, and demonstrated that utilisation of health care is reduced by any form of cost sharing compared with none, although the reduced utilisation demonstrated in that study had little impact on health status over the time scale covered. Quasi-experimental studies of low income (Medicaid) populations demonstrated reduced use of pharmaceuticals from cost sharing but with associated adverse health and expenditure effects.[7-9]

Medicaid programmes that cover some poor and disabled US individuals are state rather than federal level programmes and have varied approaches to reimbursing pharmaceuticals. Twenty-two states currently limit the drugs that doctors can prescribe for Medicaid patients, with preferred drug lists that exclude drugs such as the new branded proton pump inhibitors (for example, esomeprazole) and encourage prescription of generic H_2 antagonists (for example, cimetidine and ranitidine) instead.[10] The pharmaceutical industry is spending heavily on lobbying state legislatures to block the further use of formularies for Medicaid populations, particularly in New York.[10]

Perhaps the most significant state effort to reduce Medicaid pharmaceutical expenditure is in Maine, where manufacturers have been pressured to grant price rebates. Under the Maine prescription programme, the State assumed the role of a pharmacy benefit manager, requiring manufacturers to negotiate rebates. Manufacturers who do not cooperate face having their products subjected to a prior authorisation procedure, in which the Department of Human Services would have to approve prescriptions before pharmacies could dispense them.[11] The pharmaceutical industry challenged this policy in court, but eventually the Supreme Court gave a qualified approval to the drug cost plan. Other states have followed this case closely and are likely to experiment with similar efforts to contain pharmaceutical costs.[11]

The Medicare programme, covering Americans aged 65 years or older and some disabled younger people, currently provides very little coverage of pharmaceuticals. Unless they are veterans, and can therefore use the Veterans Administration system, elderly patients pay the whole cost of almost all outpatient drugs. This has created substantial recent debate, as policies have been proposed to provide partial coverage of pharmaceuticals and discussed in the US congress. House and Senate voted in June 2003 to expand Medicare coverage to help beneficiaries with pharmaceutical costs, but the final version of the bill is not yet agreed and debate is predicted to be "long and arduous".[4] Again, lobbyists for the pharmaceutical industry are spending millions in order to influence policy makers in this debate.[12] Their concern is that once such a programme is exacted, price controls, such as those in Medicaid, will inevitably follow, with consequent threats to their profits.

The fact that many American patients pay the full cost of their prescription drugs has highlighted the high price of drugs in the USA. Books and newspapers regularly quote patients who travel to Canada to buy pharmaceuticals there at a much cheaper price (for example, the breast cancer drug tamoxifen is reported to be eight times as expensive in Ohio as in Canada).[13] However, more general studies show that, on average, US prices for a "representative" basket of pharmaceutical products are comparable to those in other countries.[14]

While insurers and other health funders attempt to restrict patients' use of prescription drugs, manufacturers have the freedom to increase patient demand for pharmaceuticals in the USA through direct to consumer (DTC) advertising. This is well established but a matter of continuing dispute.[15,16] An investigation into DTC advertising in the USA found that companies spent $1·8 billion on such advertisements in 1999. The content of 87% of the advertisements described benefits in vague, qualitative terms, only 13% used data, and none mentioned cost.[17]

In public health care systems there is usually partial or total public reimbursement of prescribed drugs. Patient demand for pharmaceuticals, in both tax financed and social insurance systems, has been influenced primarily by user charges. Practically all European Union (EU) countries have user charges for pharmaceuticals, and this can be a significant source of revenue. There is variety in user charge systems but little analysis of their relative effects on efficiency, access, and expenditure. Payments may vary by type of drug (France, Italy), by pack size (Germany), or as a proportion of the cost (France, Spain), or there may be a standard payment (UK). Some countries have ceilings on all charges (Germany and Sweden). Others exempt the poor and elderly (UK) or particular categories of "essential" drugs (France and Italy).[18]

Evidence about cost sharing for pharmaceuticals is consistent across countries and studies, demonstrating that utilisation is reduced when patients have to pay. User charges in public or private health systems reduce efficient use of pharmaceutical products as well as "unnecessary" care, particularly in low income groups. Cost sharing policies have been as summarised as "misguided or cynical efforts to tax the ill and/or drive up the total cost of health care while shifting some of the burden out of government budgets".[19] In addressing inappropriate prescribing, it may be more suitable to target regulation at prescribing doctors, not at patients.

Recent trends in "switching" of prescription only medicines to over the counter (OTC) products has shifted some costs from government agencies to patients. OTC markets are well established in Germany, France, and the UK. In the UK a competition ruling made price fixing for OTC products illegal,[20] encouraging UK supermarkets to develop price competition for OTC products.

The European Commission is moving slowly to allow the practice of DTC advertising.[21] This is banned in some countries, such as Australia, but not in others, such as the USA and New Zealand. Even where a ban is in place, companies can run advertising campaigns that "raise awareness" of a specific condition, particularly where there is one major brand drug to treat it (for example, Pfizer's advertisements using the footballer Pele to encourage men to consult their doctors about erectile dysfunction). Also, on the internet there are many patient groups and "information" pages, with "guides to talking to your doctor", placed by the industry. The industry's covert entanglement with scientists and doctors can be illustrated by the recent debate about pharmaceutical public relations around hormone replacement therapy (HRT). Wyeth, which accounts for more than 70% of the global market for HRT, apparently surreptitiously sponsored the influential book *Feminine forever*[22] and donated large amounts of money to organisations such as the Society for Women's Health Research, which not only helped to promote HRT as a panacea for the symptoms of menopause, but also for heart disease, dementia, osteoporosis, sexual function, mood, and vitality.[23] This impression of HRT has been severely damaged by two recent studies that confirm that postmenopausal women taking combined HRT have an increased risk of heart disease[24] and a twofold greater chance of developing breast cancer.[25]

There is a risk that DTC advertising, which is common in the USA and rapidly approaching European systems, may be misleading and will certainly only be used to market new products, which may be of marginal effectiveness and high cost.[26] This could create expenditure inflation and inefficiency.

Influencing doctors

The market based approach to funding and providing US health care meant that doctors were traditionally paid a fee for service. With full reimbursement by a third party (insurers) neither doctor nor patient had any incentive to control the costs of care. More recently doctors have mixed or "blended" payment mechanisms[27,28] and are subject to the pressures of managed care. Increasingly, prescribed drugs, like other forms of health care intervention, are subject to clinical guidelines and protocols where they are reimbursed by managed care organisations. Managed care companies have also used, with varying degrees of success, mechanisms such as drug utilisation review, prior authorisation, and pharmacy benefit management to restrict expenditure on high cost pharmaceuticals.

In publicly funded systems there are three predominant mechanisms used to influence prescribing doctors: information, feedback, and guidelines; limited lists and generic prescribing; and budgetary controls.

Information and feedback systems often provide data on volume and cost of prescribing, like the UK's prescribing analysis and cost scheme (PACT).[29] This does not, however, provide any information about the appropriateness or cost-effectiveness of prescribing decisions – it aims to control costs, not improve efficiency or equity. In a number of countries clinical guidelines are provided to aid prescribing. For example, in France guidelines cover all aspects of medical care and prescribing, and are framed as statements about what doctors must not do. In theory, a lack of compliance generates a fine related to harm, cost, and the extent of deviance, although they have been described as "heavy handed and expensive"[30] and hence are little used in practice.

Prescribing guidelines were also introduced in 1995 in Germany and included a negative list of pharmaceuticals. These led to a switch in prescribing, but they were not the subject of systematic analysis and so the effects on quality, access, and expenditure are unknown. Increasingly in the UK there are prescribing guidelines, as part of the National Institute for Clinical Excellence (NICE)[31,32] and the National Service Frameworks.[33] However, NICE has created substantial cost inflation, with estimates of the cost of NICE recommendations from its inception in 2000 to 2002 of around £575 million.[34] It may be distorting clinical priorities and creating opportunity costs elsewhere in the National Health Service (NHS),[35] particularly if the "fourth hurdle" (an implied acceptable cost per quality-adjusted life year) is set too low. In addition, NICE provides recommendations that may not always be implemented, particularly when they recommend against an intervention that is already in use. A non-pharmaceutical example of this is that, in 2001, NICE recommended against laparoscopic repair of primary inguinal hernia. This apparently resulted in no change in clinical practice (Figure 4.1).[36] Other guidance often recommends

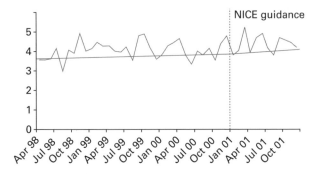

Figure 4.1 Percentage of primary inguinal hernia repairs carried out using laparoscopic techniques, before and after the publication of National Institute for Clinical Excellence (NICE) guidance. Data from Bloor *et al.*[36]

treatments for certain subgroups of the population, such as zanamavir for influenza only for "at risk" individuals, including people older than 65 years and those with chronic respiratory disease.[32] However, once the treatment is available and reimbursed on the NHS, it is extremely difficult to monitor whether it is being used only for the recommended population. "Leakage" of the treatment into other population groups is inevitable, with cost inflationary consequences.

Until recently, in the UK and around the world clinical guidelines were devised solely with regard to clinical effectiveness (with varying levels of evidence or opinion base). With ubiquitous scarce health care resources, such guidelines may be inefficient and inflationary. To promote efficiency, guidelines must be based on good evidence of relative cost-effectiveness, and they must be monitored and implemented – guidelines are pointless if they are ignored.[36]

Lists that limit reimbursement of pharmaceuticals also exist in most publicly funded health care systems, and they may be "positive" (indicating which products will be reimbursed) or "negative" (declaring those that will not). The production of a limited list of cost-effective drugs is a necessary condition for achieving efficiency in prescribing, but without monitoring and enforcement of appropriate use of medicines it is not a sufficient condition.

Generic substitution is permitted in six of the EU member states: Denmark, Finland, France, Germany, the Netherlands, and Spain. Patients' incentives to seek cheaper generic products are limited when co-payments are not related to price, and so in the absence of generic substitution by pharmacists doctors must be encouraged to prescribe generically. Generic prescribing by volume is high in some EU countries even without substitution (for example, in England 53% of prescriptions dispensed were generic[37]), but by far the biggest proportion of expenditure on pharmaceuticals is still taken up by newer branded products under patent.[38] In addition, the increasing practice of generic companies being bought out by the major pharmaceutical companies may in future limit competition and segment markets, meaning that generic prescribing may have diminishing effects on overall expenditure.

There is limited evidence about the effects of primary care budget holding. In the UK and Ireland, where practitioners were offered the opportunity to economise on prescribing and use surplus resources in other practice activities, evaluation showed some effects on prescribing expenditure,[39–41] although these may have been short term.[42] In Germany, for three years a cap on pharmaceutical expenditure was announced, with a small proportion of any overspend to be funded out of the doctor's remuneration budget. This had a much more considerable effect, with reduced volume and cost of prescribed drugs during the period of the cap.[43,44]

Although funders of health care attempt to influence doctors to contain costs and increase the efficiency of prescribing, there are substantial efforts from the industry to reverse this, in the USA and around the world.[18] Increasing international expenditure on pharmaceuticals suggests that industry marketing may be more successful than the efforts of funders. Marketing of pharmaceuticals is vigorous and often superficial, and it continues to develop, for example into product endorsement by celebrities in the media.[45] Commercial pressures lead companies to influence or even corrupt the evidence base for reimbursement and clinical decisions, and compound the choices of prescribers.[46,47] The number of major new products that have come to the market in recent decades is relatively small,[48] but new products generally show marginal improvements in effectiveness, often at high cost.[26] The industry spends more time and resources on generation and dissemination of medical information than it does on production of medicines, and such information can greatly influence clinical practice.[49] Although the industry has perfectly legitimate commercial imperatives, these may not always be in the best interests of patients and society. In contrast to the over-prescribing of new medicines, older, off-patent therapies may be under-utilised because of insufficient incentives for efficient prescribing.

Regulating industry

Efforts to influence the behaviour of patients and health professionals are focused largely on the volume of drugs prescribed. Controls on the pharmaceutical industry itself focus mostly on price, and more recently on cost-effectiveness.

In the USA, the fragmented health care system means there is no direct price control. Individual insurers and managed care organisations may negotiate discounts and rebates from pharmaceutical manufacturers, but in general pricing of prescribed drugs is left to market forces. This contrasts notably with publicly funded systems, most of which regulate prices, directly or indirectly. All EU countries have a form of direct or indirect price regulation. Denmark, Greece, Finland, Ireland, Italy, the Netherlands, Portugal, and Sweden set a maximum price by comparing prices in neighbouring countries. In Belgium, France, and Italy prices are set in relation to relative cost, prices elsewhere in the EU, and the contribution made to the national economy. In some countries (for example, Austria, France, and Spain) there are volume–cost and other rebate schemes. Spain and the UK set their prices to ensure a rate of return within a particular profit range.[18]

Use of reference price systems, where the average price within a therapeutic category is reimbursed, is increasing. These may reduce price variation across markets, but they may also prevent prices of older drugs from falling, as all therapeutic prices are driven to similar levels. In countries such as Germany, Australia, the Netherlands, New Zealand, Sweden, Denmark, and Norway, a decade of reference pricing has achieved only short-term savings.[50] Further details on pricing pharmaceuticals are discussed in Chapter 13.

Price control schemes that are not coupled with control of volume are incomplete. Physicians control prescribing volume, and attempts to limit their discretion have proved ineffective. Whatever the rigour of price control, its effects may be dissipated by volume inflation determined by doctors and influenced by industry marketing.

Throughout the EU and elsewhere, there is increasing interest in complementing pharmaceutical licensing procedures with a "fourth hurdle" of demonstrable cost-effectiveness. This was pioneered by the Australian Pharmaceutical Benefits Scheme,[51] and similar systems introduced first in Ontario[52] and later throughout Canada.[53] Since 1999, NICE[32] has issued guidance to the NHS in England. Economic data are now used to inform reimbursement and pricing decisions in a number of EU states, and this has been proposed in other countries (see Chapter 5).

Incentives and pharmaceutical expenditure

The importance of incentives is evident in this substantial and profitable market. National policy concerns often include both health objectives (cost containment, efficiency, equity) and industrial objectives (hosting an industry that contributes to investment, employment, exports, and economic growth). This potential conflict in macro-level incentives is reflected at all levels of the market. If cost containment concerns predominate, then policies are likely to discourage patients from consuming reimbursed pharmaceuticals (for example, by using co-payments) and discourage doctors from prescribing (for example, by cost feedback schemes). If efficiency concerns predominate, then policies may aim to discourage patients from consuming inefficient products (for example, by reference pricing, with a premium paid by a patient who chooses a branded drug when an equivalent generic exists) and to encourage efficient prescriber behaviour (for example, by providing a limited list of cost-effective products, or by using cost-effectiveness based guidelines). All these efforts are of uncertain effect because they are constantly undermined by private sector advertising to patients, directly or indirectly through "awareness raising", and to prescribing doctors, directly and through "conference tourism".[49]

Regulation of the pharmaceutical market in place within national health care systems clearly reflects (or perhaps is reflected by?) the size, importance, and lobbying power of the industry. In the USA there is an integrated system of research (through the National Institutes of Health), but the demand side of the market for pharmaceuticals is highly fragmented. There is no direct fixing of pharmaceutical prices, and no one purchaser is large enough to have any significant monopsony purchasing power. Currently, the federal Medicare scheme, by excluding reimbursement of prescribed drugs, makes individual patients the relevant purchasers. In recent reform proposals it is planned to include pharmaceuticals in the benefit package, but the Bush administration has proposed a fragmented system of purchasing organisations, to maintain "competition" on the demand side of the market. Policies to integrate purchasing of pharmaceuticals under Medicare have met with substantial, often industry influenced, objection. The highly imbalanced structure of market power has meant that US pharmaceutical companies, operating primarily in their own large marketplace, dominate the global pharmaceutical industry.

Outside the USA, regulatory structures also reflect industrial policies as well as health objectives. In Japan, doctors are paid a fee for each prescription, resulting in cost inflation and substantial pharmaceutical budget. It also has a strong and profitable home industry, and attracts investment from multinational pharmaceutical companies. In France, prices are directly controlled (favouring companies based in France) but the volume of prescribing is very high, maintaining high levels of expenditure. The UK Pharmaceutical Price Regulation Scheme regulates profits, leaving companies free to set prices, provided their rate of return on historical capital is between 17% and 21%.[54] This scheme favours domestic companies with a large capital base in the UK, offers little incentive for companies to be efficient, and produces confusion of goals in government. In theory, if policies such as those proposed by NICE then constrain pharmaceutical expenditure and limit company profits, then they can raise prices to return profits to an acceptable level.

A European Commission report *Global competitiveness in pharmaceuticals* raised concerns that the European pharmaceutical industry is "lagging behind" the USA.[55] Recently, the Commission has published a number of recommendations aimed at restoring the "competitiveness" of the European pharmaceutical industry.[56] Apparently, the Commission, like the industry itself, defines "competitiveness" as success (in this case, making large profits), confusing process with outcome. It could be thought that the Commission wished to regulate the market for the benefit of company profits rather than population health. It is ironic that attempts to increase "competition" and "competitiveness" appear to involve allowing companies a monopoly position while ensuring that purchasers are fragmented and have little purchasing power. These EU level recommendations mirror the Medicare debate in the USA, where purchasers are likely to be fragmented, and purchasing power is being minimised in the name of "competition". Among other suggestions, the Commission proposes that member states should allow companies more freedom in setting prices, allowing a single EU price. This risks directly undermining the success that some countries have had in controlling drug prices and profits – "while drug prices in the USA have been rising steadily over the past several years, price increases have been kept down and several European governments have actually been initiating price cuts".[56] Countries such as the Baltic States, which have cooperated in implementing pharmaceutical policies in the interest of the health of their population, could have their policies undermined or even prohibited when they join the EU, by the so-called "competition" policy that operates in the interests of industry.

Conclusions

A number of lessons can be learnt from international experience of regulating pharmaceutical expenditure, in terms of achieving the policy objectives of cost containment, efficiency, and equity, but all involve trade-offs – there is no "best" regulatory system. Influencing patient behaviour by user charges and co-payments contributes to cost containment, but unless user charges are related to the cost-effectiveness of products they are potentially inefficient, and they contravene equity goals by taxing people who are poor and sick. DTC advertising, if permitted by the EU, is likely to result in marketing of new and expensive products to individual patients, which could undermine cost containment and efficiency goals.

In terms of influencing doctor behaviour it is necessary to provide not just information and feedback on prescribing, but also more active incentives to prescribe efficiently, fairly, and with an awareness of costs. Budget holding schemes have had some limited impact,[41] and guidelines, if they are based on evidence of cost-effectiveness and are actively implemented, may also be worthwhile.[57,58] However, providing good information to prescribing doctors about cost-effective products is an uphill struggle when faced with the pervasive marketing efforts of the pharmaceutical industry. The relationship between doctors and drug companies has recently been described as the two groups being "entwined in an embrace of avarice and excess, an embrace that distorts medical information and patient care".[59] Redefining and disentangling relationships between doctors and the pharmaceutical industry[60,61] is a necessary challenge if prescribing efficiency and equity is to be improved.

Finally, to achieve health policy goals it is essential to regulate the pharmaceutical industry, in terms of both price and volume of products. Rationing health care is inevitable and should be undertaken explicitly, on the basis of prioritising the most cost-effective products and targeting them at those who benefit the most, without the pretence that simply spending more money is any kind of solution to scarcity in health care budgets.

There is a clear trade-off between health creation and wealth creation in the pharmaceutical industry, which should also be explicitly addressed. In countries with a strong industry there is evidence of "capture" of the regulatory system[62] so that it operates in the interest of industry rather than patients. This regulatory capture is evident in the USA, where purchasers are fragmented and their power limited, and in the EU, where recent policies to allow DTC advertising and permit companies to set prices suggest that wealth creation is of higher priority than health creation. To maintain a real competitive industry, where markets pressure companies to improve efficiency, it is necessary to balance the monopoly market power of the multinational companies with, where possible, strong purchasers of health technologies with clear health objectives of promoting cost-effective pharmaceutical use, and hence promoting population health. Without explicitness about the goals of trade and health policies, pharmaceutical expenditure is likely to continue to inflate in ways that enhance profits and wealth but not the efficient improvement in population health.

Acknowledgement

The authors would like to thank Anne Burton for valuable administrative assistance.

Summary

- All health care systems face the same policy objectives relating to pharmaceuticals: expenditure control, efficient use of products, and equitable access to them.
- To achieve their objectives, policy makers regulate to varying degrees the three main groups of decision makers within the pharmaceutical market: patients, doctors, and the manufacturing industry.
- There is a clear trade-off between health creation and wealth creation in the pharmaceutical industry, which should be explicitly addressed.
- To maintain a competitive industry it is necessary to balance the market power of the multinational companies with strong purchasers of health technologies who have clear health objectives of promoting cost-effective pharmaceutical use, and hence promoting improvements in population health.
- Without explicitness about the goals of trade and health policies, pharmaceutical expenditure is likely to continue to inflate in ways that enhance profits and wealth but not the efficient improvement in population health.

References

1 Editorial. Global 500 by sector. *Financial Times*, 23 March 2003.
2 Bosely S, Pratley N. In the time it takes you to read this article Pfizer will make $250,000. So does it have a duty to provide cheap drugs to the poor? *The Guardian*, 24 April 2003.
3 Organisation for Economic Co-operation and Development. Health data 2002. Paris: OECD, 2002.
4 Anonymous. Senators firm up on Medicare drug benefit. *New York Times*, 1 August 2003.
5 Freemantle N, Bloor K. Lessons from international experience in controlling pharmaceutical expenditure I: influencing patients. *BMJ* 1996;**312**:1469–71.
6 Newhouse JP. *Free for all? Lessons from the RAND Health Insurance Experiment*. Cambridge, MA: Harvard University Press, 1993.
7 Soumerai S, Avorn J, Ross-Degnan D, Gortmaker S. Payment restrictions for prescription drugs under Medicaid. *N Engl J Med* 1987;**317**:550–6.
8 Soumerai S, Avorn J, Ross-Degnan D, *et al*. Effects of Medicaid drug-payment limits on admission to hospitals and nursing homes. *N Engl J Med* 1991;**325**:1072–7.

9 Soumerai S, McLaughlin TJ, Ross-Degnan D, Bollini P. Effects of limiting Medicaid drug reimbursement benefits on the use of psychotropic agents and acute mental health services by patients with schizophrenia. *N Engl J Med* 1994;**331**:650–5.

10 Pérez-Peña R. 22 states limiting doctors' latitude in Medicaid drugs. *New York Times*, 16 June 2003.

11 Greenhouse L. The Supreme Court: the ruling; justices allow drug-cost plan to go forward. *New York Times*, 20 May 2003.

12 Pear R. Drug companies increase spending on efforts to lobby congress and governments. *New York Times*, 1 June 2003.

13 Greider K. *The big fix: how the pharmaceutical industry rips off American consumers*. New York: Public Affairs, 2003.

14 Danzon PM, Chao LW. Cross-national price differences for pharmaceuticals: how large, and why? *J Health Econ* 2000;**19**:159–95.

15 Wolfe SM. Direct to consumer advertising: education or emotion promotion? *N Engl J Med* 2002;**346**:524–6.

16 Holmer AF. Direct to consumer advertising: strengthening our health care system. *N Engl J Med* 2002;**346**:526–8.

17 Woloshin S, Schwartz LM, Tremmel J, Gilbert Welch HG. Direct-to-consumer advertisements for prescription drugs: what are Americans being sold? *Lancet* 2001;**358**:1141–6.

18 Maynard A, Bloor K. Dilemmas in regulation of the market for pharmaceuticals. *Health Affairs* 2003;**22**:31–41.

19 Stoddart G, Barer M, Evans RE. *User charges, snares and delusions: another look at the literature*. Ontario: Premier's Council on Health and Well Being and Social Justice, 1994.

20 Office of Fair Trading. *Price fixing of medicaments ends: press release*. London: Office of Fair Trading, 2001.

21 Anonymous. Europe on the brink of direct-to-consumer advertising [editorial]. *Lancet* 2002;**359**:1709.

22 Wilson RA. *Feminine forever*. London: WH Allen, 1966.

23 Clark J. A hot flush for big pharma. *BMJ* 2003;**327**:400.

24 Herrington DM, Howard TD. From presumed benefit to potential harm: hormone therapy and heart disease. *N Engl J Med* 2003;**349**:519–21.

25 Million Women Study Collaborators. Breast cancer and hormone-replacement therapy in the Million Women Study. *Lancet* 2003;**362**:419–27.

26 Garattini S, Bertele V. Efficacy, safety, and cost of new anticancer drugs. *BMJ* 2002;**325**:269–71.

27 Robinson JC. Blended payment methods in physician organizations under managed care. *JAMA* 1999;**282**:1258–63.

28 Robinson JC. Theory and practice in the design of physician payment incentives. *Milbank Q* 2001;**79**:149–77.

29 Prescription Pricing Authority. *Annual report 2001–2002*. Newcastle-upon-Tyne: PPA, 2002.

30 Dixon J. France seeks to curb health costs by fining doctors: heavy handed and expensive [editorial]. *BMJ* 1997;**315**:895–6.

31 Department of Health. *Faster access to modern treatment: how NICE appraisal will work*. London: Department of Health, 1999.

32 National Institute for Clinical Excellence (NICE). http://www.nice.org.uk/ (accessed 29 January 2004).

33 Department of Health. National service frameworks. http://www.doh.gov.uk/nsf/index.htm (accessed 29 January 2004).

34 Mayor S. NICE estimates that its recommendations have cost the NHS £575m. *BMJ* 2002;**325**:924.

35 Cookson RF, McDaid D, Maynard A. Wrong SIGN, NICE mess: is national guidance distorting allocation of resources? *BMJ* 2001;**323**:743–5.

36 Bloor K, Freemantle N, Khadjesari ZCS, Maynard AK. Impact of NICE guidance on laparoscopic surgery for inguinal hernia: interrupted time series. *BMJ* 2003;**326**:578.

37 Department of Health. *Statistical bulletin: prescriptions dispensed in the community, statistics for 1992 to 2002, England.* London: Department of Health, 2003.

38 Kaufman DW, Kelly FP, Rosenberg L, *et al.* Recent patterns of medication use in the ambulatory adult population of the United States. *JAMA* 2002;**287**:337–44.

39 Bradlow J, Coulter A. Effect of fundholding and indicative prescribing schemes on general practitioners' prescribing costs. *BMJ* 1993;**307**:1186–9.

40 Walley T, Murphy M, Codd M, *et al.* Effects of monetary incentives on primary care prescribing in Ireland: changes in the prescribing patterns of one health board 1990–1995. *Pharmacoepidemiol Drug Saf* 2000;**9**:591–8.

41 Dusheiko M, Gravelle H, Jacobs R, Smith PC. *The effect of budgets on doctor behaviour: evidence from a natural experiment. Department of Economics discussion paper 03/04.* York: University of York, 2003.

42 Stewart-Brown S, Surender R, Bradlow J, *et al.* The effects of fundholding in general practice on prescribing habits three years after the introduction of the scheme. *BMJ* 1995;**311**:1543–7.

43 Schulenberg M. The German health care system at the crossroads. *Health Econ* 1994;**3**:301–4.

44 Editorial. Price levels still good in Germany. *Scrip* 1994;**3**.

45 Petersen M. Heartfelt advice, hefty fees. *New York Times*, 11 August 2002.

46 Freemantle N, Maynard A. Something rotten in the state of clinical and economic evaluations? *Health Econ* 1994;**3**:63–7.

47 Morgan S, Barer M, Evans R. Health economists meet the fourth tempter: drug dependency and scientific discourse. *Health Econ* 2000;**9**:659–67.

48 National Institute for Health Care Management Research and Educational Foundation. Changing patterns of pharmaceutical innovation. Washington, DC: National Institute for Health Care Management Research and Educational Foundation, 2002. http://www.nihcm.org/innovations.pdf (accessed 29 January 2004).

49 Chren MM, Landefeld CS. Physicians' behaviour and their interactions with drug companies. *JAMA* 1994;**271**:684–9.

50 Kanavos P, Reinhardt U. Reference pricing for drugs: is it compatible with US health care. *Health Affairs* 2003;**22**:16–30.

51 Australian Pharmaceutical Benefits Scheme (PBS). http://www.health.gov. au/pbs/ (accessed 29 January 2004).

52 Ontario Ministry of Health. *Ontario guidelines for economic analysis of pharmaceutical products.* Toronto: Drug Programs Branch, 1994.

53 Canadian Coordinating Office for Health Technology Assessment (CCOHTA). http://www.ccohta.ca (accessed 29 January 2004).

54 Department of Health. *The pharmaceutical price regulation scheme.* London: Department of Health, 1999.

55 Gambardella A, Orsenigo L, Fammolli F. *Global competitiveness in pharmaceuticals: a European perspective. Enterprise Papers No 1.* Brussels: European Commission, 2001.

56 Anonymous. What price competitiveness in the drugs industry? [editorial]. *Lancet* 2003;**362**:257.

57 Freemantle N, Nazareth I, Eccles M, *et al.* A randomised controlled trial of the effect of educational outreach by community pharmacists on prescribing in UK general practice. *Br J Gen Pract* 2002;**52**:290–5.

58 Mason JM, Freemantle N, Nazareth I, *et al.* When is it cost-effective to change the behaviour of health professionals? *JAMA* 2001;**286**:2988–92.
59 Abassi K, Smith R. No more free lunches. *BMJ* 2003;**326**:1155–6.
60 Moynihan R. Who pays for the pizza? Redefining the relationships between doctors and drug companies 1: entanglement. *BMJ* 2003;**326**:1189–92.
61 Moynihan R. Who pays for the pizza? Redefining the relationships between doctors and drug companies 2: disentanglement. *BMJ* 2003;**326**:1193–6.
62 Stigler G. The theory of economic regulation. *Bell J Econ Man Sci* 1971;**2**:3–21.

5: Development of fourth hurdle policies around the world

ROD S TAYLOR, MIKE F DRUMMOND, GLEN SALKELD, SEAN D SULLIVAN

Introduction

This chapter discusses the issue of "the fourth hurdle", providing an historical overview of the development of the fourth hurdle up to the present day; an analysis of the impact of the fourth hurdle policies on health care systems and the pharmaceutical industry; and finally an examination of the key challenges and potential future directions for the fourth hurdle.

Emergence of the fourth hurdle

The Australian health care system was the first to develop formal regulations governing the use of cost-effectiveness evidence in reimbursement decisions. Since 1993, the Australian Pharmaceutical Benefits Scheme (PBS) will not authorise the public funding of a new drug unless appropriate economic evidence is provided. The first step toward reimbursement of a drug is the application by a drug manufacturer to the PBS (the "sponsor"). Submissions are required to follow specific guidelines that have been developed in consultation with international experts in pharmaceutical evaluation and the pharmaceutical industry.[1] Submissions include reports describing key trials that establish the effectiveness of the drug, and economic analyses that bring together estimates of the probable benefits of the introduction of a drug with the costs involved.

Once it is received by the PBS, a submission is appraised in an explicit process that deconstructs the evidence provided by the manufacturer. A detailed and systematic appraisal is conducted by the secretariat that supports the PBS Advisory Committee. Where the submission contains good evidence that a drug provides benefits similar to those of an existing available drug, and the manufacturer is requesting a lower price (cost minimisation analyses), the submission is passed directly to the Committee. However, where the analyses are flawed or where they suggest additional benefits at added costs, the technical aspects of the submission are considered by the Economics Subcommittee. After consideration by the Economics Subcommittee the submission proceeds to the main PBS Advisory Committee, along with a summary of technical quality. The Advisory Committee considers the evidence on cost-effectiveness as one of a number of potentially important factors when advising the Health Minister on whether to list the drug for reimbursement. These include the importance of the clinical area, the availability of alternative therapies, the probable impact of listing on the health care system and on other therapeutic activities, and the investment of the sponsor in primary research. This may lead to acceptance of a higher price for a "breakthrough" product, in which the sponsor has invested substantially in relevant primary research, than the price given to subsequent "me-too" drugs, where these are listed on the basis of an equivalent "group" effect. However, relative cost-effectiveness is considered the most important criterion.

In September 1994, the Canadian province of Ontario followed the Australian lead in issuing guidelines for the economic evaluation of drugs, and since September 1995 submissions for listing of new drugs on the Ontario provincial formulary have been deemed to be incomplete if they do not contain an economic analysis or provide justification for its absence. In November 1994, the Canadian Coordinating Office for Health Technology Assessment (CCOHTA) issued economic guidelines that were proposed to provide a common framework for adoption across all Canadian provinces.[2] Despite the CCOHTA guidelines and unlike the Australian national system, the restriction of new drugs on the basis of cost-effectiveness remained solely a requirement of the province of Ontario.

Industry, academics, and governments alike have watched these early "roots" of fourth hurdle policies develop in Australia and Ontario with an interest that extends far beyond their local importance to those markets.[3,4] Nevertheless, we were to wait almost a decade to see these roots of fourth hurdle development take hold across the world.

Global development

Somewhat belatedly, a number of countries are now following the example of Australia and Ontario. Since 1997, many countries, particularly in Europe, have begun to introduce the use of economic evidence in selected national reimbursement decisions. These recent fourth hurdle developments are outlined in further detail below.

However, let us first consider the reasons for the recent proliferation of fourth hurdle systems. Increasingly, health care payers view economic evaluation as a key device in containing costs, particularly with respect to new drugs.[5] New drugs have driven costs up in three main ways. First, the unit cost of new drugs has been startlingly higher than those of the drugs they replace. Selective serotonin reuptake inhibitors, for example, cost six times as much as the older tricyclic antidepressants;[6] taxanes are several thousand pounds per patient more expensive than previous anticancer drugs;[7,8] and two drugs for severe rheumatoid arthritis (i.e. etanercept and infliximab) can cost nearly £10,000 per patient for every year that they are treated.[9] However, although decision makers may regard cost-effectiveness considerations as a cost containing device, it is important to appreciate that economists would argue that their goal is efficiency. Second, drugs are being developed for many conditions for which therapies were not previously available. Such "novel" therapies, range from what might be regarded as "lifestyle drugs", such as sildenafil (Viagra) for the treatment of erectile dysfunction and bupropion for smoking cessation, through to growing number of high cost "designer" drugs that are often produced by the biotechnology industry to treat uncommon ("orphan") diseases. Third, the introduction of a drug can result in demand for the use of other expensive technologies.[10] For example, the effective use of the antiflu drug zanamivir may be aided by the use of a near patient diagnostic test to confirm flu-like illness. Moreover, drug delivery may depend explicitly on other medical technologies, such as insulin pumps for diabetic persons, intrathecal morphine pumps that are used in the treatment of chronic back pain, and, more recently, drug eluting coronary artery stents that are coated with anticoagulant glycoproteins.[11]

Europe

Probably the single most significant fourth hurdle development in Europe has been the establishment in UK of the National Institute for Clinical Excellence (NICE), although its remit spans consideration of clinical effectiveness and service impact, and not cost-effectiveness alone. Although established in April 1999, the arrival of NICE was announced to the world by its first decision not to recommend the antiflu drug zanamivir on the grounds of insufficient evidence of clinical impact and cost-effectiveness to date. In its first few years NICE has attracted much attention and criticism, and it has even been seen as a potential model for a pan-European fourth hurdle agency.[12–15] Although NICE has cost-effectiveness as its central goal, as does its Australian counterpart, there are number of notable differences between the two models (Tables 5.1 and 5.2).

The UK is not the only European country to take an interest in the use of economic evaluation to assist in decisions about the value for money from the use of pharmaceuticals. Guidelines for the conduct and reporting of pharmacoeconomic studies exist in most Western European countries, although there are various degrees of official recognition. These were reviewed by Hjelmgren *et al.*,[16] who found a reasonable level of agreement among the requirements of the various guidelines, especially the official ones.

A smaller number of countries have introduced a formal requirement for the consideration of economic evidence as part of the pricing or reimbursement decision. These include Belgium, Finland, Norway, Portugal, and Sweden. Another country, the Netherlands, has indicated its intention to introduce a formal requirement but has postponed this until 2005. Just recently Hungary became one of the first Eastern European countries to introduce a formal requirement for economic evidence.[17]

Table 5.1 Requirements of fourth hurdle: comparison of PBS and NICE

Requirement	Details
1: Statement of information needs of decision maker	This is usually achieved by promulgation of guidelines (see Table 5.2).
2: Submission of evidence dossier	The submission of economic evidence can be either initiated by the drug company (or companies) themselves (such as in the Australian PBS system) or it can be initiated by the decision making body (such as NICE). An advantage of the former is that it puts both the responsibility for the timing of assessment and onus of proof on the sponsor
3: Critical assessment of dossier	Technical assessment of the validity, relevance, strength, and interpretation of the sponsor's economic submission is a critical requirement. Such an assessment can take various forms, such as the two-stage process in Australia, which involves both a university based evaluation team plus a technical (economic) subcommittee; in the UK, the assessment and critique of the sponsor's submission is undertaken by an academic team alone
4: Appraisal or decision making	Following assessment of the economic evidence, a policy decision must be formulated regarding whether to fund (or not) the drug. Such decision making is often achieved by a formally convened independent standing committee with clinical and patient (and occasionally industry) stakeholder representation, such as PBAC in Australia or the NICE Appraisal Committee in the UK
5: Issuance of guidance policy	The funding decision must be communicated to the clinical community. Such policy decisions can range from either mandatory, as is the case in Australia, to "advisory", as are the decisions of NICE to the NHS in England and Wales

NICE, National Institute for Clinical Excellence; PBAC, Pharmaceuticals Benefits Advisory Committee; PBS, Pharmaceutical Benefits Scheme. Modified from Mitchell[28] and Taylor et al.[45]

Table 5.2 Comparison the key methodological issues in national guidelines

	Australia (PBS)	Canada (CCOHTA, 1997)	England and Wales (NICE, 2001)
Perspective of analysis	Societal	Societal	NHS and personal social services
Comparator	Most frequently used alternative	Existing best practice and minimum practice	Most frequently used alternative
Source of medical evidence	Effectiveness rather than efficacy	Effectiveness rather than efficacy	Any source, but must be justified
Analytical techniques	CEA and CUA encouraged; CBA discouraged	CUA or CEA preferred, but CBA acceptable	CEA or CUA only
Outcomes	Intermediate or long term	–	Preferably long-term clinical effectiveness
Discounting	5% on costs and outcomes	5% on costs and outcomes	6% on costs and 1·5% on outcomes
Equity	Not addressed	No equity weights should be used but results should reflect equity issues	Provide information on clinical and social status of patients most likely to benefit

CBA, cost-benefit analysis; CCOHTA, Canadian Coordinating Office for Health Technology Assessment; CEA, cost-effectiveness analysis; CUA, cost-utility analysis; NICE, National Institute for Clinical Excellence; PBS, Pharmaceutical Benefits Scheme.
Adapted from McDaid et al.[38] and Taylor et al.[45]

In several other countries, including Denmark, France, and Italy, the submission of economic evidence (by companies) is voluntary, but it is considered as and when it is submitted. However, it is difficult to assess what role this evidence plays under these circumstances.

Finally, two of the larger European countries, Germany and Spain, do not as yet have any arrangements at the central level for considering economic evidence for pharmaceuticals. However, Germany is establishing an institute that may have an evaluating function, and there is some activity in health technology assessment at the regional level in Spain.

Much less has been written about experience with the use of economic evidence in other European countries as compared with the UK. However, it is possible to identify several common issues. First, whereas in some countries evidence is required for all new drugs (as in Australia), in others only certain products are evaluated. In the Netherlands the plan is to request economic evidence only for drugs that are not covered by the reference price system. In Portugal, the national drug evaluation agency determines when an economic assessment is required.[18] As with NICE in the UK, this begs the question as to how the priorities for assessment are set. Second, in most European countries drugs are assessed individually; this is in contrast to NICE, which often assesses groups of similar drugs. Individual assessments lessen the problem of making indirect comparisons of efficacy, in situations where head to head clinical studies do not exist. However, individual assessments may mean that, on occasions, relevant clinical and health policy choices will not be explored. Third, there exist different approaches to evaluating the economic evidence submitted. In some countries the agency evaluates the evidence in-house. In others a committee of appointed academics conducts the evaluation. Only rarely is an independent assessment report commissioned (the normal procedure for NICE). One explanation for differences in the approach may be constraints on the availability of trained health service researchers, including health economists. This has been identified as a problem in some of the smaller countries.[17]

USA

Like in Europe, the emergence of economic evaluation in drug listing decisions in the USA is very recent. In 1998

Regence BlueShield, a health maintenance organisation in Seattle, Washington with 1·1 million members, began requesting clinical and economic evidence from pharmaceutical and biopharmaceutical manufacturers as a condition for formulary review.[19] In 2000 the Academy of Managed Care Pharmacy (AMCP), a national professional society of managed care purchasers, developed its own version of the guidelines – the AMCP Format for Formulary Submission.[20,21]

The AMCP Format represents a shift for managed care purchasers who are accustomed to being passive recipients of information and promotional materials submitted by drug companies to support formulary adoption decisions. The AMCP Format specifies that purchasers formally request data from pharmaceutical manufacturers in a standardised dossier. In response to this unprompted request from a purchaser, the manufacturer could provide individualised and detailed information on efficacy, safety, and economic impact beyond what it historically provided. The AMCP Format prescribes the layout for the submission, recommending that companies include unpublished data, off-label information, and economic models that support cost-effectiveness or budget impact promotional statements. The Food and Drug Administration's remit in this process is to ensure that the request for information is strictly unsolicited and that the information provided through the product dossiers is not false or misleading.

Although the exact figure is not known, over 50 private and public sector health care purchaser organisations, covering well over 120 million lives, have adopted the AMCP Format or a similar process. Awareness of the AMCP Format among pharmaceutical purchasers is high, although small studies suggest broad variation in the adherence of plans to guideline recommendations, as well as poor quality in submitted information.[22,23]

The rest of the world

Little has been written about experience with the use economic evaluation outside Australia, Europe, and North America. For example, despite it having the second largest health care economy in the world, in Japan little economic evaluation appears to be undertaken, and there is currently no system for limiting market entry of drugs based on their cost-effectiveness.[24] The situation in the so-called emerging economies (such as the former East/Eastern block communist countries, South America, and many parts of Asia) is immensely variable.[17,25,26]

Unlike the industrialised and emerging economies, the priority for low income developing economies is one of drug affordability, particularly for treatment of common diseases, rather than the fourth hurdle goal of value for money for new and more expensive innovative drugs. A key development was the introduction in 1977 of the World Health Organization Essential Medicines List, which seeks to make available a basket of necessary drugs to developing countries at affordable prices.[27]

Summary

From this global overview it appears that, after a slow start, many countries now have some form of fourth hurdle system that reflects the local health economy. Mitchell[28] has proposed a three-tier framework for the organisation of fourth hurdle systems (see Table 5.1). This framework not only allows us to characterise current fourth hurdle agencies systems but also provides a basis template for those countries developing fourth hurdle systems in the future.

Impact of the fourth hurdle

Although achieving the criteria of "value for money" or cost-effectiveness for new drugs may be intuitively appealing, little has been published on the impact of national fourth hurdle systems.[29] It could be argued that an analysis of the impact of fourth hurdle systems should consider effects both on the health care system and on the pharmaceutical industry, but what do we mean by "impact" and how should it be assessed? The ultimate goal of economic evaluation is to maximise health for a given health care budget, but this is very difficult to assess in practice. Instead, we examine the impact of the fourth hurdle according to three outcomes: impact on the quality of economic evidence produced by the pharmaceutical industry; impact on evidence on access to more cost-effective drugs; and impact on drug costs. Given that most of the experience is from Australia, much of the evidence on impact is drawn from that setting.

Quality of pharmacoeconomic evidence

The problem of quality and related biases of pharmacoeconomic studies has long been recognised. Friedberg *et al.*[30] found that studies funded by the pharmaceutical industry were one-eighth as likely to reach unfavourable qualitative conclusions and 1·4 times more likely to reach favourable quantitative conclusions as were non-profit funded studies. The industry related bias in economic evaluation reports has been confirmed in a number of subsequent publications.[31,32] It has been argued that any biases in the outcomes of commercially sponsored economic analyses is inevitable and due to the fact that published economic analyses concentrate on those drugs that remain following the weeding out process of development. This does not, however, explain why a higher proportion of non-profit sponsored cost-effectiveness analyses of drugs already on the market are negative; neither does it account for why head to head economic analyses funded by commercial agencies demonstrate a consistent favourable bias in comparison with those funded by non-profit agencies.

Is the quality of pharmaceutical industry economic submissions to fourth hurdle agencies any better than that of published studies? Hill and colleagues[33] examined all 326 submissions made to the Australian PBS between 1994 and 1997. Of these submissions, 216 (67%) were considered to present serious problems with interpretation. Sometimes no randomised controlled trials were available, or the randomised controlled trials were of poor quality or low power; the analysis was defective or made ill-justified claims; assumptions were unsubstantiated; and calculations of costs and outcomes were not transparent. The drug benefit plan committees in British Columbia and Ontario have confirmed this Australian experience. Anis *et al.*[34] reported that, out of the 32 pharmacoeconomic study submissions made to the two committees in 1996, recommendations were only possible for 21, the remainder being rejected because they contained incomplete or pending information. Of 21 submissions used to make drug plan recommendations, 16 were described as "non-compliant" with Canadian (CCOHTA or Ontario) guidelines for pharmacoeconomic evaluation.

That these Canadian and Australian experiences paint such a gloomy picture of the quality of pharmacoeconomic analyses emphasises that an independent technical assessment of industry submissions is a central requirement of any fourth hurdle system (see Table 5.1). We were unable to find more publications of more recent experience of fourth hurdle agencies regarding the quality of pharmacoeconomic studies to assess whether quality has improved in more recent years; anecdotal commentaries suggests not! Indeed, rather than focusing on quality and transparency, industry economic submissions are increasingly being supported by highly complex decision analytic models to support the acceptable clinical and cost-effectiveness of their drugs.

Access to more cost-effective drugs?

A central premise of the fourth hurdle approach is that those drugs that are deemed to achieve "acceptable" cost-effectiveness are recommended while those that fail to meet to acceptable levels of cost-effectiveness are rejected. What might constitute "acceptable" cost-effectiveness is beyond the scope of this chapter and is discussed elsewhere.[35] Here we focus on the evidence as to whether the existence of a fourth hurdle agency will increase the likelihood that cost-effective drugs will enter the market and prevent access to drugs with unattractive cost-effectiveness. This issue has been examined both in Australia and in the UK (NICE).

George et al.[36] examined 355 submissions to the Australian PBS system between 1991 and 1996, and they identified 26 that used cost per life year gained (LYG) and nine that used cost per quality-adjusted life year (QALY). Raftery[37] conducted a similar exercise based on the decisions of the NICE Appraisal Committee up to March 2001. From these two studies it is possible to compare the cost per LYG or QALY of drugs that have been recommended for funding with such costs for those drugs that have been rejected. In both the PBS and NICE case series of decisions, there appears to a cost per LYG or QALY threshold above which drugs were regarded as "good value for money". This threshold was $AU76,000 per LYG and $AU42,000 per QALY, and £30,000 per LYG or QALY. Although broadly supportive of the objective of efficiency, both case series demonstrate that decision makers do not appear to operate against a fixed willingness to pay threshold. Possible explanations for these apparent inconsistencies include the overall budget impact of the drug (i.e. the overall cost of introducing a drug to the health system), "rule of rescue" (i.e. funding a drug for serious clinical indication on the grounds that there are is a lack or inadequacy of alternative therapies), and decisions around so-called lifestyle drugs such as sildenafil (Viagra).

A related consequence of the impact of the fourth hurdle is that of defining (more carefully) the indications for which a drug should be used. For example, few of NICE's decisions have recommended that a particular drug (or group of drugs) should not be funded by the NHS, but rather that the NHS should limit the indications in which that drug should be used.[37]

Reduced drug costs?

Drugs listed in the Australian PBS have consistently been priced below the world average. The Bureau of Industry Economics estimated that, in 1991, the prices of drugs in Australia were 30% below the EU average and about 50% below the world average.[39] Today, Australia has had more than a decade of subjecting drugs to the fourth hurdle cost-effectiveness requirements. By 2001–2002, 42% of a total of 644 entities listed on the PBS had been subjected to the cost-effectiveness requirements. A key question is whether the drug price differentials observed in 1991 between Australia and the rest of the world has widened or narrowed as a result of the fourth hurdle requirement.

In 2000, the Australian Government commissioned the Productivity Commission to undertake a research study examining the differences between the prices of pharmaceutical benefit items in Australia (those listed on the PBS) and the prices of the same items in comparable overseas countries, and to identify as far as possible the reasons for any differences.[40] Australian prices were compared with those in countries with similar and dissimilar subsidy arrangements. The seven comparison countries included in this study are the USA,

Canada, the UK, France, Spain, Sweden, and New Zealand. The review was based on the PBS listed price of 150 drug entities, representing 80% of government expenditure on PBS listed pharmaceuticals. Prices were compared for new and innovative, "me-too", and generic pharmaceuticals.

For the purposes of the international comparison, a weighted average price was calculated. This ensured that the results were not distorted by the inclusion of forms that have a large price differential but a small market share. Australian sales volumes were used to weight manufacturer prices. The price comparisons are reported using a ratio of prices between Australia and each comparison country. An average exchange rate for June 2000 was used for the price comparison. No attempt was made to adjust price by gross domestic product, and hence the study cannot be used to draw inferences about price levels across the comparison countries. Full details of the methodology are available in the Productivity Commission report.[39]

The results are shown in Figures 5.1–5.3. Overall, the greatest price differentials between Australia and other countries are for me-too and generic drugs. Price differentials are smaller for innovative drugs, with the exception of the USA (where prices are 104% higher). This is at least consistent with the objective of the fourth hurdle cost-effectiveness requirements, where price is set in relation to the value of the additional benefit of the drug. Clinically superior drugs are rewarded with a higher price.

The Productivity Commission report[39] concludes that, "in very broad terms, it is difficult to find any obvious associations between the observed price differences and the types of subsidy and cost-containment policies adopted in the comparison countries." It is hard to disagree with that conclusion, particularly where prices in Sweden and France were also higher than in Australia, even though they have similar subsidy arrangements. Other factors must come into play.

The most obvious factor is that the Australian government is a monopolist purchaser of pharmaceuticals. This has allowed the government to negotiate lower prices consistently over a long period of time. Also, the use of reference pricing, namely setting a maximum reimbursement price for a group of therapeutically equivalent pharmaceuticals based on the price of the cheapest product in the group, will keep prices

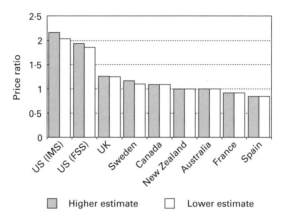

Figure 5.1   Results for new, innovative pharmaceuticals. Because the bilateral comparisons are based on Australian consumption patterns and different bundles of pharmaceuticals for each country comparison with Australia, conclusions about relative price levels across countries cannot be drawn. FSS, Federal Supply Service; IMS, IMS Health. Adapted with permission from Productivity Commission.[39]

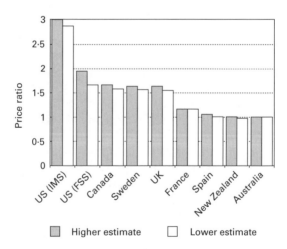

Figure 5.2   Results for "me-too" pharmaceuticals, using IMS data. Because the bilateral comparisons are based on Australian consumption patterns and different bundles of pharmaceuticals for each country comparison with Australia, conclusions about relative price levels across countries cannot be drawn. FSS, Federal Supply Service; IMS, IMS Health. Adapted with permission from Productivity Commission.[39]

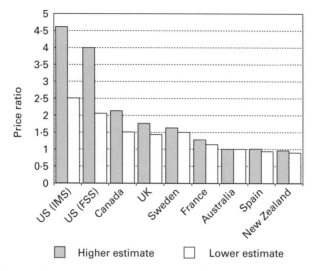

Figure 5.3   Results for generic pharmaceuticals, using IMS data. Because the bilateral comparisons are based on Australian consumption patterns and different bundles of pharmaceuticals for each country comparison with Australia, conclusions about relative price levels across countries cannot be drawn. FSS, Federal Supply Service; IMS, IMS Health. Adapted with permission from Productivity Commission.[39]

down in Australia. Although a similar approach is used in New Zealand and British Columbia, it has not been applied in the other comparison countries.

The Productivity Commission report[39] goes on to speculate that, "the overall results also may reflect the influence of factors affecting the prices of particular pharmaceuticals, or therapeutic groups, including differences in demand conditions, volume controls, patent arrangements, and competition from therapeutically similar molecules." It concludes that, "Australia's cost-containment arrangements may have contributed to keeping prices relatively low."

It is difficult to draw any conclusions about the impact of the fourth hurdle cost-effectiveness requirements because we do not know enough about the counterfactual (what would have happened otherwise). We do know that up until 2001 about 30% of all drug submissions for listing on the PBS were rejected. In recent times, the rejection rate for drugs has risen dramatically. However, not enough is known about the factors that influence the listing decision to warrant any firm conclusion to be drawn regarding the impact of the scheme on Australian drug prices. Until such time as there is quantitative information about the relative weight attached to all of the factors that influence decisions (such as the cost-effectiveness ratio, equity, perceived importance of the drug including severity and prevalence of disease, availability of alternatives, leakage, preference for certain population groups, and the operation of the "rule of rescue"), it would be premature to attribute the comparatively low pharmaceutical prices in Australia to fourth hurdle requirements.[41]

The future

The concept of the fourth hurdle appears to be here to stay. Spiralling health care budgets and the development of increasingly more expensive drugs will mean that policy makers need more, not less, information on those therapies that are likely to be clinically beneficial and cost-effective. Nevertheless, the use of economic evaluation in the funding of drugs poses a number of challenges. We close this chapter by highlighting three of these challenges and possible ways forward.

Harmonising fourth hurdle systems

An evitable consequence of the global growth of the fourth hurdle has been the development of a wide range of differing systems. This is well illustrated by the proliferation of guidelines for economic submissions, with a recent review identifying over 25 different guidelines being issued across Europe, North America, and Europe.[16] Table 5.2 compares current Australian (PBS), Canadian (CCOHTA), and UK (NICE) guidelines.

Differences in the collection and use of both cost and outcomes data can lead to undesirable effects. Perhaps the most significant effect is that the presentation of different economic studies on the same new drug can lead to different decisions being made. There have recently been a number of drugs (zanamivir for the treatment of flu and riluzole for motor neurone disease, among others) that have been deemed to have acceptable cost-effectiveness in one jurisdiction but rejected in another. A lesser but nevertheless potentially important effect of the differing fourth hurdle requirements across countries has been the inefficiency of a pharmaceutical manufacturer investing in often substantially differing submissions for a new drug in order to meet local fourth hurdle requirements. The time seems right for some degree of harmonisation.

Within Europe, one response has been to call for the European Medicines Evaluation Agency to incorporate cost-effectiveness requirements (or at least common economic data gathering requirements) into its licensing decisions.[42] One major difficulty with any such proposal for a pan-European fourth hurdle, however, is that cost-effectiveness can vary substantially between countries because of differences in resource utilisation patterns, costs, acceptable cost thresholds, and national policy goals. Forms of harmonisation that are more acceptable and easier to implement would appear to be international consensus on the requirements of economic submissions from the pharmaceutical industry, and exchange of information on specific drug decisions between fourth hurdle agencies.

Confidentiality and openness

A lack of confidentiality and openness presents challenges to the fourth hurdle.[43] The Australian PBS is probably one of the starkest examples of a closed system that affords the industry a high level of confidentiality. Not only is the basis of listing decisions of the PBS Advisory Committee not made available in the public domain, but also, and of even more concern, is that its negative decisions are not published at all. However, problems of confidentiality and openness are not limited to Australia alone. For example, although developed to be an open and transparent process, NICE allows manufacturers to submit confidential effectiveness and economic data. As a result (although to a lesser extent than with the PBS), NICE can make decisions on the cost-effectiveness of a drug based on information that cannot be shared in the public domain. Should pharmaceutical companies be allowed to continue to submit data in confidence to public funding systems including licensing? Also, openness encourages collaboration between countries that are undertaking fourth hurdle evaluation of pharmaceuticals.

Risk sharing models

Two key problems that must be addressed by the fourth hurdle approach are inadequate economic information for a drug and "indication leakage". Often at the time of launch of a new drug, the necessary evidence to assess its cost-effectiveness is not available. By implication, it is argued that there is a degree of uncertainty in fourth hurdle decisions made at such a time. A second important problem is indication leakage. In other words, as the result of a fourth hurdle assessment, a drug is introduced and licensed for a precisely defined group of patients, but once its use becomes widespread its indications are (unofficially) extended to include a broader group of patients.

So-called "risk sharing" systems of new drug entry are seen as a potential solution to both of these fourth hurdle problems. In such systems, a new drug is entered into the health care system on the condition that outcomes of the new drug are formally assessed in the defined population group. The risk of the implementation is shared between the health service provider and drug manufacturer, based on the drug achieving its outcome targets and its use not broadening to patients who do not have the specific indication. If the drug meets the outcome target then the government pledges to fund its long-term availability; if it does not then the drug is withdrawn and the manufacturer must pay for the drug costs to date. Additionally, the price of the drug is agreed on a cost–volume basis. If the drug diffuses to patient groups outside the indication, then the volume is exceeded and a reduction in drug price is mandated.

Despite their apparent attractiveness, risk sharing schemes for new drugs appear to be relatively uncommon. There is considerable global interest in the outcome of the ongoing UK risk sharing scheme for multiple sclerosis patients in the National Health Service in England and Wales with the manufacturers of β-interferon and glatiramer acetate.[44]

Conclusion

Although the fourth hurdle (i.e. market access based on evidence of clinical efficacy and cost-effectiveness, in addition to the quality, safety, and efficacy of a drug) has existed in Australia and Ontario for over 10 years, its introduction to other national health care systems is relatively recent. Driven by increased health care costs, particularly of drugs, many countries, particularly in Europe, have now implemented formal or informal fourth hurdle systems, with the structure of such systems varying widely. Experience to date, particularly that gained in Australia, shows that a fourth hurdle system can broadly achieve its central objective of efficacy. Moreover, it may result in some reduction in drug costs. Nevertheless, more robust evidence of the impact of fourth hurdle is needed. Inevitably, many challenges lie ahead and much depends on the pharmaceutical industry working with health care decision makers in their goal to make available treatments that provide good value for money to patients.

Summary

- Australia and Ontario introduced the formal requirement for cost effectiveness (fourth hurdle) in drug market access over a decade ago.
- Driven by increasing drug costs, other countries have began to adopt fourth hurdle systems, such as the NICE in UK.
- Inspite of its global development, the impact of the fourth hurdle on the quality of pharmacoeconomic evidence, access to more cost-effective drugs and drug prices, remains relatively limited.
- The future of the fourth hurdle systems is likely to depend on increased harmonisation of systems across countries and clear evidence of impact.

References

1 Commonwealth Department of Health, Housing and Community Services. *Guidelines for the pharmaceutical industry on preparation of submissions to the Pharmaceutical Benefits Advisory Committee.* Canberra: AGPS, 1992.
2 Canadian Coordinating Office for Health Technology Assessment. *Guidelines for economic evaluation of pharmaceuticals: Canada, 2nd ed.* Ottawa: CCOHTA, 1997.
3 Bloor K, Maynard A, Freemantle N. Lessons from international experience in controlling pharmaceutical expenditure III: regulating the industry. *BMJ* 1996;**313**:33–5.
4 Kanavos P, Trueman P, Bosilevac A. Can economic evaluation guidelines improve efficiency in resource allocation? The cases of Portugal, The Netherlands, Finland, and the United Kingdom. *Int J Technol Assess Health Care* 2000;**16**:1179–92.

5 Ess SM, Scvhneesweiss S, Szucs TD. European healthcare policies for controlling drug expenditure. *Pharmacoeconomics* 2003;**21**:89–103.

6 Mason J, Freemantle N, Young P. The effect of the distribution of effectiveness health care bulletins on prescribing selective serotonin reuptake inhibitors in primary care. *Health Trends* 1998;**30**:120–2.

7 NICE. *Guidance on the use of taxanes for ovarian cancer. Technology appraisal guidance no. 3.* London: NICE, 2000.

8 NICE. *Guidance of the use of taxanes for breast cancer. Technology appraisal guidance no. 6.* London: NICE, 2000.

9 NICE. *Guidance on the use of etanercept and infliximab for the treatment of rheumatoid arthritis. Technology appraisal guidance no. 36.* London: NICE, 2002.

10 Haffner ME, Whitley J, Moses M. Two decades of orphan product development. *Nat Rev Drug Discov* 2002;**1**:821–5.

11 Park SJ, Shim WH, Ho DS, *et al.* A paclitaxel-eluting stent for the prevention of coronary restenosis. *N Engl J Med* 2003;**348**:1537–45.

12 NICE. *Guidance on the use of zanamivir for the treatment of influenza. Technology appraisal guidance no. 15.* London: NICE, 2002.

13 Hutton J, Maynard A. A NICE challenge for health economics. *Health Econ* 2000;**9**:89–93.

14 Benjamin I, Poston G, Sherlock D. Is the NICE process flawed? *Lancet* 2002;**359**:2120.

15 McKee M, Maclehose L, Mossialos E. After NICE: where now for health policy in the European Union? *J R Soc Med* 2003;**96**:1–2.

16 Hjelmgren J, Berggren F, Andersson F. Health economic guidelines: similarities, differences and some implications. *Value Health* 2001;**4**:225–50.

17 Gulácsi L, Boncz I, Drummond MF. Issues for countries considering introducing the "fourth hurdle": the case of Hungary. *Int J Technol Assess Health Care* 2004 (in press).

18 Gouveia Pinto C, Teixeira I. Pricing and reimbursement of pharmaceuticals in Portugal. *Eur J Health Econ* 2002;**3**:267–70.

19 Mather DB, Sullivan SD, Augenstein D, *et al.* Incorporating clinical outcomes and economic consequences into drug formulary decisions: a practical approach. *Am J Manag Care* 1999;**5**:277–85.

20 Sullivan SD, Lyles A, Luce B, Gricar J. AMCP guidance for submission of clinical and economic evaluation data to support formulary listing in U.S. health plans and pharmacy benefits management organizations. *J Manag Care Pharm* 2001;**7**:272–82.

21 Academy of Managed Care Pharmacy. AMCP format for formulary submissions; version 2.0 (October 2002). http://www.fmcpnet.org/data/resource/formatv20.pdf (accessed 22 August 2003).

22 Jstreetdata Fast Alert Study. *Attitudes towards adoption of the AMCP formulary guidelines.* Washington, DC: Jstreetdata.com; 2 November 2001.

23 Robinson AM. AMCP's format for formulary submissions: an evolving standard. Results of two recent surveys. Presentation at the 15th Annual Meeting of the Academy of Managed Care Pharmacy; Minneapolis, MN; 9–12 April 2003.

24 Oliver A. Health economic evaluation in Japan: a case study of one aspect of health technology assessment. *Health Policy* 2003;**63**:197–204.

25 de Joncheere K, Paul T. Providing affordable medicines in transitional countries. *Int J Risk Saf Med* 2002;**15**:127–35.

26 Freemantle N, Behamane D, de Joncheere K. Pricing and reimbursement in the Baltic States. *Lancet* 2001;**358**:260.

27 Laing R, Waring B, Gray A, *et al.* 25 years of the WHO essential medicines list: progress and challenges. *Lancet* 2003;**361**:1723–9.

28 Mitchell AS. Measures relating to use of drug subsidy lists and to regulation. *Int J Risk Saf Med* 2002;**15**:77–9.
29 Guillen AM, Cabiedes L. Reforming pharamaceutical policies in the European Union: a "penguin effect"? *Int J Health Serv* 2003;**33**:1–28.
30 Friedberg M, Saffran B, Stinson TJ, *et al*. Evaluation of the conflict of interest in economic analyses of new drugs used in oncology. *JAMA* 1999;**282**:1453–7.
31 Lexchin J, Bero LA, Djulbegovic B, Clark O. Pharmaceutical industry sponsorship and research outcome and quality: systematic review. *BMJ* 2003;**326**:1167–70.
32 Barbui C, Percudani M, Hotopf M. Economic evaluation of antidepressive agents: a systematic critique of experimental and observational studies. *J Clin Psychopharmacol* 2003;**2**:145–54.
33 Hill SR, Mitchell AS, Henry DA. Problems with the interpretation of pharmacoeconomic analyses. A review of submissions to the Australian Pharmaceutical Benefits Scheme. *JAMA* 2000;**283**:2116–21.
34 Anis AH, Rahman T, Schechter MT. Using pharmacoeconomic analysis to make drug insurance coverage decisions. *Pharmacoeconomics* 1998;**13**:119–26.
35 Olsen JA, Smith RD. Theory versus practice: a review of "willingness to pay" in health and health care. *Health Econ* 2001;**10**:201–8.
36 George B, Harris A, Mitchell A. Cost-effectiveness and the consistency of decision-making. Evidence from pharmaceutical reimbursement in Australia (1991 to 1996). *Pharmacoeconomics* 2001;**19**:1103–9.
37 Raftery J. NICE faster access to modern treatments? Analysis of guidance on health technologies. *BMJ* 2001;**323**:1300–3.
38 McDaid D, Mossialos E, Mrazek MJ. Methods for evaluating and monitoring and evaluating processes and outcomes. *Int J Risk Saf Med* 2002;**15**:67–76.
39 Productivity Commission. *International pharmaceutical price differences*. Canberra: AusInfo. Research report, 2001.
40 Bureau of Industry Economics. *The pharmaceutical industry: impediments and opportunities, Bureau of Industry Economics Program Evaluation Report 11*. Canberra: Bureau of Industry Economics, 1991.
41 Salkeld G, Mitchell A, Hill S. Pharmaceuticals. In: Mooney G, Scotton R, eds. *Economics and Australian health policy*. Sydney: Allen and Unwin, 1999. pp. 115–36.
42 Drummond MF. Will there ever be a European drug pricing and reimbursement agency? *Eur J Health Econ* 2003;**4**:67–9.
43 Drummond M. Should commercial-in-confidence data be used by decision makers when making assessments of cost effectiveness? *Appl Health Econ Health Policy* 2002;**1**:53–4.
44 Sudlow CIM, Counsell CE. Problems with UK government's risk sharing scheme for assessing drugs for multiple sclerosis. *BMJ* 2003;**326**:388–92.
45 Taylor RS, Hutton J, Culyer AJ. Developing the revised NICE appraisal technical guidance to manufacturers and sponsors: opportunity or threat? *Pharmacoeconomics* 2002;**20**:1031–8.

6: Economic modelling in drug reimbursement

GLENN SALKELD, NICK FREEMANTLE,
BERNIE O'BRIEN

Introduction

Evidence on the safety and efficacy of a new medicine is a
formal requirement for the licensing of a new product in
many countries, and it is a well established part of
pharmaceutical regulation and consumer protection.[1] A series
of randomised controlled trials (RCTs) in humans has become
the rigorous evidentiary standard for regulatory approval of
new medicines. The RCT is a cornerstone of evidence based
medicine, and the merits of such experiments in terms of
making unbiased inferences on treatment efficacy and on
safety between treatments have been summarised many times,
including in this book (see Chapter 3).

However, RCT evidence on safety and efficacy, although
necessary for regulatory approval, is seldom sufficient
evidence for health care payers who wish to determine the
cost-effectiveness of a new product for the purpose of deciding
whether a drug should be reimbursed on a local or national
formulary. There are numerous ways in which evidence from
premarketing RCTs is inadequate, unhelpful, or even
misleading for addressing the question of cost-effectiveness.
Buxton et al.[2] have catalogued many of these points and they
are summarised in Box 6.1.

One immediate reason why decision analytic modelling
should play a role in the analysis of cost-effectiveness is
therefore to adapt, adjust, or extrapolate trial based evidence
that was gathered to address often narrowly defined questions
of safety and efficacy within the context of a tightly controlled
experiment that may have limited generalisability. This is a
somewhat passive and narrow view of modelling – as an
adjunctive and corrective activity aimed at reworking

Box 6.1 Uses of models in economic evaluation

- Extrapolating beyond the data observed in a trial
- Linking intermediate clinical end-points to final outcomes
- Generalising to other settings
- Synthesising head to head comparisons where relevant trials do not exist
- Informing decisions in the absence of hard data

Data from Buxton et al.[2]

premarketing RCT evidence to address the reimbursement question of cost-effectiveness. A more active and broader view of modelling arises, however, if one recognises that evidence gathering and synthesis must be set in the context of a decision problem, and therefore a coherent decision analytic model provides an overall quantitative framework for the organisation and analysis of evidence from trials and other sources.[3,4] Early construction of a decision model for the treatment and disease will provide a means to identify gaps in the existing evidence on effects and costs, and will indicate where key uncertainties exist. This larger view of modelling affords it a primacy in the evaluation process, such that trials and other pieces of evidence are inputs into the specified evaluative model.

The purpose of economic modelling is not to test hypotheses or make inferences about scientific "truth". Rather it is a pragmatic tool for the mathematical synthesis of the best, currently available data for the purpose of informing a health policy decision.[5] Although evidence based medicine seeks to establish a scientific truth (or inference), the modelling approach has a deliberately instrumental concept of the value of new information. It is valuable to collect information to the extent that it reduces decision uncertainty and changes decisions.

So which comes first – the model or the evidence? One cannot exist without the other if the purpose is to make resource allocation decisions. Evidence is necessary, but a decision analytic framework is needed in which the implications of funding a drug can be made explicit. In this way policy makers can see the impact of drug reimbursement on resources across the health and community sectors, and on patients themselves (by eliciting utility values), and they can therefore quantify the uncertainties that exist for any given resource allocation decision. Thus, the role of evidence (data gathering) should be to update a pre-existing model of cost-effectiveness and to give more precise estimates of model parameters. Using the Bayesian reasoning of observed data being used to update prior information, new evidence should be used to reduce both structural (related to the model structure itself) and parameter (related to the estimated values of the parameters in the model) uncertainty in a cost-effectiveness model. We characterise this process as an iterative loop in which the value of new information in reducing decision uncertainty plays a key role in the decision to conduct further data collection.

One of the advantages of models is that they offer high external validity and the potential to generalise findings. However, models also increase the likelihood of bias. It is the trade-off between internal and external validity that Buxton *et al.*[2] argue is a key part of the modelling debate. As Weinstein *et al.*[6] argue, however, decisions will be made with or without the model: "To reject a model because of incomplete evidence would imply that a decision with neither the data nor the model is better than a decision with the model but without the data." Like any technology, we must recognise when it is appropriate to use it and do so in a transparent way that reduces uncertainty, not increase it. Using models for decision making requires the same degree of scepticism that would be applied to any claim for cost and effect. Are the claims valid, reliable, and reproducible?

The key issue is the quality of decision making (and hence the risk of making wrong decisions). We suggest that the iterative loop for evidence synthesis provides a logical framework for adaptive cost-effectiveness analysis and efficient data collection. In doing so we hope to move the debate from the value of information *per se* to how this information is used in decision making.

In this chapter we describe the components of modelling – designing a model structure, data incorporation, data modelling, and model validation – and concentrate on issues relating to the appropriate use of economic models in drug reimbursement policy. We aim to provide a guide on what constitutes good practice in decision analytic modelling.

What is a model?

A model is a means of representing the complexities of the real world in a simple and comprehensive form. The

International Society for Pharmacoeconomic and Outcomes Research (ISPOR) Task Force on Good Research Practice – Modelling Studies[6] define a health care evaluation model as "an analytic methodology that accounts for events over time and across populations, that is based on data drawn from primary and/or secondary sources, and whose purpose is to estimate the effects of an intervention on valued health consequences and costs." In defining "what is a model", the ISPOR Task Force makes clear that cost-effectiveness models are an aid to decision making, in which the relationship between assumptions and outcomes are explicit and transparent. The nature of those assumptions is discussed under the heading Data incorporation and modelling, below.

Components of modelling

Model structure

The starting point in the design of a decision model is a decision tree (Figure 6.1), which is a systematic and quantitative method for representing, in schematic form, all of the important outcomes of a decision and explicitly estimating the expected value of each alternative.[7,8] Decision trees are appropriate for modelling interventions where events occur over a relatively short time period and the required structure is not too complex; the disadvantage of using trees to model longer durations or more complex structures is that they become too "bushy" and difficult to manage.[9-11] A common approach to the design of models over longer periods of time, and where a complex disease history must be characterised, is the use of stochastic compartment models such as Markov State Transition models. In a typical Markov model the analyst defines a finite number of "states" that a patient can be in over time. Each state might have quality-adjusted life year (QALY) weights and costs associated with a sojourn time, and the model proceeds by taking the expectation of these outcomes to be conditional upon the specified probabilities for transitions between states. The most common analytic procedure is the Markov Cohort simulation method described by Sonnenberg and Beck[12] and Briggs and Sculpher.[13] An example of a Markov model used to estimate

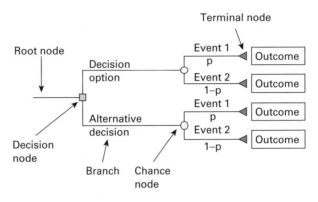

Figure 6.1   Example of a decision tree. p, probability of an event.

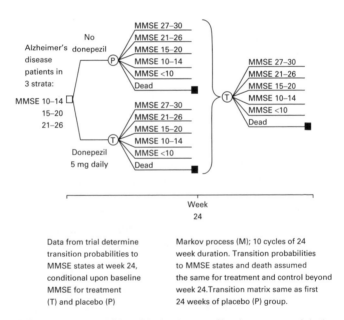

Data from trial determine transition probabilities to MMSE states at week 24, conditional upon baseline MMSE for treatment (T) and placebo (P)	Markov process (M); 10 cycles of 24 week duration. Transition probabilities to MMSE states and death assumed the same for treatment and control beyond week 24. Transition matrix same as first 24 weeks of placebo (P) group.

Figure 6.2   A state transition (Markov) cost-effectiveness model: the case of donepezil and Alzheimer's disease. MMSE, Mini-Mental State Examination. Source: O'Brien et al.[14]

the cost-effectiveness of a medicine is illustrated in Figure 6.2 and ISPOR guidelines for good practice are described in Box 6.2.

O'Brien et al.[14] estimated the incremental cost-effectiveness of donepezil relative to no therapy for treatment of patients

---

Box 6.2 Selected ISPOR guidelines for good practice: model structure

- The model structure (inputs and outputs) should reflect the decision making context and should be as simple as possible
- Structure of the model should be consistent with a coherent theory of the health condition being modelled and with causal linkages between variables
- Limitations in underlying assumptions should be acknowledged and tested in a sensitivity analysis
- The time horizon of the model should be long enough to reflect valued and important differences between the long term costs and outcomes of alternative options and strategies

For further details on all 13 ISPOR guidelines for good practice in model structure, see the report by Weinstein et al.[6]

---

with mild-to-moderate Alzheimer's disease, defined as having a Mini-Mental State Examination (MMSE) score in the range 10–26. The analysts had efficacy data from placebo-controlled phase III randomised trials of duration 24 weeks, in which change in cognition (measured using the Alzheimer's Disease Assessment Scale–cognition subscale and the MMSE) was the primary end-point. MMSE score ranges are from 0 (worst) to 30 (best). To extrapolate beyond 24 weeks the analysts constructed a state transition model (see Figure 6.2) in which, at every 24 week cycle of the model, patients could transition into (or remain in) one of five mutually exclusive MMSE score ranges, with death being a competing risk to form a sixth absorbing state. The observed MMSE data for the first 24 week transitions were used for treatment and control groups, and a further nine cycles of the model were run to a time horizon of just over five years. For cycles two to nine of the model, both treatment groups where assigned the transition matrix for the placebo group.

The clinical outcome for the cost-effectiveness analysis was specified as the cumulative time per patient over the 5 years in non-severe Alzheimer's disease (MMSE score > 10). Patients treated with placebo were expected to spend 2·21 years in non-severe Alzheimer's disease, as compared with 2·41 years for patients treated with donepezil. Data from patients with Alzheimer's disease in the Canadian Study on Health and Aging[15] were used to estimate costs as a function of MMSE score. Over the five year period, the model forecasted that that health care costs per patient would be lower by C$929 per patent in the treated group, due mainly to reduced nursing home admissions. However, the model also forecasted an increase by C$48 per patient in care giver costs, for an overall cost saving of C$882 per patient.

Data incorporation and modelling

The philosophy guiding the incorporation of data into models is that of "the best available data". Models synthesise evidence from many different sources of empirical data, including clinical trials, observational studies, and public health statistics, into a logical framework to answer clinical and policy questions.[3-5] Data modelling is defined as the mathematical steps that are taken to transform empirical observations into a form that is useful for decision modelling.[5] Virtually every economic evaluation includes some form of data modelling to generate the results, and some examples are as follows:

- transforming interval probabilities into an appropriate format and time interval for use in a model
- combining disease specific and all-cause mortality into the model
- modelling survival using an underlying parametric or non-parametric distribution function
- modelling the effect of risk factors on baseline probabilities or rates of disease incidence or mortality
- estimating multiattribute utilities from domain specific utilities
- transforming available price and charge information into estimates of cost
- adjusting costs for changes in purchasing power over time and among countries.

Sensitivity analysis

All of the parameters listed above are subject to some degree of uncertainty. For many years the conventional approach to assessing parameter uncertainty in a cost-effectiveness analysis has been by one-way or multiway sensitivity analyses.[16,17] In a one-way sensitivity analysis, the analyst identifies the key model parameters to which it is anticipated that the model results will be sensitive. In an exploration of "what if", each of these parameters is then changed one at a time to determine the effect on the results. The values of the parameters are varied through the range of feasible values. A multiway sensitivity analysis proceeds in a similar way, but the analyst varies more than one parameter at the same time.

More recently, probabilistic approaches to evaluating uncertainty have been advocated so that the results of a sensitivity analysis convey information about both the range of possible results and the probability of each result.[18,19] Probabilistic sensitivity analysis makes it possible to assign ranges and distributions to uncertain variables in a model. The parameters to consider might include estimates related to the probabilities of a pathway in a decision tree or transition probabilities in a Markov model, estimates of resource use and health outcomes, and estimates of the values associated with the resource use (costs) and health outcomes (utility weights). By assigning a distribution, a probabilistic sensitivity analysis can be undertaken by sampling from each of these parameter distributions simultaneously in a (second order) Monte Carlo simulation.[16] Such an approach provides the simulated joint density between costs and effects, and permits the analyst to compute analogues of conventional measures of precision for parameters such as 95% confidence intervals. A detailed illustration of how probabilistic sensitivity analysis can be applied to a model of alternative treatments for reflux disease can be found in the report by Briggs et al.[20] An example of a cost-effectiveness model with both conventional and probabilistic sensitivity analysis is the study of oseltamivir for treatment of influenza by O'Brien et al.,[21] and this is summarised in Figure 6.3.

O'Brien et al.[21] used a probabilistic decision tree model with a time horizon of seven days to estimate the cost-effectiveness of treatment for influenza in otherwise healthy adults and relative to no treatment. Of key relevance to this model is an understanding that the new drug works by inhibiting viral replication and must be used within 48 hours of symptom onset. Model parameters such as probabilities where encoded into the model as β distributions based on event data from the phase III trials and other sources. Outcomes were based on

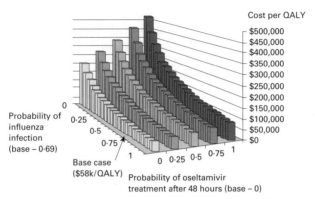

Figure 6.3 An illustration of conventional and probabilistic sensitivity analysis with a cost-effectiveness model: the case of oseltamivir for treatment of influenza. QALY, quality-adjusted life year. Reproduced with permission from O'Brien *et al.*[21]

time free from symptoms and associated visual analogue scores to estimate QALYs. Monte Carlo simulation was used to create 1000 simultaneous draws from each parameter distribution to permit the estimation of a bivariate density of incremental costs and QALYs, and a 95% credible interval for incremental cost-effectiveness. The estimated cost per QALY for oseltamivir was C$57,863, with a 95% credible interval from C$48,919 to C$70,149.

An interesting part of that study was the traditional two-way sensitivity analysis that showed the cost per QALY as a function of two key variables that have an impact on effectiveness: the proportion of patients presenting with flu-like symptoms who actually have the influenza virus; and the proportion of patients who receive the drug after 48 hours. As is clear from Figure 6.3, the cost per QALY increases exponentially if the drug is used in patients who do not have the influenza virus and beyond the 48 hour therapeutic window.

Advances have also been made in methods for statistical analysis of data on observed costs and effects from trial based cost-effectiveness studies. Non-parametric resampling methods such as bootstrapping have become a popular method for estimating standard errors and confidence intervals for cost and effect means.[22] Parametric methods such as Fieller's Theorem, in which cost and effect differences are assumed to follow a bivariate normal distribution, have also been shown to have good coverage properties in computing confidence intervals for cost-effectiveness.[23,24] A comprehensive review of statistical methods in cost-effectiveness analysis can be found in the paper by Briggs *et al.*[19]

Model validation

Model validation refers to tests to confirm the internal and external consistency of the model with known facts, and it includes both debugging and calibration.[5] Validation may include ensuring the face validity of the model, corroboration or convergent validity to compare the results of models that were developed independently, and predictive validity to determine whether a model produces results that actually occur. Models can only be built on the best available evidence at the time, and sometimes that evidence proves to be inaccurate. Weinstein *et al.*[5] noted that, in the areas of HIV and hyperlipidaemia, early models assumed that outcomes were mediated by risk factors (CD4+ cell counts, serum cholesterol). Data from subsequent clinical trials were found to be at variance with the estimates from the early models. This emphasises the importance of approaching model development as an iterative loop in which new evidence can be incorporated into a model in order to reduce decision uncertainty.

In the following sections we use some recent examples of economic modelling in pharmaceuticals to highlight the technical and conceptual issues that confront the user of models.

The use of trial based evidence in models

Clinical data on the effectiveness and safety of an intervention play a central role in economic modelling, essentially driving estimates of cost-effectiveness. It stands to reason that if everything else is equal, then a more (or less) effective intervention will be more (or less) cost-effective. In the review by Hill *et al.*[25] of 326 submissions by the pharmaceutical industry for product funding by the Australian Pharmaceutical Benefits Scheme, 218 (67%) of

Table 6.1   Problems in estimates of comparative clinical efficacy

Details of problem	Number (%) of problems
Availability of trials	12 (7·8)
Poor quality of trials	31 (20·1)
Interpretation of trial results	32 (20·8)
Use of surrogate outcomes	15 (9·7)
Determining therapeutic equivalence	64 (41·6)
Total	154 (100)

submissions had 249 serious problems of interpretation and 154 (62%) had problems related to uncertainty on the analysis of clinical efficacy. The sources of uncertainty and types of problems found are described in Table 6.1.

Randomised trials undertaken before licensing of a new pharmaceutical are aimed primarily at achieving a licence, and thus the modest proportion of problems associated with the (lack of) availability of trials (7·8%) could be considered surprising. By contrast, the number of problems identified that were associated with poor quality of trials (20·1%) may be considered high. The quality of trials to address their original purpose (e.g. the effect of treatment on the primary outcome) may not be the same as the quality of trials for the purpose that they are used in an economic analysis. Hill et al.[25] described a submission for a new drug that claimed lower adverse events but was based on a small open label trial with subjective end-points.

Problems in the interpretation of trial results included inappropriate subgroup analyses and adjustment of event rates, and problems with the statistical pooling of data. When reviewing economic analyses it is often quite difficult to identify why specific data were chosen. For example, in a cost-effectiveness analysis of celecoxib in the treatment of arthritis, Burke et al.[26] included a relative risk for symptomatic ulcer between celecoxib and standard non-steroidal anti-inflammatory drugs (NSAIDs) based on 5643 patients from seven randomised trials of 12 weeks' duration and one trial of 24 weeks' duration. This list of trials does not include the Celecoxib Long-term Arthritis Safety Study (CLASS), which was specifically designed to "determine whether celecoxib … is associated with a lower incidence of significant upper GI [gastrointestinal] toxic effects and other adverse effects compared with conventional NSAIDs", and which randomised 8059 patients among whom over half completed six months of treatment.[27]

The two sources of data provide very different results. For example, the relative risk of symptomatic ulcer for celecoxib versus conventional NSAID is described by Burke et al.[26] as 0·28 (95% confidence interval 0·17–0·45). However, in the CLASS trial, only 19 out of 3987 patients taking celecoxib had symptomatic ulcer compared with 29 out of 3981 taking a conventional NSAID, yielding a relative risk of 0·65 (95% confidence interval 0·37–1·16).[27,28] Given that the aim of the CLASS trial was to identify differences in "significant" events, it seems likely that the more extreme estimate with tighter confidence intervals identified by Burke et al.[26] had a lower threshold for inclusion of events, and included many that were (in the CLASS trial definition at least) not of clinical importance. The presentation of the results of CLASS was controversial,[29] and likely to present the results of the study in the best possible light, further questioning the choice of data included in the economic analysis by Burke et al.[26]

Surrogate outcomes that are designed to support the licensing of new pharmaceuticals are commonly used in clinical trials, and it is therefore unsurprising that 9·7% of problems related to this phenomenon. The importance of some surrogate outcomes is relatively well established (for example, reduction in blood pressure in stroke prevention, or HbA1c in the management of diabetes), but others remain controversial. For example, trials intended to support the licensing of newer NSAIDs used endoscopically detected lesions as an outcome measure even though, as the data sheet acknowledged, "the correlations between the findings of endoscopic studies, and the relative incidence of clinically serious upper GI events with different products, has not been fully established."[29]

Most new drugs are not so-called "block busters" but "me-too"s that provide alternatives to existing compounds, often with the questionable prospect for clinical advantage. The most common problem identified by Hill et al.,[25] that of inappropriate claims for equivalence, presents problems in clinical epidemiology as well as health economics, and is addressed in detail in Chapter 3.

Preference elicitation in models

Translating clinical end-points from trials into measures valued by patients, providers, and the community is yet another area of controversy in modelling. Few would argue with the notion that quality of life (QoL) is an important and worthwhile consideration in deciding which drugs to fund, or that an economic framework such as QALYs[30] is an appropriate tool for quantifying the opportunity cost of survival and QoL outcomes relative to cost. However, there is disagreement about the best measurement approach. A generic health measure covers a range of QoL domains and combines preferences in a multiattribute utility index. Condition specific measures include QoL domains relevant to the condition and use measurement techniques such as time trade-off or standard gamble to elicit utility weights for the condition specific health states being valued. The choice of approach should be guided by what yields information that produces the best decision. Proponents of generic health measures, such as Dowie,[31] argue that only generic instruments are useful for decision making. Proponents of condition specific measures, such as Guyatt,[32] argue that generic health measures are insensitive to important but small changes in clinical outcome. For that reason, Guyatt argues that condition specific measures are the preferred approach. The guiding principle for modelling preference based outcomes should be to determine, from the decision maker's viewpoint, what are the relevant domains of QoL and whether the measurement tool will allow comparisons to be made across competing health care programmes or pharmaceuticals. All too often, this consideration appears to be missing from preference elicitation studies.

Stolk *et al.*[33] used the time trade-off technique to elicit preferences for the outcomes of treatment with sildenafil compared with papaverine–phentolamine injections for erectile dysfunction. Using a random sample of the local population, 169 men and women aged 18–80 years were asked to value 24 disease specific health states. By applying the mean utility values for these states to the clinical outcomes achieved in a separate trial of sildenafil, the authors concluded that the "social tariff" or mean utility gain attributable to sildenafil was 0·11 (on a scale in which 0 = death and 1 = full health with no erectile dysfunction).

As the purpose of that study is to assess the value of sildenafil to society, it is appropriate to elicit preferences using a random sample of men and women from the community. If the purpose had been as an aid to the clinical management of patients with erectile dysfunction, then there would be a strong argument to use only the values of patients enrolled in the trial. What is not clear is the appropriateness of using a disease specific approach in the valuation exercise. This depends on what Dowie[31] calls the "decision validity", that is, "does it measure what it is necessary to measure for the decision which is to be made using it?" In the context of study conducted by Stolk et al.,[33] the issue of decisional validity is not addressed and there is no way of knowing whether the disease specific approach captures the full range of health outcomes that would otherwise be captured by a generic or multiattribute scale. Although the disease specific approach may be more sensitive to those domains of health that are most affected by sildenafil, we do not know which aspects of health are not covered by this measure.

In the context of a constrained drug budget, decision makers need a standardised approach to preference elicitation to ensure comparability of QALY estimates. Without this, it is impossible to compare the relative value for money across classes of drugs. Also, within a class of drugs, non-standardisation may call into question the value of going beyond the clinical outcomes in the first place.[34]

Conclusion

Economic modelling is an inevitable part of the information technology needed to support decision making in pharmaceuticals. It provides a logical framework in which the best available evidence can be used to inform the decision. The theoretical framework, decision analysis, is well developed and represents the paradigm for rational decision making in health care. Despite this, the use of models in drug reimbursement is viewed with scepticism. Is this view misplaced? There is no need to fear the decision analytic approach if we accept that the primary goal of resource allocation in pharmaceuticals is to maximise outcome within a constrained budget. There is some justification, however, for being sceptical about the application of economic models in cost-effectiveness submissions for pharmaceuticals. It is the same justification that we apply to the search for truth in information assessment. Bias moves us away from the truth. Sources of bias must be assessed in terms of their importance to how we interpret the results of a trial or other clinical effectiveness study. Whether accidental or deliberate, errors and other sources of bias in economic models must be identified and assessed within the context of decision making through a process of critical appraisal. That is asking no more than would be expected when assessing the value of a clinical trial.

Economic models offer a means by which the basis for decisions can be laid bare for all to see. For that potential to be realised, economic models in the public domain should be freely available, as should the decision weights that funders attach to the key factors that influence drug reimbursement decisions.

Summary

- Economic models provide a logical framework in which the best available evidence can be used to inform a decision on the selection and reimbursement of pharmaceuticals.
- The process of modelling should be seen as an iterative loop whereby the value of new information in reducing decision uncertainty plays a key role in the decision to collect further data.
- Cost-effectiveness models should be transparent, so that the assumptions, evidence, and structure of the model can be verified and reproduced by others.
- Probabilistic approaches to evaluating uncertainty surrounding variables in models enhance the usefulness of results to decision makers.

References

1 Salkeld G, Mitchell A, Hill S. Pharmaceuticals. In: Mooney G, Scotton R, eds. *Economics and Australian health policy.* Sydney: Allen and Unwin, 1999. pp. 115–36.
2 Buxton MJ, Drummond MF, Van Hout BA, *et al.* Modelling in economic evaluation: an unavoidable fact of life. *Health Econ* 1997;6:217–27.

3 Sculpher M, Fenwick E, Claxton K. Assessing quality in decision analytic cost-effectiveness models. *Pharmacoeconomics* 2000;**17**:461–77.

4 Brennan A, Akehurst R. Assessing quality in decision analytic cost-effectiveness models. *Pharmacoeconomics* 2000;**17**:445–9.

5 Weinstein MC, Toy EL, Sandberg EA, *et al.* Modelling for health care and other policy decisions: uses, roles and validity. *Value Health* 2001;**4**:348–61.

6 Weinstein MC, O'Brien B, Hornberger JC, *et al.* Principles of good practice for decision analytic modelling in health-care evaluation: report of the ISPOR task force on good research practices–modelling studies. *Value Health* 2003;**6**:9–17.

7 Weinstein MC, Finberg HV, Elstein AS, Fraser HS, Neuhauser D, Neutra RR. *Clinical decision analysis.* Philadelphia: W.B. Saunders Company, 1980.

8 Petitti DB. *Meta-analysis, decision-analysis, and cost-effectiveness analysis: methods for quantitative synthesis in medicine.* New York: Oxford University Press, 1994.

9 Detsky AS, Naglie G, Krahn MD, Naimark D, Redelmeier A. Primer on medical decision analysis: part 1 – getting started. *Med Decis Making* 1997;**17**:123–5.

10 Redelmeier A, Naglie G, Krahn MD, Naimark D, Detsky AS. Primer on medical decision analysis: part 2 – estimating probabilities and utilities. *Med Decis Making* 1997;**17**:136–41.

11 Naimark D, Krahn MD, Naglie G, Redelmeier A, Detsky AS. Primer on medical decision analysis: part 5 – working with Markov processes. *Med Decis Making* 1997;**17**:152–9.

12 Sonnenberg A, Beck J. Markov models in medical decision making: a practical guide. *Med Decis Making* 1993;**13**:322–38.

13 Briggs A, Sculpher M. An introduction to Markov modelling for economic evaluation. *Pharmacoeconomics* 1998;**13**:397–409.

14 O'Brien BJ, Goeree R, Hux M, *et al.* Economic evaluation of donepezil for the treatment of Alzheimer's disease in Canada. *J Am Geriatr Soc* 1999;**47**:570–8.

15 Hux MJ, O'Brien BJ, Iskedjian M, *et al.* Relation between severity of Alzheimer's disease and costs of caring. *CMAJ* 1998;**159**:457–65.

16 Briggs A. Handling uncertainty in cost-effectiveness models. *Pharmacoeconomics* 2000;**17**:479–500.

17 Briggs A, Sculpher M, Buxton MJ. Uncertainty in economic evaluation of health care technologies: the role of sensitivity analysis. *Health Econ* 1994;**3**:95–104.

18 Doubilet P, Begg CB, Weinstein MC, Braun P, McNeil BJ. Probabilistic sensitivity analysis using Monte Carlo simulation. A practical approach. *Med Decis Making* 1985;**5**:157–77.

19 Briggs A, O'Brien B, Blackhouse G. Thinking outside the box: recent advances in the analysis and presentation of uncertainty in cost-effectiveness studies. *Annu Rev Public Health* 2002;**23**:377–401.

20 Briggs A, Goeree R, O'Brien B. Probabilistic analysis of cost-effectiveness models: choosing between treatment strategies for gastro-oesophageal reflux disease. *Med Decis Making* 2002;**22**:290–308.

21 O'Brien BJ, Goeree R, Blackhouse G, Smieja M, Loeb M. Oseltamivir for treatment of influenza in healthy adults: pooled trial evidence and cost-effectiveness model for Canada. *Value Health* 2003;**6**:116–25.

22 Briggs A, Wonderling DE, Mooney CZ. Pulling cost-effectiveness analysis up by its bootstraps: a non-parametric approach to confidence interval estimation. *Health Econ* 1997;**6**:327–40.

23 Willan A, O'Brien B. Confidence intervals for cost-effectiveness ratios in clinical trials: a new method using Fieller's Theorem. *Health Econ* 1996;**5**:297–305.

24 Willan A, O'Brien B. Sample size and power issues in estimating incremental cost-effectiveness ratios from clinical trials data. *Health Econ* 1999;**8**:203–11.

25 Hill S, Henry D, Mitchell A. Problems in pharmacoeconomic analyses. *JAMA* 2000;**284**:1922–4.

26 Burke TA, Zabrinski RA, Pettitt D, Maniadakis N, Maurath CJ, Goldstein JL. A framework for evaluating the clinical consequences of initial therapy with NSAIDS, NSAIDs plus gastroprotective agents, or celecoxib in the treatment of arthritis. *Pharmacoeconomics* 2001;**19**:33–47.

27 Silverstein FE, Faich G, Goldstein JL, Simon LS, Pincus T, Whelton A. Gastrointestinal toxicity with celecoxib vs nonsteroidal anti-inflammatory drugs for osteoarthritis and rheumatoid arthritis. The CLASS study: a randomised controlled trial. *JAMA* 2000;**284**:1247–55.

28 Deeks JJ, Smith LA, Bradley MD. Efficacy, tolerability and upper gastrointestinal safety of celecoxib for treatment of osteoarthritis and rheumatoid arthritis: systematic review of randomised controlled trials. *BMJ* 2002;**325**:619.

29 Juni P, Rutjes AWS, Dieppe PA. Are selective COX 2 inhibitors superior to traditional non steroidal anti-inflammatory drugs? *BMJ* 2002;**324**:1287–8.

30 Drummond MF, O'Brien B, Stoddart GL, Torrance GW. *Methods for the economic evaluation of health care programs.* Oxford: Oxford University Press, 1997.

31 Dowie J. Decision validity should determine whether a generic or condition-specific HRQOL measure is used in health care decisions. *Health Econ* 2002;**11**:1.

32 Guyatt G. Commentary on Jack Dowie, "Decision validity should determine whether a generic or condition-specific HRQOL measure is used in health care decisions". *Health Econ* 2002;**11**:9–12.

33 Stolk EA, Busschbach JJV, Caffa M, Meuleman EJH, Rutten F. Cost utility analysis of sildenafil compared with papaverine-phentolamine injections. *BMJ* 2000;**320**:1–6.

34 Freemantle N. Valuing the effects of sildenafil in erectile dysfunction. Strong assumptions are required to generate a QALY value. *BMJ* 2000;**320**:1156–7.

7: Priority setting in health care: matching decision criteria with policy objectives

GINA BRINSMEAD, ALAN WILLIAMS

A too great disproportion among the citizens weakens any state. Every person, if possible, ought to enjoy the fruits of his labour, in a full possession of all the necessaries, and many of the conveniences of life. No one can doubt, but such an equality is most suitable to human nature, and diminishes much less from the happiness of the rich than it adds to that of the poor.

David Hume[1]

Introduction

As new and increasingly expensive technologies contend for reimbursement in a climate of concern about rising health care budgets, the need for appropriate and accountable priority setting at all levels in the health care system has become increasingly evident and urgent. Within the context of this book, we are directly concerned with decisions about the reimbursement of pharmaceuticals at a national or institutional level, made by bodies such as the National Institute for Clinical Excellence (NICE) in the UK and the Pharmaceutical Benefits Advisory Committee (PBAC) in Australia. However, the principles and approaches explored in this chapter apply equally to decisions about any health technology at any level within the health system.

To be appropriate, priority setting must reflect the objectives of the health care system. Most public health care systems have two primary goals. The first is to improve the overall health of the population as much as possible, and the second is to bring about a more equitable distribution of health within that population. For brevity, we will call the first the health maximisation or efficiency objective, and the second the inequality reduction or equity objective.

Neither of these objectives has an unequivocal, universally accepted meaning. The main problem with the first objective is finding a suitable definition of health. For our purposes it is argued that the best concept of health to use is a person's lifetime experience of health, as measured by their health history to date plus their quality-adjusted life expectancy from today onward. This composite measure takes into account both the duration of a person's life and any disability or distress they may suffer during its course. The main problem with the second objective is that there are many different concepts of equity. In this chapter we give a central role to reduction in inequalities in people's lifetime experience of health, because in our view this is the most important equity objective for public health care systems. It will serve as a yardstick against which we assess the implications and comparative merits of other possible equity objectives. The alternative formulation to which we give particular attention is the "rule of rescue", because this has been given a practical policy incarnation within the Australian context.

At an empirical level the evidence base for priority setting is currently highly skewed in favour of the health maximisation objective. This is because clinical trials have concerned themselves solely with health maximisation, and the economic studies that draw on and extend them have the same preoccupation. There has been no such tradition of rigorous quantitative evaluation of matters to do with equity. Here it is important to draw a distinction between description and evaluation. There has been plenty of statistical work describing inequalities in health, much of it based on the implicit assumption that all inequalities are inequitable. However, before an inequality can be declared "inequitable", some ethical principle must be adduced and brought to bear. It is highly likely that such a principle will lead to the view that some inequalities are more inequitable than others. If it fails to do this then it will be of little use for priority setting, because the essence of priority setting is the judgement that some situations merit more urgent redress than others. So although descriptive data on the existence of health inequalities may usefully tell us where we are at present, it does not tell us where we want to go or the best way to get there. For this we need to move on to the evaluative phase.

However, just as priority setting is about more than health maximisation, so it is about more than simply reducing health inequities. With these two broad objectives in competition for limited resources, the issue of how to make trade-offs between them in an appropriate and accountable manner becomes crucial. Very few data exist about this key policy variable. This is an important theme in this chapter, in the course of which we offer some tentative ideas as to how this void in the current evidence base might be filled.

The structure of the rest of this chapter is as follows. We first discuss the underlying principles that lead us to seek decision criteria other than those based on health maximisation (such as cost-effectiveness). We then propose the "fair innings argument" as an equity principle to operate alongside (but not to replace) the health maximisation objective. Attention is then focused on the trade-offs that will be required in order to accommodate simultaneously both health maximisation and the reduction of inequalities in health. A possible method of eliciting these trade-offs is described, together with preliminary data obtained from convenience samples of health professionals. Finally, the "rule of rescue" is examined as a potential alternative or supplement to the fair innings argument. The ethical claim of its traditional formulation is found to be rather weak in the policy context in which priority setting agencies for health care systems operate. The variant of the rule of rescue that has been adopted by the Australian PBAC may serve as a reasonable compromise between the claims of rescue, fair innings, and health maximisation. We conclude that more empirical work is needed to specify the policy trade-offs that the general public would support, in order to ensure that priority setting in health care is appropriate and accountable to those it serves.

Going beyond health maximisation

Principles

As indicated earlier, the evaluation (as opposed to the description) of inequities requires the adoption of some principle of distributive justice. The philosophical literature offers a wide choice of such principles. The dominant ideological position in the health care field has been some form of egalitarianism, which has variously been defined in terms of resources, access, utilisation, health gains, and lifetime health. The position adopted here is that it is lifetime health that is fundamental, while the other factors listed are instrumental. In order to reduce inequalities in people's lifetime experience of health, it may be in fact be necessary to accept, or even to create or worsen, inequalities in resources, access, utilisation, and distribution of health gains from the health care system.[2]

On this basis, the "fair innings argument" is proposed as the best approach to the fundamental equity goal of reducing inequalities in people's lifetime experience of health. Its essence is encapsulated in the following extract from John Harris's book *The value of life*:[3] "while it is always a misfortune to die when one wants to go on living, it is not a tragedy to die in old age; but it is … both a tragedy and a misfortune to be cut off prematurely."

The fair innings argument comes in two variants. The first concentrates exclusively on life expectancy, of which about 70 years seems to be the popularly conceived norm (perhaps influenced by the biblical "threescore years and ten"). The second variant of the fair innings argument also takes into account the disability and distress that people have suffered during their lives. Thus, someone disabled from birth and in lifelong pain would not be regarded as having had a fair innings even if they did live to be 70 years old. In this case the norm is more difficult to define, but it would be measured in quality-adjusted life years (QALYs) rather than in simple life years and would be less than, say, 70 years because most people do not expect to live a life free from disability and distress. The total lifetime QALYs held to constitute a fair innings may, for example, be around 60 (judging from population norms such as those reported by Kind *et al*.[4]). Ultimately, what constitutes a fair innings in either variant of the fair innings argument is a matter for social judgement within each community. The quality-adjusted variant of the fair innings argument is adopted as the preferred version here.

Key characteristics of the fair innings argument that deserve particular attention in the present context and which distinguish it from alternative prioritising principles are as follows.

- It reflects a societal aversion to inequality (unlike simple maximisation)
- Its formulation is quantitative and amenable to decision making at the margin (unlike simple needs based allocation)
- It takes a person's whole lifetime experience as the fundamental unit of analysis (not how they happen to be at the moment).

The latter characteristic is an important point of departure from other approaches to priority setting. The health maximisation approach looks only at expected future possibilities, taking past and current situations as irremediable and given, respectively. Needs or rescue based approaches look only at the exigencies of present ill health. In contrast, past, current, and expected future possibilities are weighed in trying to judge whether a person is likely to enjoy a fair innings. A person who is deemed unlikely to achieve a fair innings would get some priority over someone who looks very likely to do so.

Following this way of thinking, the most immediate implication is that someone who has already had a fair innings (for example, a fit elderly person) will get lower priority in the distribution of health gains than a young person who, without treatment, will certainly not reach the societal norm (through premature death and/or lifelong disability). This reflects what most surveys of public opinion on this matter show, namely that most people (even old people) would give priority to the young where there is a limited number of extra life years to be distributed.

It should be noted here that the fair innings argument is not proposed as replacing the health maximisation objective but as operating alongside it. Neither the maximisation objective nor the equity objective "trumps" its rival; rather, each is weighed carefully within some more general context. Within this context there will be some trade-off between the two, such that, in the preceding situation, if the gain to the young person were very small, and that to the older person very large, then the balance might swing in favour of the old person despite the fair innings argument working in favour of the young person. The extent of the trade-off depends on the strength of society's aversion to the particular circumstances of the inequality. An aversion to inequality implies a sense of solidarity, of fellow feeling, of sympathy and even possibly of moral duty. The fair innings argument asks whether this sense of community is sufficiently strong in each situation to warrant a tangible sacrifice. That is, to what extent are people willing to sacrifice improvements in average population health in order to reduce inequality?

A subsidiary issue is whether everyone is entitled to the same fair innings, or whether there is a different fair innings for different sorts of people. Is it differentially unfair that women live longer than men, that non-smokers live longer than smokers, or that the rich live longer than the poor? When the members of a given community are determining what constitutes a fair innings in a particular context, they also must consider just how inequitable each inequality is, and to what extent sacrifices are to be made to reduce it.

Evidence

The existing literature provides limited practical guidance to decision makers on the important question of how to balance the equity and efficiency objectives when they pull in opposite directions. A number of theoretical solutions have been proposed,[5–7] most along the lines of applying equity weights to QALYs. Empirically, studies[8–10] as well as policy experience[11] have shown the public to be dissatisfied with allocation based only on health maximisation, and have suggested other potential bases for priority setting (Box 7.1).

As shown in Box 7.1, few studies have gone beyond simply identifying the factors that might be considered in priority setting, to making a quantitative trade-off between them. Interpretation of those studies that do specify a trade-off is hampered by the lack of a representative population sample and, in some cases, contradictory results. Overall, the available theory and empirical evidence stop short of providing a satisfactory method for quantifying the strength of community aversion to various inequalities, and thereby capturing the extent to which gains in overall population health should be sacrificed to reduce them. Algebraically, we have the variables but we do not have the equation that precise decision making requires.

Box 7.1 In search of an empirical basis for rationing

Who should decide?

A key issue is the extent to which the views of the general public should be explicitly sought and applied to health care rationing. Consulting the general public seems required by a commitment to democratic process, although some have raised concerns that this could lead to a "dictatorship of the uninformed".[12] For their own part, how eager are the citizenry to be engaged in this type of decision? Studies generally find the public willing to participate, to an extent that may vary depending on the level at which priorities are being set.[13,14]

How should we ask them?

Various study types have been used to elicit the views of the public, including questionnaire surveys, interviews, focus groups, and citizens' juries.[15] Key methodological issues include framing effects,[16] and allowance for reflection and discussion,[17] both of which have been shown to influence participant views.

What factors have been identified as relevant for priority setting?

Although participants' attitudes vary across settings and studies,[8,18] consistent concerns include age,[19,20] severity of illness,[21] and perceived personal responsibility for unhealthy lifestyles.[22] Prior receipt of health care is less frequently identified as important.[23] In Australia it appears that whether a patient has dependants is not regarded as relevant,[9] whereas other data indicate that having children of school age is very relevant.[10] Factors that have been generally regarded as unimportant include whether he/she is engaged in paid work.[24]

From decision factors to quantitative trade-offs

A number of studies have quantified a trade-off between efficiency and equity. Using a "veil of ignorance" approach, Andersson and Lyttkens[25] elicited a median trade-off of one year lost by the "long lived" (better off) for 0·11–0·35 years gained by the short lived. In a similar study, Johannesson and Gerdtham[26] found a willingness to trade one year lost by the better off for 0·45 years gained by the worse off. Schwappach[23] used a conjoint analysis approach to specify trade-offs between a number of factors (including age, socioeconomic status, prior health care, and lifestyle choices). The results of the latter study were surprising in that respondents wanted to preferentially allocate more resources to those who had embraced unhealthy lifestyles. The subjects in these three studies were convenience samples of students. Lindholm *et al.*[27] used a study sample of politicians; in a simple binary choice between programmes, two-thirds of respondents were prepared to sacrifice overall health gain to reduce inequity (the more efficient choice was given an "equity weighting" of less than 0·9).

Box 7.2 describes the preliminary results of a questionnaire designed to start filling this gap in the priority setting literature. The aim is to quantify the sacrifices in efficiency that respondents would be prepared to make for the sake of increasing equity. In the context of the questionnaire, achieving efficiency means maximising overall population life expectancy, whereas achieving equity means reducing inequality in life expectancy. Of all the inequalities in health that feature in discussions of public policy, the most commonly mentioned is that between rich and poor (or between the social classes). This is accordingly the first inequality that respondents are asked to consider. Two additional inequalities examined are the differential life expectancies between smokers and non-smokers, and between men and women. The questionnaire thus explores the strength of the respondents' aversion to different inequalities.

The results presented in Box 7.2 were obtained from convenience samples of (mostly) public health professionals, and so like previous exercises of this kind (see Box 7.1) they cannot claim to represent the view of the general public. Even within this professional group there were widely divergent views regarding the policy weight to be attached to health inequalities, suggesting that the task of generating agreement on such policies is likely to be formidable.

Importantly, these preliminary results show that it is possible, within the general framework of the fair innings argument, to distinguish between different degrees of aversion to different inequalities, depending on their nature and context. (The degree of aversion is likely also to be influenced by the size of the inequality and its trend over time.) However, can the fair innings argument handle other equity concerns that people have? Before considering other possible approaches, it is important to remember that the health maximisation objective is always at work alongside the equity objective. Every departure from the simple maximisation rule will mean that the average health of the population as a whole is being reduced below what it might have been. Being equitable has a cost – giving higher priority to one group necessarily means giving lower priority to others. Favouring the young implies discriminating against the old. In what follows it is important to stress who is losing out in order that others may gain; otherwise, the moral dilemma is not fully captured.

Box 7.2 A questionnaire designed to capture trade-offs between efficiency and equity*

Questionnaire design

Respondents are told that there is a five year difference in life expectancy at birth between social classes, between smokers and non-smokers, and between men and women. They are initially asked which of two policies they would prefer: policy A (which improves the life expectancy of each group, equally, by two years), or policy B (which gives all four extra years to the worse off group). Those who initially choose policy B are then questioned further to see how small the gain to the worse off can get before they regard the equal distribution as a better option. Those who initially choose policy A are first given an opportunity to make the inequality larger rather than smaller. The remaining questions test their indifference between the equal distribution of four years in total, and an unequal distribution of less than four years in total, but one in which both groups get some gains (which is not what happens if policy B is chosen).

Preliminary sample

The questionnaire was administered to convenience samples of public health professionals/trainees in the UK, Italy, Spain, the Netherlands, Australia, and New Zealand, as well as to attendees at the European Philosophers Forum and an International Society for Pharmacoeconomics and Outcomes Research (ISPOR) workshop.

Results

- Social classes (n = 416): 16 (4%) respondents would favour the better off social class, 72 (17%) preferred an equal distribution, 56 (13%) would favour the worse off but felt that the better off should also benefit, and 272 (65%) would favour the worse off even if the better off got nothing. The median respondent was willing to sacrifice two extra years for the better off in order to obtain one extra year for the worse off.
- Smokers versus non-smokers (n = 214): 97 (45%) favoured an equal distribution, and the median respondent fell within this group; 59 (28%) would favour non-smokers.
- Men versus women (n = 132): a bimodal distribution occurred for respondents of both sexes. Roughly speaking, one-third favoured doing nothing, one-third saw the difference in life expectancies as just as inequitable as the social class difference, and the median respondent was in the moderate middle outnumbered by both.

*This questionnaire was developed by Paul Dolan, Rebecca Shaw, Aki Tsuchiya, and Alan Williams, and is available on request from the Alan Williams at ahw1@york.ac.uk

Going beyond the fair innings argument

One of the principal contenders here is the so-called "rule of rescue". In a recent comprehensive review of this position by McKie and Richardson,[28] this is summarised as "the imperative people feel to rescue identifiable individuals facing avoidable death". The key features of this imperative are described as neglect of opportunity costs, identifiability of the potential beneficiaries, a focus on the life-threatening aspect of the situation, and a belief that an imminent death is avoidable by prompt action. There may also be a sense of shock or horror, which generates a suspension of cool calculating modes of response.

If haste and neglect of opportunity cost are momentarily set aside, then the key difference between the fair innings and McKie and Richardson's rule of rescue lies in their perspective. Whereas the fair innings argument adopts the longitudinal perspective of overall health experience (so that the relevant units are expected lifetime QALYs), the rule of rescue's view is cross-sectional, focused only on the severity of the present threat to life. Like the fair innings argument, the cross-sectional view has some empirical support.[21] These preferences might reflect methodological problems in their elicitation, such that participants did not fully appreciate the implications of their choices. However, they also reflect a very human gesture of caring. It is in the making of this gesture, if anywhere, that McKie and Richardson conclude that the moral justification for the rule of rescue must lie.

If this is indeed the socially valuable aspect of the application of the rule of rescue, then we should still be seeking ways of minimising its opportunity costs. We would not want to see a lifeboat launched in circumstances where the crew is almost certain to perish. To what extent, then, do we allow the lives of individuals, identifiable or otherwise, to be put at risk by the diversion of health care resources to rescue? (Although the issue of the identifiable beneficiary may not be applicable to the level of decision making under present consideration, it is important to opine in passing that being identifiable *per se* should not have any moral relevance in priority setting.) Consider, too, the purpose of bodies such as NICE or the PBAC; if these institutions are given the task of allocating resources in a deliberative manner, then should we expect from them the type of personal, impulsive response we might expect from a friend or indeed a health care professional in an emergency situation? What seems an admirable humanitarian response on a personal level may constitute unthinking, irresponsible behaviour at an institutional level.[29]

It could be argued that the rescue situation described by McKie and Richardson[28] is in some respects quite different from that in which a public body like NICE or the PBAC finds itself; there is no threat to the survival of a named individual, and so there is no shock/horror on the part of the decision makers (although this aspect of rescue may become relevant when the shock/horror dimension is felt by their constituents). Instead, there is time to think. A reasoned decision must be reached and justified, and part of the justification comes from demonstrating that the decision is one that will on the whole improve social welfare. Opportunity costs cannot be ignored. In the present context relevant opportunity costs will be not only a reduction in the average level of population health (the only opportunity cost considered in the McKie and Richardson formulation) but also a reduction in the capacity of the system to reduce inequalities in individuals' lifetime experience of health (because the fair innings argument is also in play here).

One approach to reducing the opportunity costs in terms of the capacity to reduce inequalities in lifetime health is to limit the rule of rescue so that it is activated only by the threat of unexpected "premature" death. McKie and Richardson[28] appear to have had this lurking in the back of their minds too, because at one point they exclude from rule of rescue eligibility "the very elderly, or those who have had cancer for an extended period and we [sic] have come to accept the inevitability of death". In this case, the priorities of the fair innings argument and rule of rescue are similar (although the former would not apply until potential costs had been counted).

The Australian PBAC has recognised that its decisions have been influenced by a variant of the rule of rescue with just such a focus on the avoidance of premature death. Two additional criteria must be met before this variation on the rule of rescue can be said to apply; the patients in question must have no treatment alternatives, and their number must

Box 7.3 "Rule of rescue" and a summary of a proposal for discussion by the PBAC

In deciding whether to recommend subsidy, the PBAC not only considers comparative cost-effectiveness. Instead, a number of relevant factors are likely to be considered. Among these may appear a well defined set of factors that the PBAC has dubbed the rule of rescue. These factors are as follows.

1 There are no alternative treatments, pharmacological or otherwise, available in Australia to the patients in question.
2 The condition in question is "severe, progressive, and expected to lead to premature death".
3 The number of patients to be treated is very small.

Factor 1 is an absolute requirement, whereas factors 2 and 3 will, by virtue of increased intensity, increase the influence of the combined set of factors. That is to say, the more severe the patients' condition or the more prematurely they are likely to die, and likewise the smaller the patients are in number, the more influential will be the rule of rescue in decision making.

The process whereby the rule of rescue enters into the decision process is also clearly defined. Importantly, the rule of rescue supplements rather than supplants the consideration of comparative cost-effectiveness (and other relevant factors).

The PBAC's approach to the incorporation of factors such as the rule of rescue into a decision process that must remain consistent and defendable continues to evolve.

be small. This combination of factors is considered alongside comparative cost-effectiveness (and other relevant factors), and may be sufficiently influential to reverse a decision that would have arisen based solely on a consideration of comparative cost-effectiveness (Box 7.3).

Does the PBAC's rule of rescue withstand scrutiny of its underlying principles? That a person has a rare, as opposed to a common, condition does not seem a good moral basis for accepting higher opportunity costs (meaning additional health sacrifices imposed on others) when both conditions leave the sufferer in identical circumstances. Stipulating that the number of beneficiaries must be small serves, rather, as another way of limiting the opportunity costs of rescue; the extra costs of meeting their needs will be small on aggregate and can therefore be spread thinly over the rest of the population. Similarly, restricting the rule of rescue to patients who lack treatment alternatives and thus any hope of alleviation allows a tangible but relatively low-cost caring gesture to be made. It could, however, be argued that to overstep the fair innings argument in favour of those who lack treatment alternatives is to introduce morally invidious distinctions between people who have reached that terminal phase in their lives in different ways, for which no blame or credit can be assigned to the affected individual.

Overall, it seems that the PBAC's approach to the rule of rescue owes more to the fair innings argument than to McKie and Richardson's rescue formulation. If denial has a cost, and rescue has a cost, then the PBAC's approach may represent a satisfactory compromise between maximisation, rescue, and the fair innings argument. Indeed, it may represent one that allows institutions such as the PBAC to retain the popular support necessary for their continued deliberative role. Nevertheless, its application means that the health of the community on aggregate will be poorer than it would otherwise have been, and/or inequalities in lifetime health will be greater than they would otherwise have been. One caring gesture competes with another.

The question remains, then, as to whether the rule of rescue retains elements that an informed public, fully cognizant of the sacrifices involved, would support? Specifically, are there elements that public priority setting bodies should take on board so that no particularly deserving groups of people slip through the net, despite careful balancing of the fair innings argument and maximisation principles? This remains a question for careful empirical research, perhaps with an approach similar to the trade-off exercise described above. It will be of fundamental importance to test the strength of preference for each principle by confronting respondents with the opportunity cost in terms of other health gains sacrificed. Also, if it turns out that more than one equity principle should be in play, then we have multiple trade-offs to consider, which include trade-offs between different equity principles. It may be that measuring the acceptable efficiency loss associated with each equity principle separately will provide the "triangulation" required, if interdependence and process concerns can be ignored. There is much empirical work to be done here.

Conclusion

The evidence base to support priority setting in health care is at present severely unbalanced, with very few data available on the trade-offs that the general public (or even health professionals) would be prepared to make between equity and efficiency, or between different equity principles when more than one is in play. We have attempted to demonstrate that this void can be filled, although at present the pilot work reported here is no more than an exploration of feasibility and has yet to tackle the general public as respondents. However, it is important to recognise that it is dangerous to take the important step from looking at factual information about inequalities in health to making ethical judgements about how inequitable they are, without making explicit the value judgements that are being made, and testing whether they conform to the views of those in whose name they are being made. There can, and should, be an evidence base for incorporating equity into decision making that is as rigorous as the evidence base supporting the pursuit of efficiency. Otherwise, priority setting in health care will be neither appropriate nor accountable.

Summary

- Priority setting must reflect the objectives of the health system.
- Broadly, these objectives encompass the dual (and often competing) goals of efficiency and equity.
- The "fair innings argument" is proposed as the ideal approach to the equity objective.
- The "rule of rescue" may provide an alternative or supplement to the fair innings argument.
- Evidence is needed as to the trade-offs that the general public would be prepared to make between equity and efficiency, and/or between competing equity principles.

References

1 Hume D. *Hume: political essays*. Cambridge: Cambridge University Press, 1994.
2 Culyer AJ, Wagstaff A. Equity and equality in health and health care. *J Health Econ* 1993;12:431–57.
3 Harris J. *The value of life: an introduction to medical ethics*. London: Routledge, 1985.

4 Kind P, Hardman G, Macran S. *UK Population Norms for EQ5D, Discussion Paper 172*. York: University of York, Centre for Health Economics, 1999.

5 Nord E, Pinto JL, Richardson J, Menzel P, Ubel P. Incorporating societal concerns for fairness in numerical valuations of health programmes. *Health Econ* 1999;8:25–39.

6 Wagstaff A. QALYs and the equity-efficiency trade-off. *J Health Econ* 1991;10:21–41.

7 Dolan P, Olsen JA. Equity in health: the importance of different health streams. *J Health Econ* 2001;20:823–34.

8 Schwappach DL. Resource allocation, social values and the QALY: a review of the debate and empirical evidence. *Health Expect* 2002;5:210–22.

9 Nord E, Richardson J, Street A, Kuhse H, Singer P. Maximising health benefits vs egalitarianism: an Australian survey of health issues. *Soc Sci Med* 1995;41:1429–37.

10 Williams A. Conceptual and empirical issues in the efficiency equity trade-off in the provision of health care. In: Culyer AJ, Maynard A, eds. *Being reasonable about the economics of health*. Cheltenham, UK: Edward Elgar Publishing, 1997.

11 Hadorn DC. Setting health care priorities in Oregon: cost-effectiveness meets the rule of rescue. *JAMA* 1991;265:2218–25.

12 Robinson R. Limits to rationality: economics, economists and priority setting. *Health Policy* 1999;49:13–26.

13 Litva A, Coast J, Donovan J, *et al*. "The public is too subjective": public involvement at different levels of health-care decision making. *Soc Sci Med* 2002;54:1825–37.

14 Wiseman V, Mooney G, Berry G, Tang KC. Involving the general public in priority setting: experiences from Australia. *Soc Sci Med* 2003;56:1001–12.

15 Lenaghan J, Mitchell E. Setting priorities: is there a role for citizens' juries? *BMJ* 1996;312:1591–3.

16 Ubel PA. How stable are people's preferences for giving priority to severely ill patients? *Soc Sci Med* 1999;49:895–903.

17 Dolan P, Cookson R, Ferguson B. Effect of discussion and deliberation on the public's views of priority setting in health care: focus group study. *BMJ* 1999;318:916–19.

18 Shickle D. Public preferences for health care: prioritisation in the United Kingdom. *Bioethics* 1997;11:277–90.

19 Nord E, Street A, Richardson J, Kuhse H, Singer P. The significance of age and duration of effect in social evaluation of health care. *Health Care Anal* 1996;4:103–11.

20 Bowling A. Health care rationing: the public's debate. *BMJ* 1996;312:670–4.

21 Nord E. Health status index models for use in resource allocation decisions. A critical review in the light of observed preferences for social choice. *Int J Technol Assess Health Care* 1996;12:31–44.

22 Cookson R, Dolan P. Public views on health care rationing: a group discussion study. *Health Policy* 1999;49:63–74.

23 Schwappach DLB. Does it matter who you are or what you gain? An experimental study of preferences for resource allocation. *Health Econ* 2003;12:255–67.

24 Nord E, Richardson J, Street A, Kuhse H, Singer P. Who cares about cost? Does economic analysis impose or reflect social values? *Health Policy* 1995;34:79–94.

25 Andersson F, Lyttkens CH. Preferences for equity in health behind a veil of ignorance. *Health Econ* 1999;8:369–78.

26 Johannesson M, Gerdtham U-G. A note on the estimation of the equity-efficiency trade-off for QALYs. *J Health Econ* 1996;15:359–68.

27 Lindholm L, Rosen M, Emmelin M. An epidemiological approach towards measuring the trade-off between equity and efficiency in health policy. *Health Policy* 1996;**35**:205–16.
28 McKie J, Richardson J. The rule of rescue. *Soc Sci Med* 2003;**56**:2407–19.
29 Goodin R. *Utilitarianism as a public philosophy*. Cambridge: Cambridge University Press, 1995.

8: Tensions in licensing and reimbursement decisions: the case of riluzole for amytrophic lateral sclerosis

STIRLING BRYAN, JOSIE SANDERCOCK,
PELHAM BARTON, AMANDA BURLS

Introduction

The decision to license a pharmaceutical product and the decision to reimburse the manufacturer for its use in a public health care system do not necessarily run parallel. By definition, the two decisions are taken for different reasons and, as such, employ different criteria. This chapter considers these processes, using the case of the drug riluzole for the treatment of amyotrophic lateral sclerosis (ALS) as an example. The licensing and reimbursement decisions examined are those relating to the UK. The decision by the National Institute for Clinical Excellence (NICE) is viewed as being somewhat unusual in that the drug was approved despite the weakness of the evidence for effectiveness and the fact that the cost-effectiveness ratio is higher than that normally considered to be affordable by the National Health Service.[1]

Riluzole for amyotrophic lateral sclerosis

The disease

ALS is a form of motor neurone disease that is caused by degeneration of the motor neurones of the brain and spinal cord. Symptoms include spasticity, muscle weakness and paralysis, and impaired speaking, swallowing and breathing. It is a very distressing disease for sufferers, who experience rapid, progressive, and profound loss of their ability to move and function. This leads to an erosion in their autonomy – a problem compounded by the involvement of the muscles used for speech (which eventually affects some 80% of patients), resulting in impaired communication, isolation, and frustration. The disease is therefore very distressing for family and carers also.

ALS is relentlessly progressive and death nearly always occurs within three to five years, usually from respiratory infection or respiratory failure. Survival time is significantly reduced when the disease starts with bulbar symptoms or at an older age. There is no cure and most interventions are directed at practical support and palliative care. The quality of life experienced by patients with ALS varies greatly, even among those with the same objective functional impairment. This is in part due to the individual's attitudes and values, and in part to the degree of social support and care they receive.

The prevalence of ALS is around five to six per 100,000. At any one time there are around 3000 people in the UK with ALS.

The licensing of riluzole

Riluzole was granted a licence for use in ALS by the European Agency for the Evaluation of Medicinal Products on 10 June 1996. The Committee for Proprietary Medicinal Products (CPMP) concluded that:

Clinical trials designed to investigate Rilutek have demonstrated that it induces a modest extension to life or the time taken for the progression of the disease to require mechanical ventilation, in ALS patients other than those who are in the late stages of the disease ... There is no evidence that Riluzole exerts a therapeutic effect on motor function, lung function, fasciculations, muscle strength and motor symptoms.

The CPMP, on the basis of the efficacy and safety data submitted, considered that Rilutek showed adequate evidence of efficacy for the approved indication, as well as a satisfactory risk/benefit profile and therefore recommended that the Marketing Authorisation should be granted.

The original authorisation was based on three trials, with a total of 1382 patients randomised (Meininger V, Lacomblez L, Bensimon G; unpublished study report).[2,3] All three trials were conducted by the same trialists and were similar in design. The trial by Lacomblez et al.[3] was designed to confirm the positive results of the earlier trial by Bensimon et al.,[2] with the trial by Meininger et al. (unpublished data) conducted in parallel for patients who were ineligible for inclusion in the trial by Lacomblez et al. (Broadly, the patients studied by Meininger et al. were older or had a longer prior duration of disease.)

In their discussion the CPMP expressed concern at the lack of concordance in the trials between effects on survival, with the findings reported by Bensimon et al. and Lacomblez et al. suggesting a benefit from riluzole, and functional status, for which no clear differences between groups were apparent in any of the trials. It is clear from the discussion in the Public Assessment Report[4] that this was an issue of some concern both on ethical and scientific grounds, with the CPMP questioning the clinical relevance of extending survival in this devastating disease without improving functional status.

Although marketing authorisation was granted on the basis of these trials, the CPMP requested that the results of a fourth study be presented when available. On reviewing the results of that study,[5] with a further 195 patients meeting similar eligibility criteria to those employed by Bensimon et al. and by Lacomblez et al., along with a further meta-analysis of all four studies, the CPMP stated that:

> Following evaluation of the meta-analysis, the CPMP concluded that the statistical evidence for the efficacy of riluzole is less secure. Nevertheless, given the high levels of statistical significance achieved in [two of the four trials] and the overall results of the new meta-analysis, the balance of probability is still in favour of riluzole.

The results of these four trials are discussed in more detail below.

The reimbursement decision

The guidance issued by NICE[6] in January 2001 states that, "Riluzole is recommended for the treatment of individuals with the amyotrophic lateral sclerosis (ALS) form of motor neurone disease (MND)." The evidence and economic analyses that were considered by NICE in reaching its decision are summarised below (see Stewart et al.[7] for a detailed report, which is downloadable from http://www.ncchta.org).

The review of effectiveness evidence

No additional studies were identified beyond the four trials on which the marketing authorisation was based. All four trials compared riluzole with placebo. Three trials used riluzole at 100 mg/day and one (Lacomblez et al.[3]) randomly assigned patients to three different doses (50, 100, and 200 mg/day), in addition to a placebo arm. Three of the trials had broadly similar eligibility criteria; the other one (Meininger V, Lacomblez L, Bensimon G; unpublished study report) recruited patients who were older, had a longer prior duration of disease, or had a forced vital capacity below 60%. All trials had tracheostomy-free survival (time to death or life support) as a primary outcome. In all four trials, most patients were prevalent rather than incident cases.

Two of the trials (Bensimon et al.[2] and Lacomblez et al.[3]) had been published in full in high profile English language journals, the trial conducted by Yanagisawa et al.[5] had been published only in Japanese, and the trial by Meininger et al. remained unpublished. The Bensimon and Lacomblez trials had been included in all three previous published systematic reviews, Meininger in one, and Yanagisawa in none.

The results of the trials are summarised in Figure 8.1. Note that the results for Yanagisawa et al.[5] were obtained from the unpublished meta-analysis performed at the request of the European Medicines Evaluation Agency (EMEA); these results had never been made public before inclusion in the assessment report prepared for NICE.[7]

The estimated pooled hazard ratio reported in the full meta-analysis performed by the manufacturer of riluzole for the EMEA was 0·89 (95% confidence interval 0·75–1·05). Before these data were obtained, our estimate based on the combined results of the other three trials was 0·83 (95% confidence interval 0·69–0·99). The differences between these results are of no practical importance; the upper limit of the confidence interval is still compatible with little or no benefit. However, with the inclusion of the Yanagisawa data the impression

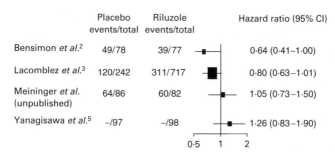

Figure 8.1 Trial results for riluzole in terms of tracheostomy-free survival. Note that the number of events for the trial by Yanagisawa *et al.*[5] are not available. The boxes are centred on the reported estimates for each trial, with the area of the boxes indicating the amount of information contributed by the trial. The lines indicate the 95% confidence interval (CI) for the trial. (The left pointing arrow indicates that the line extends off the scale.)

of heterogeneity is strengthened, with a p value for heterogeneity of 0·09 (as compared with 0·39 previously). Although not reaching conventional levels of significance, this heterogeneity is of some concern because it reflects a qualitative, rather than merely quantitative, difference in the results of these trials, with one of the four trials suggesting no benefit and another giving weak evidence of possible harm. These trials are too small to allow a firm conclusion to be drawn concerning the extent and importance of heterogeneity in their results.

It is worth noting that the hazard ratio for all four trials quoted above excludes half of the patients from the trial by Lacomblez *et al.*,[3] specifically those assigned to 50 or 200 mg/day riluzole (as opposed to the eventual licensed dose of 100 mg/day). It has been asserted that the exclusion of these patients is based on an incorrect interpretation of the results, which the company claimed indicated a dose–response relationship, with 50 mg/day being less effective than 100 mg/day, and 200 mg/day being similarly effective but more toxic. Although toxicity does appear to rise with dose, there is no clear indication of a dose–response relationship, as can be confirmed by a cursory glance at the published estimates for each dose level.[7] We therefore repeated the meta-analysis of the four trials, combining the data from the 50, 100 and 200 mg/day arms of the trial by Lacomblez et al.[3] for comparison against placebo. The results are very similar but with slightly tighter confidence intervals, giving an estimated hazard ratio of 0·88 (95% confidence interval 0·75–1·02) and a p value for heterogeneity of 0·09.

Data on functional status were available from three of the four trials (Bensimon et al.,[2] Lacomblez et al.,[3] and Meininger et al. [unpublished study report]). When these results were combined, a small reduction in the rate of deterioration in functional status was observed. We included results from all arms of the trial by Lacomblez et al. for this analysis, substantially increasing the sample size compared with the meta-analysis that had been presented to the licensing authorities. Our results thus provide somewhat stronger statistical evidence of a benefit in terms of functional status than was previously reported. However, the analysis is incomplete because there are no data available from the trial by Yanigasawa et al.,[5] and the estimated differences based on the three other trials are small and of questionable clinical significance.

A large proportion of patients in both groups reported adverse events, but there was little overall difference between riluzole and placebo.

There was no evidence available about longer term treatment outcomes, beyond the 18 month follow up period of the trials. Both trials that suggested a benefit from riluzole were suggestive of diminishing benefit over time, but the sample sizes concerned are far too small to investigate this reliably.

The review of existing cost-effectiveness evidence

At the time the work was carried out, there were four original economic evaluations of riluzole published in peer reviewed journals.[8–11] All studies compared treatment with riluzole against service provision without riluzole, either "standard therapy" or "best supportive care". The base case incremental cost-effectiveness ratios (ICERs) varied widely between studies (Table 8.1).

One of the main drivers of the observed variation in results was the variation in the estimates of mean survival gain from the use of riluzole. In all trials, patients on placebo were

Table 8.1 Existing economic evaluations	
Study	**Base case ICER**
Gray[8]	£44,890/life year gained
Ginsberg and Lev[9]	$12,013/life year gained
Messori et al.[10]	$62,609/life year gained
Tavakoli et al.[11]*	£8587/life year gained
Aventis NICE submission*	£20,906/QALY

*These are the published results from the Tavakoli model, which contained an undiscovered error (described in the text). The Aventis submission to NICE was based on the Tavakoli model with utilities incorporated to provide a cost-utility analysis; the submission was corrected when the original error came to light, and it is this corrected result that is used in this table.

switched to riluzole at the end of follow up and so no longer term survival data for placebo patients are available. The implication of this is that, for the purposes of estimating the full survival gain associated with the use of riluzole, extrapolation beyond the follow up data observed in the trials is required.

Gray[8] did not extrapolate beyond trial data, and Ginsberg and Lev[9] made no reference to the issue of survival extrapolation. Messori et al.[10] applied a Gompertz model to the survival curves, which allowed survival curves to be extrapolated and mean lifetime survival to be estimated (as area under the survival curve). Their base case analysis indicated a difference in mean lifetime survival between trial arms of 2·4 months (undiscounted).

Tavakoli et al.[11] constructed a Markov model to estimate survival from the point of entry into the trial through to death, with transition probabilities based on the data from two arms (placebo and 100 mg/day riluzole) of the trial by Lacomblez et al.[3] The paper reports observed survival (in the trial) and predicted survival (using the Markov model) through the presentation of survival curves. The estimated difference in mean lifetime survival between the riluzole and placebo groups appears to be about 12 months in this analysis. (Note that this survival gain is not reported in the paper – this estimate is derived from visual inspection of two figures in the report by Tavakoli et al.) As detailed by Stewart et al.,[7] this result arose from a serious error in the logic of the constructed model. The error had the effect of preventing riluzole patients in the terminal state of ALS from dying without their health improving initially and their condition then returning to the severe state. Thus, the death rate in the riluzole arm was seriously underestimated; this error was not present in the "usual care" arm of the model. The Tavakoli model was used as the basis for the company's submission to NICE; this submission was corrected when the error in the original model came to light.

The review of existing economic analyses suggested that the existing published estimates of the cost-effectiveness of riluzole must be viewed very cautiously, and so a new analysis was undertaken. The key uncertain parameter appeared to be the estimated gain in life expectancy for patients who take riluzole.

Further economic analysis

We used the "numbers at risk" and "number of events", reported at three month intervals in the trial publications, to combine the published survival curves from the trials by Bensimon et al.[2] and Lacomblez et al.[3] only. It should be noted that this analysis thus ignores the evidence from the two trials that did not suggest any benefit from riluzole. It was not possible to use the combined data from all four trials to inform the economic analysis, in part because survival curves were not available for the trial by Yanagisawa et al.[5] and because the median survival for the patients in the trial by Meininger et al. (unpublished study report) was so much shorter than for those in the Bensimon and Lacomblez trials as a result of patient selection criteria; combining these survival curves would be meaningless. It is important to note that because the data from both excluded trials were the least favourable to riluzole, the economic analysis is based on a highly optimistic selection of trial data and has a default "worst case" of dominance by placebo, regardless of other parameter values.

Extrapolation beyond the observed survival in the two trials was undertaken using a Weibull model.[12] The survival curves resulting from this analysis are shown in Figure 8.2. The mean survival for patients in each group was estimated as the area under the survival curve. On the basis of the reanalysis of trial

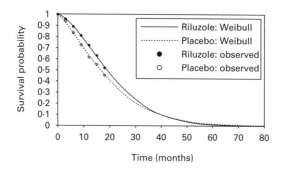

Figure 8.2 Survival curves with Weibull extrapolation.

data reported by Munsat *et al.*[13] on time spent in each ALS health state, the assumption for the base case analysis was that the increase in survival brought about by riluzole is experienced in ALS health state II (state I being mild disease and IV being terminal).

The economic analysis adopted a health service perspective and so it considered only those costs incurred within the health sector. These included costs associated with the drug itself, the associated serum alanine aminotransferase testing, and the general costs of caring for patients with ALS over the extended period of survival. For the base case all future costs and benefits were discounted at a rate of 6%. In the trials it was observed that 25% of patients who began on riluzole withdrew from treatment. The cost analysis has assumed that such a withdrawal rate would be seen in routine practice and cost estimates have been adjusted accordingly.

The parameters used in the base case economic analysis undertaken for this review are reported in Table 8.2.

The economic evaluation includes both cost-effectiveness analyses (cost per life year gained) and cost-utility analyses (cost per quality-adjusted life year [QALY] gained), both using an incremental approach with a focus on the increase in costs and increase in effectiveness. Data on quality of life were taken from the standard gamble utility estimates reported in the Aventis NICE submission (cited by Stewart *et al.*[7]). The results of the base case economic analysis were that riluzole is associated with an increase in expected lifetime survival of

Table 8.2 Base case parameters for the economic analysis

Parameters	Value	Source
Undiscounted survival (months) with riluzole	21·38	Stewart et al.[7] (Weibull extrapolation)
Undiscounted survival (months) with placebo	19·67	
Discounted survival (months) with riluzole	20·85	
Discounted survival (months) with placebo	19·24	
Proportion of patient withdrawals from riluzole	0·25	Trials by Bensimon et al.[2] and Lacomblez et al.[3]
Riluzole cost per daily dose (£)	10·21	£286 per 56 50-mg tablets
Patient monitoring cost per month (£)	17	Tavakoli et al.[11]
Annual care cost (£)		Munsat et al.[13]
ALS health state I	1236·61	
ALS health state II	834·28	
ALS health state III	1771·42	
ALS health state IV	3263·17	
Discount rate	6%	UK Treasury
Utility		Aventis NICE submission
ALS health state I	0·79	
ALS health state II	0·67	
ALS health state III	0·71	
ALS health state IV	0·45	

Price base: 1999. ALS, amytrophic lateral sclerosis; NICE, National Institute of Clinical Excellence.

0·13 years, which translates into 0·09 QALYs. The expected additional discounted cost to the health service is £5200 per patient over the remainder of the patient's life.

The robustness of the base case results was explored through the use of sensitivity analysis. Table 8.3 indicates the parameters that were varied and the results.

Overall, the sensitivity analysis indicates that the base case results are reasonably robust to variation in the health state assumptions and to discount rate variation. The cost-effectiveness of riluzole is unsurprisingly more attractive when a dosage of 50 mg/day is used, assuming a simple 50% decrease in drug costs and no reduction in effectiveness; there

Table 8.3 Results: base case and sensitivity analyses

Parameter	Gain in life-years	Gain in QALYs	Increase in cost (£)	ICER (cost per life-year; £)	ICER (cost per QALY; £)
Base case result	0·13	0·09	5200	39,000	58,000
Riluzole given to incident population*					
Assuming the same absolute gain in life years as in the base case	0·13	0·09	9700	72,000	107,000
Assuming that the absolute gain in life years is greater by the same proportion as the increase in duration of therapy	0·27	0·18	10,700	39,000	58,000
Variation in survival estimates					
Using a Gompertz model for survival extrapolation for both placebo and riluzole	0·08	0·05	4500	59,000	88,000
Using a Gompertz model for placebo and Weibull model for riluzole extrapolation	0·31	0·21	5300	17,000	25,000
Using a Weibull model for placebo and Gompertz model for riluzole extrapolation	−0·10	−0·07	4300	−42,000†	−62,000†
Assuming one month survival gain for riluzole (as an estimate of the upper bound 95% CI)	0·08	0·05	5000	66,000	98,000
Assuming six month survival gain for riluzole (as an estimate of the lower bound 95% CI)	0·47	0·32	6400	14,000	20,000
Variation in health state assumption					
Survival gain distributed evenly across all four ALS health states	0·13	0·09	5300	40,000	60,000
All survival gain experienced in health state IV	0·13	0·06	5500	41,000	91,000
Discount rate					
Benefits undiscounted, costs discounted at 6%	0·14	0·10	5200	37,000	54,000
Costs and benefits discounted at 3%	0·14	0·09	5200	38,000	56,000
Variation in dose of riluzole 50 mg/day	0·13	0·09	2800	21,000	31,000

*Assuming that patients start taking riluzole two years earlier, on average, than trial patients. †Riluzole associated with higher cost and lower survival than placebo. ALS, amyotrophic lateral sclerosis; CI, confidence interval; ICER, incremental cost-effectiveness ratio; QALY, quality-adjusted life year.

is no evidence to suggest that there is any difference in effectiveness between these two doses, although there are insufficient data to rule out the possibility of a moderate dose–outcome relationship. The use of riluzole in an incident population is associated with a marked increase in costs, given the longer period of time over which the drug is taken. The impact of this on the ICER depends on the extent to which the gain in life years might be influenced by the earlier use of riluzole; there are no adequate published data that address this question.

The sensitivity analysis confirms that the key driver of the cost-effectiveness result is the survival gain associated with riluzole. Different methods of extrapolating beyond observed survival in the trials give widely varying results.

Most scenarios considered suggest an ICER (or cost per QALY) in excess of £50,000/QALY. The most optimistic ICER is around £20,000, based on an optimistic reading of an already optimistic selection of trial data; the more pessimistic scenarios suggest that riluzole is dominated by placebo (being both less effective and more expensive).

Tensions between licensing and reimbursement decisions

Licensing versus reimbursement

Licensing and reimbursement decisions are fundamentally different. The licensing authorities establish, essentially, that it is not unreasonable to use a treatment for a specific condition. This is usually assessed in terms of the impact the treatment appears to have on the disease process or outcomes, the extent to which the side effects are viewed as acceptable given the nature and severity of the disease, and the quality and product consistency of the manufacturing processes.

Once a product is licensed, decision makers must determine whether it is appropriate that the treatment should be used, both for the particular patient group in whom the treatment would be applied and within the wider context of a health service with a limited budget. This reimbursement decision requires quite different information than that required for licensing. A prerequisite for reimbursement is that a treatment is considered clinically appropriate for use in at least some circumstances. This judgement typically requires different, and generally rather more, data than are required for licensing, and involves an explicit consideration of the extent of all clinical benefits and disadvantages, weighted appropriately to their importance to the patient. To inform a reimbursement decision, information is required on a range of clinical outcomes, including quality of life, preferably measured over an extended period of follow up, and conducted in a "real world" patient population. Importantly, although regulatory decisions are ideally based on placebo controlled trials (it would be counter-productive to demand that every new treatment is better than the best available current treatment) and rarely against "real world" alternatives, reimbursement decisions must be based on comparisons with the most effective available alternatives. Riluzole is unusual in this respect in that there are as yet no alternative comparator treatments to consider.

With some estimate of the likely benefit to be obtained through the use of a particular treatment, ideally expressed in a generic measure such as the QALY, the reimbursement decision must then examine the treatment within the context of the health service as a whole. If a treatment is more expensive than the alternatives and produces zero or negative QALYs, then its use is clearly not desirable. The more difficult situation is where one treatment is both more expensive and more effective, offering the possibility of greater health gain but at some cost. At this point the reimbursement decision must consider the "value for money" that the treatment offers as compared with treatments used in other diseases. Within a limited budget for health care, the adoption of a more expensive treatment necessitates paying less for treatment elsewhere in the system.

This is of course where the tension between licensing and reimbursement decisions is most acute. If a treatment is licensed for use and provides clinical benefits, then denial on the grounds of cost might appear hard to justify. However, recognition that there is a fixed budget, within which there is a responsibility to distribute resources efficiently and fairly, may make such a decision seem more reasonable; in these circumstances the decision is made not on grounds of cost to the health service but in terms of the opportunity cost to other patient groups whose care would be compromised by the diversion of resources. Arguing that the budget should be increased does not resolve this problem. If the budget is increased, the point at which a treatment is no longer considered cost-effective is raised, but there is still, of necessity, a threshold beyond which treatment cannot be justified.

The tension in the case of riluzole

When considered alongside other treatments appraised by NICE, riluzole appears to be an expensive outlier.[1] There are a number of additional factors that may have influenced the reimbursement decision in this case. Broadly, these can be categorised either as concerns relating to equity issues or as budget impact considerations. The latter is simply the acknowledgement that the condition is rare and so the overall financial impact (and thus the opportunity cost) resulting from a positive reimbursement decision is likely to be fairly small.

There are two components to the equity concerns: the fact that there is no other active treatment for ALS and the simple fact that this is a devastating disease. The absence of alternatives does not, of course, make riluzole any more effective, nor does the severe nature of the disease. However, in the absence of alternatives, withholding riluzole is equivalent to denying any disease modifying treatment to a patient who is destined to a certain, rapid physical decline and untimely death. In such circumstances a criterion driven by efficiency might be downgraded by decision makers who wish to see ALS patients given access to the therapy despite it not reaching accepted levels of cost-effectiveness. In such cases, life conserving considerations may be given more weight in decision making – a social imperative known as the "rule of rescue".[14,15] That this appears to have played some role in the Appraisal Committee's decision appears to be suggested in the guidance:

> The Committee took account of the severity and relatively short life span of people with ALS and in particular, as directly reported to it, of the values which patients place on the extension of tracheostomy free survival time.

NICE guidance on riluzole for ALS (January 2001)[6]

Riluzole for ALS is not very cost-effective largely because it is not very effective,[7] and so if we choose to reimburse largely on equity grounds there might be criticism that we are simply offering an expensive illusion of hope. However, others point to the intangible benefits from being able to do something rather than nothing:

This is a disease over which we have no control. It takes hold of people and removes their ability to live life as they choose. At the very least this drug gives people with motor neurone disease the sense that they are doing something, and it offers hope.

Tricia Holmes, Director of Care Development at the
Motor Neurone Disease Association

There is one final consideration that may have had an impact on the reimbursement decision. When the reimbursement decision was made riluzole was not a particularly new drug, and it was very unlikely that there would be any further research addressing the role of riluzole in such a rare disease, and so there was little hope that the uncertainties in the clinical and cost-effectiveness results could be reduced. A decision to "wait and see" would effectively have been a decision to wait indefinitely.

Uncertainty, the need to make a decision, and the need for further research: the final tension

Neither the decision to license nor the decision to reimburse riluzole for ALS were clear-cut. Both the EMEA and NICE expressed reservations about the quality, strength, and clinical relevance of the evidence available. Both decisions were positive, however, and appear to have been heavily influenced by the nature of the disease and the lack of any alternative for this patient group.

Although the licensing authorities may request more primary research before making a decision, the key difficulty for bodies such as NICE is that the treatments they consider are often already on the market and usually in use to some extent. Even if the evidence base is encouraging but nevertheless inadequate to inform the reimbursement decision, some sort of decision still must be made. To what extent should treatments be given the "benefit of the doubt" at the reimbursement stage?

One option is to make the treatment available in the interim while better evidence is being gathered. This approach is attractive in that it does not deny patients access to a potentially valuable treatment, but there are some important problems that must be noted. First, if the treatment becomes a part of "standard practice" then it will, in practical terms, be very hard to withdraw should further evidence suggest that it is not an appropriate use of resources. Second, the "benefit of the doubt" may in itself act as a disincentive to the conduct of the research that is needed. It is hard to see industry being routinely willing to invest in research that has little potential for direct benefit.

This places a great onus of responsibility on decision makers. Although there are cases in which it is simply not efficient or necessary to conduct more research, we will often require more information than is available through regulatory trials in order to make rational health care choices. Without a clear commitment to such research, and adequate funds committed at a sufficiently early stage in the development of new treatments, the need to make a decision in the short term may, in effect, prevent us from making the right decision for the longer term.

Conclusion

The licensing decision and the reimbursement decision are fundamentally different and do not necessarily run parallel. Because the two decisions are taken for different reasons, they quite appropriately employ different criteria. This chapter considered these processes in the UK context using the case study of the drug riluzole for the treatment of ALS. Neither the decision to license nor the decision to reimburse riluzole for ALS was clear-cut. Both the EMEA and NICE expressed reservations about the quality, strength, and clinical relevance of the evidence available. In the event, both decisions were positive, and appear to have been heavily influenced by the nature of the disease and the lack of any alternatives for this patient group.

Summary

- The decision to license a pharmaceutical product and the decision to reimburse the manufacturer for its use in a public health care system do not necessarily run parallel.
- By definition, the licensing and reimbursement decisions are taken for different reasons, and as such they employ different criteria.
- The licensing authorities establish that it is *not unreasonable* to use a treatment for a specific condition, whereas the reimbursement decision is driven by whether it is *appropriate* that the treatment should be used, both for the particular patient group in whom the treatment would be applied and in the wider context of a health service with a limited budget.
- In the case of riluzole for patients with ALS, both the licensing and reimbursement decisions in the UK were positive and appear to have been influenced, in part, by equity concerns relating to the severe nature of the disease and the lack of any alternative treatments for this patient group.

References

1 Raftery J. NICE: faster access to modern treatments? Analysis of guidance on health technologies. *BMJ* 2001;**323**:1300–3.
2 Bensimon G, Lacomblez L, Meininger V. A controlled trial of riluzole in amyotrophic lateral sclerosis. *N Engl J Med* 1994;**330**:5855–91.
3 Lacomblez L, Bensimon G, Leigh PN, Guillet P, Meininger V, for the Amyotrophic Lateral Sclerosis Study Group II. Dose-ranging study of riluzole in amyotrophic lateral sclerosis. *Lancet* 1996;**347**:1425–31.
4 Committee for Proprietary Medicinal Products. *European Public Assessment Report (EPAR): Rilutek (CPMP/290/96).* The European Agency for the Evaluation of Medicinal Products, 1999.
5 Yanagisawa N, Tashiro K, Tohgi H, *et al.* Efficacy and safety of riluzole in patients with amyotrophic lateral sclerosis: double-blind placebo-controlled study in Japan. *Igakuno Ayumi* 1997;**182**:851–66.
6 National Institute for Clinical Excellence. NICE guidance on the use of riluzole (Rilutek) for the treatment of motor neurone disease. http://www.nice.org.uk/article.asp?a=14490 (accessed 3 February 2004).
7 Stewart A, Sandercock J, Bryan S, *et al.* The clinical effectiveness and cost-effectiveness of riluzole for motor neurone disease: a rapid and systematic review. *Health Technol Assess* 2001;**5**:1–97.
8 Gray AM. ALS/MND and the perspective of health economics. *J Neurol Sci* 1998;**160(suppl 1)**:S2–5.
9 Ginsberg GM, Lev B. Cost-benefit analysis of riluzole for the treatment of amyotrophic lateral sclerosis. *Pharmacoeconomics* 1997;**12**:578–84.
10 Messori A, Trippoli S, Becagli P, Zaccara G, on behalf of the Italian Cooperative Group for the Study of Meta-Analysis and the Osservatorio SIFO sui Farmaci. Cost effectiveness of riluzole in amyotrophic lateral sclerosis. *Pharmacoeconomics* 1999;**16**:153–63.

11 Tavakoli M, Davies HTO, Malek M. Modelling the long-term cost effectiveness of riluzole for the treatment of amyotrophic lateral sclerosis. *J Drug Assess* 1999;2:219–32.
12 Cox DR, Oakes D. *Analysis of survival data.* London: Chapman & Hall, 1984.
13 Munsat TM, Riviere M, Swash M, Leclerc C. Economic burden of amyotrophic lateral sclerosis in the United Kingdom. *J Med Econ* 1998;1:235–45.
14 McKie J, Richardson J. The rule of rescue. *Soc Sci Med* 2003;56:2407–19.
15 Freemantle N, Bloor K, Eastaugh J. A fair innings for NICE? *Pharmacoeconomics* 2002;20:389–91.

9: Relationships between stakeholders: managing the war of words

SUZANNE HILL, KEES DE JONCHEERE

Introduction

The contribution of pharmaceuticals to improving health outcomes is indisputable. It is impossible to talk about pharmaceuticals in the current world order without considering the view, roles, and capacity of their producer, which is for the most part the pharmaceutical industry. The aims of this chapter, therefore, are as follows:

- To define the current pharmaceutical industry and its contribution to medicine development
- To consider the views and expectation of the various groups that are involved in making choices about which pharmaceuticals to use and purchase
- To define some of what is known about how the industry interacts with these other stakeholders
- To describe some examples of extremes of this interaction
- To consider some of the possible strategies for responding to pharmaceutical industry pressures and needs, in a way that maintains as the principal outcome that of health of the community.

The pharmaceutical industry

One of the discoverers of penicillin, Howard Florey, said, "Too high a tribute cannot be paid to the enterprise and energy with which the American manufacturing firms tackled the large-scale production of the drug. Had it not been for their efforts, there would certainly not have been sufficient penicillin by D-Day in Normandy to treat all severe casualties, both British and American."[1]

Although the pharmaceutical industry has been described as the "devil",[1,2] it is undoubtedly true that they are the drivers behind development of many of the effective drugs that are now widely available.[3] One way of measuring the impact of the industry is to look at diseases in which the multinationals have not been involved, such as some of the neglected tropical diseases; where there is no industry interest, there are very few drugs.[4]

So what is the "pharmaceutical industry" today? For many of us, when the pharmaceutical industry is mentioned the term stimulates a vision of "big pharma" – multinational corporations such as Pfizer and GlaxoSmithKline that, on certain scales, have net values greater than those of many countries. After Pfizer completed its merger with another multinational, namely Pharmacia, in April 2003 (which in turn was a combination of Pharmacia and Upjohn), it became the largest privately funded biomedical organisation in the world, with more than 200 products in its development pipeline.[5] It is not alone; there are a number of other mega-companies that are competing for the market share.

The other side of the pharmaceutical industry that is perhaps less well recognised, but especially important in terms of supplying lower priced products, is the generic pharmaceutical industry. Again, this industry is not monolithic – there are large and small companies, and high quality and low quality manufacturers. In terms of policy and choice of medicines, however, generic manufacturers are becoming increasingly important. Often generic companies have been bought by large multinational firms.

Drugs such as antihypertensives, antibiotics, thrombolytics, and antipsychotics are products developed by the industry that have contributed to improving health outcomes in developed countries. Many of these medicines could not have been developed without the major clinical trials that have been to a large extent sponsored by the manufacturers. It has been suggested, however, that this success in a few key disease areas has led to some of the current difficulties with the industry in relation to its perceived aggressive marketing polices and pressure to increase profits.[6] Because the development of new medicines has been concentrated in a small number of disease areas, the pipeline of "blockbuster" drugs in relation to these diseases is now starting to dry up; this creates more pressure and uncertainty but it is also perhaps starting to stimulate interest in other health problems. One downside of this that has been of particular concern is the marketing of "lifestyle diseases" such as "erectile dysfunction" at the expense of investment in developing treatments for health problems in developing countries.[4,7,8]

In addition to the development of drugs for diseases that have large and prosperous markets, drug development is also determined by the level of risk. Compounds that may be effective but have an associated level of risk that may be problematic are less likely to proceed through the full process of development. Although safety of the public is the key reasons for drug regulatory authorities to exist at all, the downside of assessing safety is that sometimes compounds that are promising for severe diseases may not proceed through full development because of the potential for adverse events. The regeneration of thalidomide for use in the treatment of leprosy and some HIV/AIDS related skin diseases is one unusual example of an otherwise damned product remerging for a second and probably much more important indication.

The other contribution of industry is that of its input to the economic development and growth of countries. The UK, for example, has a flourishing local industry that contributed an estimated £0·7–2·0 billion to the economy in 2001.[9] Europe likewise gains a great deal from the economic boost provided by pharmaceutical companies.[10]

Tensions between views and expectations of users and producers

Given the size, growth, and value of the pharmaceutical industry, and the rise in expenditure on pharmaceuticals internationally, it is hardly surprising that there are increasing tensions between the manufacturers and those involved in the consumption and purchase of pharmaceuticals. Medicines are not a "normal" economic commodity; there is not a simple and direct interaction between the seller and the consumer. In relation to pharmaceuticals, there are numerous players involved, including not only the patient and the health care professional but also medical insurance companies and government agents who make choices about which pharmaceuticals will be bought and supplied. A responsible company will very reasonably want to obtain the best possible price for its product; a responsible purchaser will also very reasonably want to obtain the best value for money. The doctor plays the role of informant between the consumer and the supplier, and therefore is subject to influence and pressure from both sides.

This tension is illustrated by the debate about drug prices and industry competitiveness. The European Commission report "Global competitiveness in pharmaceuticals"[11] indicated the Europe was generally lagging behind the USA in the development and marketing of pharmaceuticals, and recommended a number of changes to the way in which European Union (EU) countries handle pharmaceutical patents and prices. However, as pointed out in an editorial published in the *Lancet*,[12] any such reforms would pose risks to the health care systems in Europe that have sought to provide affordable health care for all.

Given that the debate and tensions cannot be avoided, and indeed are usually magnified when it comes to considering choices between pharmaceuticals for reimbursement decisions, it is important to consider what types of interactions occur between the key players and what dilemmas are faced, what can go wrong in the process of making choices, and what strategies can be adopted to maximise the likelihood of robust decisions being made.

What do we know about the interaction between industry and the other players?

In his article in the *BMJ* in May 2003,[13] Ray Moynihan described the relationship between doctors and drug companies as "twisted together like the snake and the staff". Doctors are one player with whom the pharmaceutical industry has a key interaction, through a variety of links and mechanisms. The relationship has been the subject of increasing scrutiny over the past few years, but there has also been increasing interest in relationships between the industry and other players, including consumers and health policy makers. Given that at times the needs of the industry and the community may be in conflict, what do we know about the nature and outcome of these relationships and what impact do they have on the processes of selecting pharmaceuticals for use in health systems?

The relationship between doctors and the pharmaceutical industry has probably been subjected to the most intense scrutiny, and it is undoubtedly a complex one. Doctors relate to the industry in a variety of ways, such as visits from marketing representatives, continuing education programmes, meetings, and research projects. A systematic review published in 1998 described the studies that examined the effect of the most obvious and well described interaction between doctors and industry, the question of gifts.[14] Although an extreme description of the interaction is provided by Giannakakis and Ioannidis,[15] it is clear that many doctors receive multiple gifts from drug company representatives each year, and most deny that the gifts have any effect on their practice, despite studies that point to the contrary.[16–19] The outcomes of concern in relation to acceptance of gifts are that doctors who accept gifts may show a preference for new products that have no advantages over old, and there may be a decrease in generic prescribing; as a result, there may be a rise in expensive prescribing, with perhaps less caution than is warranted. If a health care system is structured in favour of generic prescribing, then there may be tensions arising between doctors who wish to prescribe the "new" and managers who wish to supply the generic and well established "old".

The relationship between doctors and industry is not just via the marketing department. Industry sponsorship of research is another well developed mechanism for the interaction to occur and has come under increasing scrutiny. According to Moses and Martin,[20] the industry's share of total investment in research and development in the USA grew from approximately 32% in 1980 to 62% in 2000. At the same time, government support declined. Such financial support of research has led to two main questions being raised: does it lead to inappropriate conflicts of interest arising, and does it compromise the quality of the research that is carried out?

In a systematic review of the studies that examine the extent, impact, and management of financial conflicts of interest in biomedical research, Bekelman *et al.*[21] found that there was substantial evidence that a significant number of scientific investigators and academic institutions have industry affiliations and ties. In their review those investigators combined the results of the eight studies that they identified that quantified the relationship between industry sponsorship and the study outcome in research. There was a statistically significant increase in the likelihood of the outcome of the study favouring industry where there was a financial relationship (odds ratio 3·60, 95% confidence interval 2·63–4·91). In addition, industry sponsorship of research was associated with restrictions on publication and on data sharing.

In terms of the impact of industry funding on the quality of studies, Bero and Rennie[22] identified some of the things that can go awry in studies that are supported by manufacturers. The publication of the *Guidelines for Good Clinical Practice*[23] and the requirements of drug regulatory authorities have diminished the likelihood that obvious quality flaws will exist in manufacturers' studies. Indeed, in terms of compliance with key aspects of quality in randomised controlled trials, such as centralised randomisation procedures, pharmaceutical companies are more likely to have the resources to conduct this appropriately than are independent clinical investigators. It is in the more subtle aspects of clinical trial design, such as the research question being relevant to health care policy makers or the choice of the comparator drug, that the quality of sponsored studies is likely to be flawed.[24] Given that pharmaceutical manufacturers' studies often provide the key data available at the time when a purchasing decision is to be made, these flaws may present significant challenges to decision makers.

A more recent review also found that company funded studies that were negative are less likely to be published than positive studies.[25] This is discussed in more detail in Chapter 3. There is other evidence that suggests that publication bias in relation to industry funded studies may be a problem but in the opposite direction – multiple publication of the same studies. One recent example is that described by Melander *et al.*[26] who documented publications in relation to selective serotonin reuptake inhibitors. They found that there was multiple publication, selective publication, and selective reporting of results of studies that would lead to an estimate of overall effectiveness based on published studies being biased in favour of the drugs.

Because patients are the recipients of the pharmaceuticals, it is hardly surprising that there is an increasing interaction between the industry and consumers generally. Some of this interaction is via the process of direct to consumer (DTC) advertising, particularly in the USA. Rosenthal *et al.*[27] found that annual spending on DTC advertising in the USA tripled between 1996 and 2000, to nearly $2·5 billion. However, the expenditure on DTC advertising accounted for only 15% of total expenditure on promotion, and was highly concentrated on a subgroup of products. The question that needs to be answered is what is the impact of DTC advertising on prescribing patterns? There is some evidence that it puts pressure on physicians to prescribe drugs that they would not otherwise choose to use,[28,29] and the concern is that it leads to waste and unnecessary use of medications.

In the ongoing review of pharmaceutical legislation in the EU, the European Commission initially proposed to allow companies to communicate directly with patients on prescription medicines for a limited number of diseases. Critics argued that this would open the door to DTC advertising, and both the European parliament as well as the Council of Ministers rejected these proposals. In the recent Commission communication,[10] the ban on DTC advertising is currently maintained but this is likely to be subjected to continued review – as well as pressure from the pharmaceutical industry to change. The position of the International Federation of Pharmaceutical Manufacturers on promotion generally is very clear:

The promotion of prescription medicines to healthcare professionals is a vital extension of the process of searching for and developing new and better means of preventing and treating illness. Promotion and the dissemination of educational information ensures that the full benefits of the years of work and enormous expenditure of skill and money will be made available promptly to the patients of the world.[30]

In addition to obvious DTC campaigns, there are other perhaps more subtle ways, such as non-product advertising and awareness raising campaigns, through which the industry can try to influence prescribing by physicians.[31,32] Where these campaigns aim at under-treated health problems, the health benefits and the increased costs for prescribing the most appropriate drugs are becoming less clear. If the health problem is severe then, clearly, increased awareness and treatment should lead to health benefits. However, over the past few years the term "disease mongering" has been applied to "new" diseases that in some instances appear to have been identified to suit a possible market niche.[33,34]

The impact of DTC advertising on the process of choice of pharmaceuticals is fairly predictable. If there is a widespread marketing campaign, then the pressure to reimburse the product that is the subject of the campaign can be substantial. As a result, efforts to use rational choice mechanisms and evidence based purchasing decisions can be significantly undermined. The challenge overall is to balance the (very reasonable) need of the public for information with a mechanism that ensures that the information is balanced and reliable and can be appropriately evaluated by the consumers.

In addition to DTC advertising, pharmaceutical companies have developed relationships with patient support groups. As described by Herxheimer,[35] there are positive and negative aspects to this relationship. On the one hand it allows patient groups to obtain information and financial and other support from the companies, but on the other hand such relationships may be fostered by manufacturers as a means to market a new product. In an extreme example of this, namely the establishment of "Action for Access", a patient group established by Biogen to lobby for the availability of β-interferon in the UK, the activity was ruled as unlawful promotion.[32] In the USA there has been controversy about a similar issue; in this case, an organisation of senior citizens has identified significant funding support to three other organisations that were described as being "fronts" for the pharmaceutical industry.[36]

There are other parts of the "prescribing chain" that are subject to influence by the pharmaceutical industry. In particular, the community pharmacist can be an important target, especially if the pharmacist has discretion over what brand of product to dispense. This part of the supply chain includes wholesalers, who may also want to influence dispensing. Although there are anecdotes about bonuses and rebates being used to influence the choice of product dispensed, there is very little in the published literature that relates this to product specific promotion.

The interaction between industry and policy makers is also much less studied. Although most people who work in the pharmaceutical sector are aware of relationships that develop between politicians and pharmaceutical companies, it is much more difficult to find clear descriptions of the effect this interaction has on decision making. One example is the "Poggolini affair" in the early 1990s, which involved inappropriate relationships between the Italian drug regulatory authority and the pharmaceutical industry.[37] The relationship became corrupt, with the acceptance of bribes and gifts being the basis for registration decisions on individual applications. This is clearly the extreme end of the possible spectrum of influence.

More common, however, are law suits and "behind the scenes" activities. In South Africa, during the transition to democratic government and the development of a National Medicinal Drugs Policy, the local pharmaceutical manufacturers systematically engaged the major stakeholders in the new government and policy development process to try to ensure the aims of the industry would be satisfied.[38] When this approach was not successful, and what were seen as anti-industry policies including generic substitution and parallel importuning were proposed, the pharmaceutical industry (39 companies) took the Government of South Africa to court. It was not until 2001, after activism by lobby groups such as Médecins Sans Frontières, that the court case was dropped.

What has happened when industry's interests have been threatened?

The South African court case is only one of several examples in the past several years of what can happen when the interests of the pharmaceutical industry are threatened by activities that are undertaken in relation to improving access to medicines. Although it is difficult to make a case for there being a systematic and planned response from the industry, at times it appears that a pattern of activity is developing and predictable responses will occur in a given situation. A number of examples are described below to illustrate this.

The use of legal challenges to decisions is one such pattern. In Australia, the Pharmaceutical Benefits Advisory Committee was taken to the Federal Court after it refused to list Viagra on the Pharmaceutical Benefits Scheme (PBS) in 1999. The grounds for the appeal were that the Committee had failed to carry out its decisions according to due process, and that it had considered matters in the decision that it should not have, which were the estimated total costs of listing the drug on the PBS. The judge found that this was not the case.[39] The Committee subsequently reconsidered a new application to list the product and recommended listing it on the PBS. The Australian Government, however, decided that drugs for impotence should not be covered by the PBS, partially on cost grounds.[40]

Legal challenge has also been used in the UK. The National Institute for Clinical Excellence (NICE) has a clearly defined appeal structure and a process that has been thoroughly tested. Initially, the decision on Relenza – the first decision by NICE – was challenged by an appeal from the sponsor, establishing a difficult precedent. Subsequently, as processes have improved, appeals have not decreased in frequency but they have been less likely to succeed when lodged by sponsors.[41]

Legal challenge tends to operate at a national level because this is the level at which decisions about reimbursement are often made. Other strategies are also used at a national level that take advantage of national isolation. Although double standards in registering medicines in different countries have been criticised for a long time, there continue to be different practices, even among countries that are supposedly applying the same legislation. The drug sertindole that was withdrawn from the EU market because of safety concerns in 2000 continued to be marketed in one of the Baltic countries.[42]

At a national and international level, the pharmaceutical industry is increasingly making use of public relations companies to influence thinking about their products.[43] Tactics that are used are timing and issuance of press releases and news stories about "breakthrough" products in relation to key decisions about reimbursement, sponsorship of patient groups in relation to specific disease, "disease awareness" campaigns, and publication of studies at times most likely to influence decision making. The difficulty with these approaches is that there is very little that has been done to document systematically the extent and nature of the use of the various tactics, and one can only guess at the influence they have on the outcomes of decisions.

Other political international strategies are clearly aimed at influencing the macro-environment in which the pharmaceutical industry operates. This includes, for example, the debates about TRIPS (Agreement on Trade Related Aspects of Intellectual Property Rights) and patent protection and trade in pharmaceuticals. Countries that have effective strategies for controlling prices seem to be the obvious target. For example, in Australia recently the negotiations with the USA about a new free trade agreement included the discussion of whether Australia will give up its price setting system for medicines in order to gain trade advantages with the USA.[44] Canada experienced similar pressures.[45]

Strategies to respond and manage the influence of the industry

Given the diverse tactics that have been described, what are the options and approaches that have been tried to counter the influence of industry and manage the relationship? If it is accepted that the relationship is necessary to ensure the continuing availability and development of new medicines, then there needs to be some way to ensure that the interaction is productive rather than counter-productive. Again, relatively little has been published about strategies in a systematic manner, and so we shall consider some examples.

One strategy that has been tried in many environments over recent years is to develop a "partnership" with the pharmaceutical industry. In recent years, there has been concern over the lack of development of drugs for important diseases. Trouiller et al.[4] reviewed the outcomes of pharmaceutical research and development over the past 25 years and found that, out of 1393 new chemical entities marketed between 1975 and 1999, only 16 were for tropical diseases and tuberculosis. They proposed that private sector research obligations should be explored, and a public sector not-for-profit research and development capacity promoted. As one way of doing this, the World Health Organization (WHO) proposed that partnerships with the pharmaceutical industry should be established to try to encourage private sector interest in drugs for neglected diseases;[46] indeed, this has been supported by the international industry federation.[47]

What are risks associated with partnerships? Kickbusch and Quick[46] and Buse and Waxman[48] outlined principles and criteria for partnerships. These included establishing clear goals and decision making structures for the partnership, having means of monitoring and enforcing decisions, and documenting the details and process of the partnerships. However, subsequent experience with partnerships has not been straightforward.[49] One example was the publication of the guidelines on hypertension in 1999,[50] which was a document produced in partnership by the International Society for Hypertension and WHO. The guidelines recommended use of one of six classes of antihypertensive treatments as initial therapy for uncomplicated hypertension, but it did not differentiate between them or consider comparative costs. This was contrary to the clinical evidence available at the time, which, for example, was very limited in terms of clinical outcome studies of the angiotensin II receptor blockers – the most expensive new class of drugs. As a result, many countries decided that the guidelines could not be used, and there was significant public controversy. One review of the guidelines[51] stated that, "The international expert group ignored the ground rules governing clinical assessment, and clinical trial data too, taking up a stance that favours drug manufacturers."

In this case, the partnership between industry and the guidelines group was probably flawed. There were no conflict of interest statements in the first set of guidelines, but from subsequent statements it is clear that there were substantial and longstanding relationships between industry and the guideline group that were not fully considered in the formulation of the recommendations. In this case, therefore, the partnership model was probably flawed, and much work has been necessary to recover the credibility of this guideline group.

Partnership models have also been tried in other types of interventions. In Australia, when the Quality Use of Medicines programme was introduced in the early 1990s, the pharmaceutical industry was specifically included as a partner to help plan strategies to improve the use of medicines.[52] There was an industry representative on the advisory committee for the programme who contributed to the development of the interventions and studies that have been carried out. To date, however, it is not clear what impact this partnership has had, and it would be very difficult to determine this.

Kickbusch and Quick[46] point out that, in developing countries, there are not always accepted ways for public–private sector partnerships to operate effectively. If this is the case, an alternative strategy that has been used to manage the relationship with industry is regulation, particularly in relation to advertising and promotion. One current debate is to do with self-regulation of promotion, which has been adopted as the model by many countries. The effectiveness of such codes has been subjected to limited examination only. One study[53] found that there were only limited standards within such a code to control pharmaceutical representatives' presentations and no active monitoring system in place to ensure adherence to the code.

A logical response is to ensure that health professionals understand the strategies that are aimed directly at them, with the hope of perhaps "immunising" them against effects. One example of an educational intervention designed at least to educate medical students about the effects of promotion is described by Wilkes and Hoffman.[54] In that study, third year medical students were exposed to pharmacists role playing the interaction with pharmaceutical industry representatives, and the attitudes to the industry before and after the presentation were among the outcomes that were assessed. The main change in student attitudes following the intervention was that they felt more uncertain about their ability to cope appropriately with the interaction with representatives. The study did not look at long-term behaviour change, and to date it appears that no other studies have done so. We have not been able to find any other studies that examined the effect of educational interventions in relation to health professionals.

Managing the relationship and interaction has aptly been described as "dancing with porcupines".[55,56] One strategy (for avoiding the quills) that has been widely used is the development of codes of conduct for appropriate interactions between industry and doctors. The pharmaceutical industry internationally has a code of practice,[30] which is reflected in the national industry organisation documents, such as those published by the Association of the British Pharmaceutical Industry[57] and

Medicines Australia.[58] Such codes set standards for the ethical marketing and promotion of prescription pharmaceutical products, and complement the relevant drug regulatory legislation. They may cover aspects such as sponsorship of promotional and scientific meetings, activities of representatives, provision of gifts, hospitality and sample medicines, and the provision of information to the general public. In addition, many professional organisations such as specialist colleges have codes of conduct for their members that complement the industry codes, and relate particularly to the acceptance of gifts.

The question is then whether such codes are an effective way of controlling and regulating the interaction between doctors and the industry, as well as an effective way of regulating promotion. Roughead *et al.*[53] argue that it is not, which may not be surprising. If the sanctions of such codes are limited to warnings or fines that are insignificant, then their effects may well be limited.

There have been a number of suggestions for the development of codes to guide the research interaction and the interactions in other arenas such as continuing education, to encourage "disentanglement" of the medical profession from the industry.[59–61] Should such codes also be developed to guide the interaction between the pharmaceutical industry and decision makers? Many decision making bodies such as the NICE, including WHO, now require all members of its committees to sign declaration of interest forms, and some committees also have clearly stated policies on what constitutes a significant conflict of interest and how this should be handled in decision making. Most, however, do not go any further than this. It is not clear that there is a need for any further codes of conduct, but this is perhaps something that must be considered on a case by case basis.

Conclusion

If partnerships are problematic and codes are ineffective or too new to assess, then how should those making choices about reimbursement attempt to manage the war of words? A single strategy will not be effective – it is very clear that there are multiple players and multiple sources of possible tension that must be considered.

Although there are no empirical data to support these proposals, we would first suggest that, wherever possible, decisions are made in a transparent manner, including making all data available, so that all parties involved are on an equal footing when it comes to understanding the reasons for decisions going in one direction and not another. Second, fair representation in the process of all the players seems to be key, although not all parties may need the same type of role. Patient support groups, for example, might be expert informants rather than voting on the choice; consumer groups more generally might be part of the decision itself. Finally, ensuring that the media and information flow is adequately informed is critical; it is hard to counter charges in the press of "denial of life saving drugs" unless the media can also help to tell the other side of the story!

In the end, though, it is probably reasonable to expect that there will always be a degree of tension between the buyers and sellers, and perhaps that is healthy. There are different expectations on both sides, and it is not realistic to expect that there will be perfect concordance and therefore amicability when it comes down to making a choice that can affect profits on the one hand and health on the other. What is certain is that there will continue to be a need for both buyers and sellers to ensure that there is an adequate supply of appropriate medicines at a price that purchasers can afford; the days of the free market and untrammelled profits are numbered.

Summary
- Development of new medicines has been much dependent on the growth and expansion of the pharmaceutical industry but this has resulted in increasing development of drugs for chronic and lifestyle disease with increasing advertising.
- As a result there are increasing tensions between the pharmaceutical industry and purchasers and consumers.
- Industry has responded to perceived threats to its profitability by legal challenges, use of public relations campaigns, and political lobbying.
- Strategies for managing relationships with the pharmaceutical industry are essential, but none is clearly effective and all are associated with risks.
- To manage the "war of the words", multiple strategies, particularly transparent decision making, need to be adopted.

References

1 Bonaccorso S, Smith R. In praise of the "devil". *BMJ* 2003;**326**:1220.
2 Shaw J. He who sups with the devil. *Med J Aust* 1986;**144**:617.
3 Abraham J. The pharmaceutical industry as a political player. *Lancet* 2002;**360**:1498–502.
4 Trouiller P, Olliaro P, Torreele E, Orbinski J, Laing R, Ford N. Drug development for neglected diseases: a deficient market and a public health policy failure. *Lancet* 2002;**359**:2188–94.
5 Pfizer homepage. http://www.pfizer.com (accessed 17 October 2003).
6 Taylor D. Fewer new drugs from the pharmaceutical industry. *BMJ* 2003; **326**:408–9.
7 Pecoul B, Chirac P, Trouiller P, Pinel J. Access to essential drugs in poor countries: a lost battle? *JAMA* 1999;**281**:361–7.
8 Gilbert D, Walley T, New B. Lifestyle medicines. *BMJ* 2000;**321**:1341–4.
9 UK Department of Health. Value of the pharmaceutical industry to the UK economy. http://www.doh.gov.uk/pictf/value.htm (accessed 17 October 2003).
10 Commission of the European Communities. Communication from the Commission to the Council, the European Parliament, the Economic and Social Committee and the Committee of the Regions: a stronger European-based pharmaceutical industry for the benefit of the patient – a call for action. http://pharmacos.eudra.org/F3/g10/docs/G10_Comm Comm_EN.pdf (accessed 17 October 2003).
11 Gambardella A, Orsenigo L, Pammolli F. Global competitiveness in pharmaceuticals: a European perspective. http://pharmacos.eudra.org/ F3/g10/docs/comprep_nov2000.pdf (accessed 13 February 2004).
12 Anonymous. What price competitiveness in the drugs industry? [editorial]. *Lancet* 2003;**362**:257.
13 Moynihan R. Who pays for the pizza? Redefining the relationships between doctors and drug companies. 1: entanglement. *BMJ* 2003;**326**:1189–92.
14 Wazana A. Physicians and the pharmaceutical industry: is a gift ever just a gift? JAMA 2000;**283**:373–80.
15 Giannakakis IA, Ioannidis JPA. Arabian nights: 1001 tales of how pharmaceutical companies cater to the material needs of doctors: case report. *BMJ* 2000;**321**:1563–4.
16 Spingarn RW, Berlin JA, Strom BL. When pharmaceutical manufacturers' employees present grand rounds, what do residents remember? *Acad Med* 1996;**71**:86–8.
17 Orlowski JP, Wateska L. The effects of pharmaceutical firm enticements on physician prescribing patterns. *Chest* 1992;**102**:270–3.
18 Chren MM, Landefeld CS. Physicians' behaviour and their interaction with drug companies. *JAMA* 1994;**271**:684–9.
19 Sandberg WS, Carlos R, Sandberg EH, Roizen MF. The effect of education gifts from pharmaceutical firms on medical students' recall of company names or products. *Acad Med* 1997;**72**:916–18.
20 Moses H, Martin JB. Academic relationships with industry: a new model for biomedical research. *JAMA* 2001;**285**:933–5.
21 Bekelman JE, Li Y, Gross CP. Scope and impact of financial conflicts of interest in biomedical research. A systematic review. *JAMA* 2003;**289**:454–65.
22 Bero L, Rennie D. Influences on the quality of published drug studies. *Int J Health Technol Assess* 1996;**12**:209–37.
23 THe European Agency for the Evaluation of Medicinal Products. ICH Topic EG. *Guidelines for Good Clinical Practice.* http://www.emea.eu.int/ pdts/human/ich/013595en.pdf (accessed on 6 April 2004).

24 Collier J, Iheanacho I. The pharmaceutical industry as an informant. *Lancet* 2002;**360**:1405–9.

25 Lexchin J, Bero LA, Djulbegovic B. Pharmaceutical industry sponsorship and research outcome and quality: systematic review. *BMJ* 2003;**326**: 1167–70.

26 Melander H, Ahlqvist-Rastad J, Meijer G, Beermann B. Evidence b(i)ased medicine: selective reporting from studies sponsored by pharmaceutical industry: review of studies in new drug applications. *BMJ* 2003;**326**: 1171–5.

27 Rosenthal MB, Berndt ER, Donohue JM, Frank RG, Epstein AM. Promotion of prescription drugs to consumers. *N Engl J Med* 2002;**346**: 498–505.

28 Lipsky MS, Taylor CA. The opinions and experiences of family physicians regarding direct to consumer advertising. *J Fam Pract* 1997;**45**:495–9.

29 Mintzes B, Barere ML, Kravitz RL, *et al.* Influence of direct to consumer pharmaceutical advertising and patients' requests on prescribing decisions: two site cross sectional survey. *BMJ* 2002;**324**:278–9.

30 International Federation of Pharmaceutical Manufacturers Associations. Marketing code: IFPMA code of pharmaceutical marketing practices. http://www.ifpma.org/News/news_market.aspx (accessed 20 October 2003).

31 Quick JD, Hogerzeil HV, Rago L, Reggi V, de Joncheere K. Ensuring ethical drug promotion: whose responsibility? [letter]. *Lancet* 2003;**326**:747.

32 Toine P. Marketing medicines through randomized controlled trials: the case of interferon. *BMJ* 1998;**317**:1231–3.

33 Moynihan R, Heath I, Henry D. Selling sickness and disease mongering. *BMJ* 2002;**324**:886–90.

34 Moynihan R. The making of a disease: female sexual dysfunction. *BMJ* 2003;**326**:45–7.

35 Herxheimer A. Relationships between the pharmaceutical industry and patients' organizations. *BMJ* 2003;**326**:1208–10.

36 Moynihan R. US seniors group attacks pharmaceutical industry "fronts". *BMJ* 2003;**326**:351.

37 Fattore G. Jommi C. The new pharmaceutical policy in Italy. *Health Policy* 1998;**46**:21–41.

38 Gary A, Matsebula T, Blaauw D, Schneider H, Gilson L. Policy change in a context of transition: drug policy in South Africa 1989–1999. Witswatersrand, South Africa: Centre for Health Policy, School of Public Health, University of the Witswatersrand, 2002.

39 Commonwealth Department of Health and Aged Care. Annual report 1999–2000. http://www.health.gov.au/pubs/annrep/ar2000/depart/dept12. htm (accessed 21 October 2003).

40 Commonwealth Department of Health and Ageing. Government rejects Viagra listing on PBS. http://www.health.gov.au/mediarel/yr2002/kp/ kp02005.htm (accessed 21 October 2003).

41 Dickinson D, Ashcroft R. Health care and EBM in the UK. http:// perseus.isi.it/bioeth/projects/evibase-project/Report%20UK.pdf (accessed 4 December 2003).

42 Freemantle N, Behmane D, de Joncheere K. Pricing and reimbursement of pharmaceuticals in the Baltic States. *Lancet* 2001;**358**:260.

43 Burton B, Rowell A. Unhealthy spin. *BMJ* 2003;**326**:1205–7.

44 Anonymous. Medicine to escape free trade threat. *Sydney Morning Herald*, 22 March 2003.

45 Ostry AS. International trade regulation and publicly funded health care in Canada. *Int J Health Serv* 2001;**31**:475–80.

46 Kickbusch I, Quick J. Partnerships for health in the 21st century. *World Health Stat Q* 1998;**51**:68–74.
47 Dale H. WHO should build partnerships with the pharmaceutical industry to improve public health. *Lancet* 2003;**361**:4.
48 Buse K, Waxman A. Public-private partnerships: a strategy for WHO. *Bull World Health Organ* 2001;**79**:748–54.
49 Yamey G. Faltering steps towards partnerships. *BMJ* 2002;**325**:1236–40.
50 Guidelines Subcommittee. 1999 World Health Organization-International Society of Hypertension Guidelines for the Management of Hypertension. *J Hypertens* 1999;**17**:151–83.
51 Anonymous. Flawed WHO recommendations on hypertension: WHO has damaged its reputation. *Prescrire Int* 1999;**8**:121–3.
52 Murray M. Australian national drug policies: facilitating or fragmenting health? *Dev Dialogue* 1995;**1**:148–92.
53 Roughead EE, Gilbert AL, Harvey KJ. Self-regulatory codes of conduct: are they effective in controlling pharmaceutical representatives presentations to general medical practitioners? *Int J Health Serv* 1998;**28**:269–79.
54 Wilkes MS, Hoffman JR. An innovative approach to educating medical students about pharmaceutical promotion. *Acad Med* 2001;**76**:1271–7.
55 Wager E. How to dance with porcupines: rules and guidelines on doctors' relations with drug companies. *BMJ* 2003;**326**:1196–8.
56 Lewis S, Baird P, Evans RG, *et al.* Dancing with the porcupine: rules for governing the university-industry relationship. *CMAJ* 2001;**165**:783–5.
57 Association of the British Pharmaceutical Industry homepage. http://www.abpi.org.uk (accessed 21 October 2003).
58 Medicines Australia homepage. http://www.medicinesaustralia.com.au (accessed 21 October 2003).
59 Moynihan R. Who pays for the pizza? Redefining the relationships between doctors and drug companies. 2: disentanglement. *BMJ* 2003; **326**:1193–6.
60 Donnan GA, Davis SM, Kaste M. Recommendations for the relationship between sponsors and investigators in the design and conduct of clinical stroke trials. *Stroke* 2003;**34**:1041–5.
61 Johns MME, Barnes M, Florencio PS. Restoring balance to Industry-Academia relationships in an era of institutional financial conflicts of interest. *JAMA* 2003;**289**:741–6.

10: Medicine and the media: good information or misleading hype?

RAY MOYNIHAN, LISA M SCHWARTZ, STEVEN WOLOSHIN

Introduction

In this chapter we explore what impact the media has, how well it covers medicine, and how that coverage might be improved.

Cheer squad or watchdog?

The headline read "New arthritis drug called miracle".[1] The accompanying photo featured a women running across a suburban park. "Before starting on the new drug two years ago Anne ... had trouble dressing herself. She now jogs five to eight kilometres each day." In the fourth paragraph of the article the President of the Arthritis Society tells a press conference that this new drug "is truly a breakthrough" and that people "suffering from arthritis no longer have to fear the serious side effects of their medications." The jogger Anne declares that "Celebrex gave me back my life."

This story appeared on page two of a leading Canadian daily, *The Toronto Star*, on Friday 16 April 1999, at a time when celecoxib had just been approved and was about to hit pharmacy shelves. The article cited a leading researcher warning of a coming epidemic of ageing arthritic baby boomers, and heralded the timely arrival of Celebrex as a major benefit to humankind.

Although some of the religious imagery was perhaps a little overblown in this story, its starry eyed portrayal of celecoxib and its failure to reveal the financial ties of quoted experts is not atypical. Its shortcomings reflect the evidence of a much wider problem in the Canadian newspaper coverage of Celebrex,[2] and the much deeper malaise in the way in which the media around the world covers pharmaceuticals and other medical technologies.[3-5] The body of evidence examined in this chapter suggests that, not withstanding important exceptions,[6] in many medical stories benefits are overplayed, risks and costs played down, and important conflicts of interest overlooked. Put crudely, too much medical reporting looks more like promotion than journalism. As Canadian researcher Allison Gandey concludes after her qualitative analysis of six years of Celebrex coverage, too often newspaper articles simply reprint marketing messages:[7] "Reporters appeared to buy into Celebrex's marketing hype and reproduce much of it in their news stories."

One of the challenges for those seeking to promote a more rational public debate about the appropriate use of drugs and other health care technologies is to try to engender a change in the culture of media coverage. Based on our dealings with journalists,[8,9] there is a growing recognition within the media of the flawed nature of the old "miracle cure/wonder drug" formulas, and the value of developing a more informed and critical coverage of medicine. Here we explore the depth of the problem, and offer some tentative thoughts on reform.

Media coverage of medicine and health care influences the general public and physicians

The news media can have a powerful influence on public perceptions about health and health care, potentially affecting the attitudes and behaviours of consumers and practitioners alike. People pay attention to health news. A recent survey in the USA by the Pew Research Center for the People and Press[10] found that two-thirds of people read newspapers regularly, nearly 80% watch television news, almost a half tune into radio news, and a quarter read news on the internet. Health news was the third leading type of news people followed, and 26% of adults reported following health news "very closely" and 45% reported following it "somewhat closely".

Although limited, there is some evidence that the media influences how people use health services. A recent Cochrane Collaboration review identified five studies that examined the impact of news media coverage of health issues on health service utilisation (the other 64 studies in the review looked at the use of planned media campaigns to promote a specific service such as cancer screening).[11] The main findings of these papers (and a related investigation published after the Cochrane review) are summarised in Table 10.1.[12–17] In each case, more favourable publicity was associated with higher utilisation, and less favourable publicity was associated with lower use. Whereas the Cochrane report acknowledges the weakness of the uncontrolled time series designs employed, the authors conclude that there is evidence that "[media reports] of communication have an important role in influencing the use of health care interventions".

News media coverage also appears to affect researchers. The *New England Journal of Medicine* articles that were covered in the *New York Times* were cited more frequently in the medical literature than those not covered by the *Times* (i.e. in the year following publication, articles covered by the *Times* averaged 17 science index citations per article versus 10 for those not covered).[18] Table 10.2 shows that this effect disappeared during a *New York Times* strike when editors produced an archival edition that was not distributed (i.e. comparing the *New England Journal* articles the *Times* planned to cover but did not because of the strike, with all other *New England Journal* articles in the same issue). This finding suggests that the media coverage – distinct from the scientific importance of the work – can play an important role in how knowledge is transmitted to the scientific community.

Finally, the news media affects physician decision making. Many physicians report that they have had patients asking questions or requesting tests or treatments stimulated by news reports, and many physician attitudes (or even awareness of new research findings) may come through their own exposure to the general press.

How well do medical news stories cover medicine?

Against a backdrop of soaring drug costs, and concern about misleading coverage, media stories about medicine are

Table 10.1 Selected studies of the effect of news media coverage on the public's health service utilisation

Media message	Effect Measure	Utilisation Before	Utilisation After
Hysterectomy rates may be too high in Switzerland; some hysterectomies may not be necessary[12]	Hysterectomies per 100,000 women per year	460	360
Aspirin use by children with viral infections is associated with development of Reye's syndrome[13]	Reye's syndrome cases per 100,000 children per year	6·2	1·8
Nancy Reagan chose mastectomy over breast conserving surgery[14]	% Women who had breast conserving surgery of those with early breast cancer treated surgically	27%	21%
Magic Johnson disclosed that he is HIV positive[15]	Average number of HIV blood tests per week	31·5	43·5
Increased risk of first myocardial infarction among hypertensive patients treated with calcium channel blockers noted in a case–control study	% Elderly patients receiving calcium channel blockers[16]	12%	11·4%
	% Prescription claims for calcium channel blockers of all cardiovascular drugs prescribed[17]*	19·8%	18%

*This study appeared after publication of the Cochrane Report.[11]

Table 10.2 Effect of *New York Times* coverage on medical literature citations of *New England Journal of Medicine* articles

	Citations per article in the year after publication	
New York Times coverage	No strike	During strike
Covered or planned to cover	17	8
No coverage	10	8

Adapted from Phillips *et al.*[18]

attracting increasing amounts of academic scrutiny.[2-5] Since 2000, four studies have looked at how the news media stories cover the benefits, harms, and costs of prescription medications; the two US studies focused on established drugs, whereas the Norwegian and Canadian studies looked at medicines newly introduced to the market. The studies are summarised in Table 10.3.

Benefits

To have an accurate understanding of a medication's benefit, one must know, at a minimum, what outcome is being changed and whether the magnitude of the change matters. However, many media stories that purport to inform about benefits fail to convey such basic information in a fair and accurate way. The evidence suggests that meaningful information is often missing from media stories, and when it is present it is exaggerated.

As shown in Table 10.3,[2,3,19] many news reports failed to quantify benefit information, making it very difficult for readers or viewers to judge benefits reliably. The meaning of verbal labels is too variable to substitute for numbers. For example, patients asked to assign a number to the expression "unlikely" gave responses ranging from 0% to 40%;[20] physicians given the same task gave responses with an even wider range, from 0% to 60%.[21]

When quantitative information was presented in media stories, it was often done so in a format that is prone to exaggeration. One study found that, among stories

Table 10.3 Studies on how often media reports present the benefits, harms, costs, and conflicts of interest about medications

Media	Medications	Benefit		Harms	Cost	Conflict of interest disclosed
		Quantified	Relative risk reduction only*			
US newspaper/television (n = 200 reports)[3]	Pravastatin Alendronate Aspirin	60%	83%	47%	30%	39%
US newspaper/television (n = 34 reports)[19]	Tamoxifen	82%	68%	94%	21%	N/A
Canadian newspaper (n = 193 reports)[2]	Atorvastatin Celexicob Donepezil Oseltamivir Raloxifene	20%	61%	32%	32%	3%
Major Norwegian newspapers (n = 357 reports)[4]	18 newly released medications	21%	N/A	39%	27%	1%

*Percentage among the subset of media reports where benefit was quantified.

quantifying drug benefits, 83% of stories framed benefits only in terms of the relative reduction in risk.[3] A large body of evidence suggests that presenting the benefits of medicines in relative terms only (for example, "50% fewer fractures", without specifying 50% fewer than what) leads to more enthusiasm for the medicine from consumers, physicians, and policy makers, and can thus be seen as misleading.[22,23] A good example of this problem occurred when the major US television networks reported on the results of a clinical trial of alendronate (Fosamax), a medicine used to treat osteoporosis. The stories all told their viewers that alendronate cut a woman's risk of hip fracture by 50% (described as "almost miraculous" in one news story), without explaining that in absolute terms the trial results showed the drug reduced the risk from 2% to 1%.[3]

Of the four studies of media coverage, the Canadian study was the only one to examine whether the news stories focused on clinical or surrogate outcomes (because both were known for each of the drugs studied).[2] Investigators found that 20% of stories only reported the medication's benefit on surrogate measures. The exclusive focus on surrogate measures varied widely from 47% (atorvastatin) to 4% (donepezil). Clearly, patient outcomes – what actually happens to people (for example, heart attacks) – are more important than surrogate markers of some physiological change that may predict what happens to people (for example, serum cholesterol).

Harms

The studies summarised in Table 10.3 highlight the uneven coverage of potential drug harms in the media. In the case of tamoxifen, almost all stories mentioned at least one harm and nearly half quantified the harm.[19] This attention to harm may reflect the source of the news stories; most were based on a press release issued by the National Cancer Institute announcing the early termination of a breast cancer prevention study. Alternatively, the attention given to harm may reflect journalists' perceptions about the seriousness of the harms; increased risk for uterine cancer was most frequently cited, followed by potentially fatal deep venous thrombosis or pulmonary embolism. Similarly, the Canadian study found the greatest number of mentions of harm were for the two drugs with the more serious side effects (i.e. raloxifene and oseltamivir).[2]

Harm information was much less prominent in media reports about the other 26 drugs included in the foregoing studies. Over half the media stories analysed ignored medication harms, even when the harms were potentially serious. Alendronate can result in severe gastrointestinal side effects, but half the stories on this drug were silent on this issue.[3] It has been asserted that celecoxib may be associated with an "increased incidence of serious adverse events" compared with older cheaper alternatives,[24] but its potential harms were covered in only 16% of stories.[2]

In the Norwegian study, almost two-thirds of newspaper stories were silent on potential harms.[4] In the case of zanamivir, a drug used to treat influenza, only 24% of stories mentioned potential harms, and only two of a total of 34 articles described the drug's side effects as serious. This is despite the fact that from 1999 the drug's label carried a warning about the risk for bronchospasm in patients with underlying respiratory disease; and, in 2000, following reports that several people had died after taking the drug, warnings noted the existence of potentially fatal side effects.[25]

Balance of benefits and harms

Overall, the media appears much more focused on benefits than on harms. The Canadian researchers found that the benefits of the five study drugs were mentioned almost five times more frequently than their potential harms.[2] The Norwegian study looked explicitly at the balance of the stories.[4] Overall, the investigators found that 51% of stories were rated as giving a new drug a positive evaluation (19 used terms such as "wonder pills"), 38% gave a neutral rating, and 11% were negative. As an example, of the 34 articles on the flu drug zanamivir, 15 gave it a positive evaluation and only one gave it a negative one. Given that the largest of the pivotal randomised controlled trials of zanamivir failed to find any evidence of benefit over placebo, and that the results from European trials found benefits that were at best very modest,[26] the enthusiastic newspaper articles appear to be based more on marketing information than on medical fact.

Costs

Surprisingly, drug costs were noted in only about one third of the news reports analysed in the US, Canadian, and Norwegian studies (see Table 10.3). Some might argue that the small proportions of medical stories mentioning the issue of drug costs is understandable because these questions are more appropriately covered by the business pages of the newspapers or by finance programmes on television. However, given the increasingly political nature of drug subsidy, whether in private or public insurance systems, and widespread community interest in health care, we would argue that it is critical that reporters factor the issue of cost into their thinking when covering new drugs and medical technologies.

A related issue concerns the level of appropriate use of new, expensive drugs when older, cheaper medicines are available. Data from a pharmacy benefits manager in 2002 suggested widespread inappropriate use of the celecoxib class of drugs by those at no or low risk for gastrointestinal problems, but the findings failed to attract significant media coverage according to Canadian research.[7] Similarly, in Australia, preliminary findings from the National Prescribing Service and internal documents prepared for the federal government suggested a high level of inappropriate use of celecoxib, outside of the indication for which national subsidy was approved under the Pharmaceutical Benefits Scheme.[27,28]

Conflicts of interest

Scientific journals are making increasing efforts to disclose the role of industry in funding and/or conducting studies, and the relevant financial ties of study authors,[29] although there is much evidence that this information is not routinely included in media stories that cite those studies or their authors. For example, in the US study of pravastatin, alendronate, and aspirin, only 39% of stories citing an expert or study with financial links to the drug manufacturer disclosed the link.[3] On this measure, newspaper and television coverage appeared to differ sharply. For newspaper stories, 48% of relevant links were disclosed, but for television stories 0% were disclosed. In 1996, when the three main US television news networks (ABC, CBS, and NBC) broadcasted enthusiastic stories about alendronate (following the release of trial results at a conference), none of the stories mentioned that the study investigator being interviewed had received study funding from alendronate's manufacturer, Merck.

In the Canadian setting, among stories referring to a drug study, only 26% included information on study funding.[2] In terms of the conflicts of interest of the people quoted in the stories, after excluding government and industry spokespeople, an existing financial tie with the drug maker was disclosed on only 3% of occasions. The medical specialist quoted in the *Toronto Star* "miracle" story about celecoxib, for example, was regularly cited by the main Canadian newspapers without any mention of his financial ties to the drug's manufacturer, according to the qualitative analysis by Gandey.[7] Such disclosure occurred even less frequently in Norway, where only 1% of newspaper stories reported financial ties between their quoted experts and the drug manufacturer.[4]

Can media coverage of medicine be improved?

The excited media coverage prematurely celebrating celecoxib noted at the beginning of this chapter is emblematic of much deeper problems. The promotional machinery of the pharmaceutical manufacturers declared another miracle cure and many media stories simply echoed the message. As concerns have mounted about the real safety profile of celecoxib, and debates have raged about both its cost and widespread cost-ineffective use, the extent to which the public was misled by that initial phase of excited media coverage becomes clearer. However, what are also becoming clear are the lessons to be learnt from this case study. After such an egregious example, promotional hype need no longer be confused with medical journalism.

To date there has been limited research on the reasons behind some of the major deficiencies in media coverage of medicine. Clearly, many reporters are limited both in terms of time to prepare stories and space to run them. With often extremely short timeframes, news reporters can become very reliant on their sources of information, whether they are public relations companies, medical specialists, professional societies, or medical journal articles. In the inevitable competition to cover a breaking story, the possibility of contacting independent researchers is small. Two hours before deadline, the opportunity for rigorous evaluation of the latest revelation will be extremely limited. However, although the fact of quick turnaround news may be fixed, the culture of medical news reporting can be challenged and changed.

Many activities are currently underway to try to improve the level of healthy scepticism in media stories about medicine, both within both health care/academic institutions[8] and within journalists' organisations.[9] In this section, we describe settings in which scepticism should be particularly high, and in Box 10.1 we point to some key considerations for improving coverage of new medicines.

Box 10.1 Signs and symptoms of healthy media coverage

Drawing on previous work,[30,31] we should like to offer some brief and simple suggestions that might contribute to a healthy change in the culture of media coverage of medicine. They are offered as points to consider rather than rules to be followed in the preparation of news stories. We hope they may be helpful for those reporting on health care and those who interact with reporters.

Be clearer about the benefits

When reporting on benefits it may help to specify the outcome under consideration rather than a surrogate marker, and to whom the potential benefits apply – that is, what types of patients were studied. When covering the results of a study, presenting absolute event rates with and without a treatment may help give readers/ viewers/listeners a fairer assessment of the magnitude of its effect. On close inspection the benefits of many new therapies are extremely modest. Also, the fact that studies achieve statistical significance when comparing a medicine with a placebo (or other controls) has little bearing on whether the difference is meaningful.

Harms

Although good data on harms are often lacking for new therapies, all medicines carry potential harms, and these deserve much more attention than they currently receive in media stories.

Costs and cost-effectiveness

Increasingly, those who fund health care systems are assessing whether a new medicine or technology offers value for money, and this science offers a rich new source of story material for journalists.

(Continued)

Box 10.1 Continued

There should be caution, however, about the premature discussion of cost-effectiveness (before evidence of effectiveness has been established), because this can frame and potentially skew subsequent debate.[32]

Conflicts of interest

Relevant financial ties of quoted experts, consumer advocates, or medical societies are often missing from media stories, as are funding sources for cited studies. This is an easily fixed problem because many of these ties are now routinely disclosed in journal articles and websites, etc.

The quality of the evidence

Different sorts of evidence get closer to the truth about the value of medical therapies. Weak evidence from early studies can be misleading, but strong evidence from a systematic review of all the relevant studies can get closer to the truth. Communicating better about the "quality" of the evidence and/or its inherent uncertainty could help to reduce the amount of misleading media coverage.

When scepticism should be high

Medicalisation of ordinary experience

A number of the drugs featured in the foregoing media studies were being promoted as part of pharmaceutical industry mass marketing campaigns implicitly or explicitly targeted at relatively healthy people. Some drugs were promoted as ameliorating the symptoms of common ailments or self-limiting conditions, including pain and sexual difficulties, and others as modestly reducing the risks for future adverse events such as heart attacks and fractures. Although these studies did not explore how media stories may have promoted a process of medicalisation, we and others have raised concerns elsewhere that pharmaceutical marketing strategies are increasingly attempting to redefine normal human experiences as treatable medical conditions, and to extend the boundaries of disease definitions in order to expand markets for new products.[33,34]

Medicalisation is especially relevant in light of direct to consumer drug advertising. Although the focus of this chapter is media stories about medicines, a major part of the context for these stories, particularly in the USA, is represented by the burgeoning direct to consumer advertising campaigns. In their analysis of 67 advertisements that appeared in 10 mainstream US magazines in 1999, Woloshin et al.[33] found that 39% tried to encourage consumers to consider medical causes for their common experiences, most often urging them to consult a physician. Writing in the *Lancet*, the researchers concluded, "Our findings suggest that most prescription drugs advertised to consumers target common symptoms (e.g. sneezing, hair loss, being overweight), which many patients would have managed without a physician. Although a pharmacological approach might be appropriate for some, the danger is that by turning ordinary experiences into diagnoses – by designating a runny nose as allergic rhinitis – the boundaries of medicine might become unreasonably broad."

Industry spokespeople argue strongly that advertising provides patients with information about under-diagnosed and under-treated conditions. Bonaccorso and Sturchio[35] from Merck have written, "epidemiological evidence shows a substantial under-diagnosis of many of the major diseases and known risk factors for which effective treatments exist." Others, such as Mintzes,[36] take a different view, writing in 2002 that, "Americans on average saw nine prescription drug advertisements a day on television. To an unprecedented degree they portrayed the educational message of a pill for every ill – and increasingly *an ill for every pill*" (italics added).

In our view the issue of corporate sponsored medicalisation, or what medical writer Payer[37] described as disease mongering, deserves much closer attention from those interested in the rational use of health care resources, and from reporters covering medicine and health care. Resources spent medicalising and medicating minor ailments might be better allocated to treating or preventing the pathology of the genuinely ill.

Preliminary research findings: meetings

"News" axiomatically favours the new, but the "latest" in medical science is not always the healthiest. News coverage of medical or scientific meetings is particularly problematic in this regard because meetings are often used as platforms to promote preliminary findings heavily to the media and the public. The function of meetings is to create a forum for scientists to present work to their peers at an early stage to get feedback. The research presented is work in progress that has undergone little if any formal peer review. Nonetheless, meeting organisers, study funders, academic organisations, researchers, and reporting journalists often all have a shared interest in presenting these early study findings in the best light, exaggerating "miraculous" benefits or dramatising the frightening extent of a hidden epidemic.

In a study published in the *Journal of the American Medical Association* in 2002,[38] Woloshin and Schwartz found that current press coverage of scientific meetings can be characterised as "too much too soon". They examined US press coverage of five major medical meetings in 1998, and found that many of the abstracts that received media coverage had weak designs, were small, were based on animal or laboratory studies, and a quarter of them remained unpublished in any journal three years later. "Results are frequently presented to the public as scientifically sound evidence rather than as preliminary findings with still uncertain validity."

Cost-effectiveness before effectiveness

As many of the chapters in this book make clear, evaluating the cost-effectiveness of new medicines is an extremely important process. Unfortunately, there are also cases where cost-effectiveness analysis may sometimes precede good evidence about effectiveness, a classic example of which was documented by Welch and Mogielnicki[32] in their study of autologous bone marrow transplant for advanced breast cancer. In this case the premature emphasis on cost-effectiveness distracted people from the fact that the benefit of bone marrow transplant for this indication had not yet been established (and in fact has ultimately been refuted). Focusing on cost before benefit is established shifts the debate about drugs, procedures, and tests from "does it work" and "do the benefits outweigh the harms" to "why doesn't insurance or the government pay for it", reinforcing a latent public cynicism that assumes that policy decisions are driven more by a desire to save money rather than lives.[39]

Conclusion

Our review of studies analysing media coverage of more than 20 new medicines suggests that drug benefits are often overplayed, important harms and costs are often underplayed, and relevant conflicts of interest are often overlooked. Notwithstanding the important and rigorous reporting of many conscientious journalists, in our view there is something fundamentally unhealthy about the media culture of reporting on new drugs and other medical technologies. However, we also believe that there is a real possibility to move away from the tired old promotional formulas of miracle cures, and engender a much less misleading and far more informative culture of medical reporting.

Summary

- The media has an important influence over public perceptions about health and medicine, physician and consumer behaviour.
- Too many media stories about medicines exaggerate benefits, play down harms, ignore costs, and fail to cover the conflicts of interest of cited sources.
- Many journalists, their professional associations and academic institutions have demonstrated an interest in making medical journalism less promotional and more informative.
- We suggest those covering medicine should be particularly sceptical of attempts by vested interests to: medicalise ordinary life; hype preliminary findings; confuse debates about effectiveness and cost-effectiveness.

References

1 Boyle T. New arthritis drug called miracle. *Toronto Star*, 16 April 2003:pA2.
2 Cassels A, Hughes M, Cole C, Mintzes B, Lexchin J, McCormack J. Drugs in the news: an analysis of Canadian newspaper coverage of new prescription drugs. *CMAJ* 2003;**168**:1133–7.
3 Moynihan R, Bero L, Ross-Degnan D, *et al*. Coverage by the news media of the benefits and risks of medications. *N Engl J Med* 2000;**342**:1645–50.
4 Høye S, Hjortdahl P. New wonder pill: What Norwegian newspapers write about new medications. *Tidsskr Nor Lægeforen* 2002;**122**:1671–6.
5 Schwartz LM, Woloshin S, Baczek L. Media coverage of scientific meetings. *JAMA* 2002;**287**:2859–63.
6 Schwartz LM, Woloshin S. On the prevention and treatment of exaggeration. *J Gen Intern Med* 2003;**18**:153–4.

7 Gandey A. Media malpractice in Canadian Newspaper Coverage of the arthritis drug Celebrex: guidelines for journalists covering medical news, Master of Journalism. Ottawa, Ontario: School of Journalism and Communication, Carleton University; 9 May 2003.

8 National Institutes of Health, Office of Medical Applications of Research. Medicine in the media: the challenge of reporting on medical research. 2003. http://odp.od.nih.gov/omar/symposium/ (accessed 16 June 2003).

9 Association of Health Care Journalists. Association of Health Care Journalists Fourth National Conference, 2003: exploring the Western edge of health care. http://www.ahcj.umn.edu/files/03_confprog.pdf (accessed 18 June 2003).

10 The Pew Research Center for the People and the Press. Public's news habits little changed by September 11: Americans lack background to follow international news. http://people-press.org/reports/display.php3? ReportID=156 (accessed 4 February 2004).

11 Grilli R, Ramsay C, Minozzi S. Mass media interventions: effects on health services utilisation. *Cochrane Database Syst Rev* 2002;1:CD000389.

12 Domenighetti G, Luraschi P, Casabianca A, *et al.* Effect of information campaign by the mass media on hysterectomy rates. *Lancet* 1988;2: 1470–3.

13 Soumerai S, Ross-Degnan D, Kahn J. Effects of professional and media warnings about the association between aspirin use in children and Reye's syndrome. *Milbank Q* 1992;**70**:155–82.

14 Nattinger A, Hoffman R, Howell-Petz A, Goodwin J. Effect of Nancy Reagan's mastectomy on choice of surgery for breast cancer by US women. *JAMA* 1998;**279**:762–6.

15 Tesoriero J, Sorin M. The effect of "Magic" Johnson's HIV disclosure on anonymous HIV counseling and testing services in New York state. *AIDS Public Policy J* 1992;**7**:216–24.

16 MacLure M, Dormuth C, Naumann T, *et al.* Influences of educational interventions and adverse news about calcium-channel blockers first-line prescribing of antihypertensive drugs to elderly people in British Columbia. *Lancet* 1998;**352**:943–8.

17 Brunt M, Murray M, Hui S, Kesterson J, Perkins A, Tierney W. Mass media release of medical research results: an analysis of antihypertensive drug prescribing in the aftermath of the calcium channel blocker scare of March 1995. *J Gen Intern Med* 2003;**18**:84–9.

18 Phillips D, Kanter E, Bednarcyzk B, Tastad P. Importance of the lay press in the transmission of medical knowledge to the scientific community. *N Engl J Med* 1991;**325**:1180–3.

19 Schwartz LM, Woloshin S. News media coverage of screening mammography for women in their 40s and tamoxifen for primary prevention of breast cancer. *JAMA* 2002;**287**:3136–42.

20 Woloshin K, Ruffin M, Gorenflo D. Patients' interpretation of qualitative probability statements. *Arch Fam Med* 1994;**3**:961–6.

21 Bryant G, Norman G. Expressions of probability: words and numbers. *N Engl J Med* 1980;**302**:411.

22 Hux J, Naylor C. Communicating the benefits of chronic preventive therapy: does the format of efficacy data determine patients' acceptance of treatment? *Med Decis Making* 1995;**15**:152–7.

23 Naylor C, Chen E, Strauss B. Measured enthusiasm: does the method of reporting trial results alter perceptions of therapeutic effectiveness? *Ann Intern Med* 1992;**117**:916–21.

24 Anonymous. COX-2 inhibitors update: do journal publications tell the full story? [therapeutics letter 43]. November/December 2001, and January 2002. http://www.ti.ubc.ca (accessed on 6 June 2003).

25 US Food and Drug Administration. Retyped text of a letter from Glaxo Wellcome Inc. http://www.fda.gov/medwatch/safety/2000/relenz.htm (accessed 11 August 2003).
26 US Food and Drug Administration. Unedited transcript from a meeting of the Food and Drug Administration, Center for Drug Evaluation and Research http://www.fda.gov/ohrms/dockets/ac/99/transcpt/3496t1.pdf (accessed 11 August 2003).
27 Moynihan R. "Wonder drug" misuse blows out budget, says survey. *Australian Financial Review*, 2 April 2002:p3.
28 Moynihan R. Doctors causing a drugs cost blowout. *Australian Financial Review*, 18 March 2002:p1.
29 Davidoff F, DeAngelis C, Drazen J, *et al*. Sponsorship, authorship, and accountability. *JAMA* 2001;**286**:1232–4.
30 Schwartz LM, Woloshin S, Black W, Welch G. The role of numeracy in understanding the benefit of screening mammography. *Ann Intern Med* 1997;**127**:966–72.
31 Moynihan R, Soumerai S, Fletcher R, *et al*. A tipsheet for reporting on drugs, devices and medical technologies. http://www.cmwf.org (accessed 6 June 2003).
32 Welch G, Mogielnicki J. Presume benefit: lessons from the American experience with marrow transplantation for breast cancer. *BMJ* 2002;**324**:1088–92.
33 Woloshin S, Schwartz LM, Tremmel J, Welch G. Direct to consumer advertisements for prescription drugs: what are Americans being sold? *Lancet* 2001;**358**:1141–6.
34 Moynihan R, Health I, Henry D. Selling sickness: the pharmaceutical industry and disease mongering. *BMJ* 2002;**324**:886–91.
35 Bonaccorso S, Sturchio J. Direct to consumer advertising is medicalising normal human experience (against). *BMJ* 2002;**324**:908–11.
36 Mintzes B. Direct to consumer advertising is medicalising normal human experience (for). *BMJ* 2002;**324**:908–11.
37 Payer L. *Disease mongers: how doctors, drug companies, and insurers are making you feel sick*. Chichester: John Wiley & Sons, 1992.
38 Woloshin S, Schwartz LM. Press releases, translating research into news. *JAMA* 2002;**287**:2856–58.
39 Woloshin S, Schwartz LM, Byram S, Sox H, Fischhoff B, Welch G. Women's understanding of the mammography screening debate. *Arch Intern Med* 2000;**160**:1434–40.

11: How to promote quality use of cost-effective medicines

HANS HOGERZEIL, KATHLEEN HOLLOWAY

Introduction

A careful section of cost-effective medicines is essential but not enough. Unfortunately, there are many recorded examples of irrational use of essential medicines. In a national ambulatory medical care survey conducted in the USA,[1] involving nearly 30,000 prescriptions by 1529 physicians, it was found that 51% of patients with a common cold or upper respiratory tract infection received antibiotics, as well as 66% of patients with common bronchitis. This involved 12 million antibiotic prescriptions. Assuming that a large proportion of these prescriptions were not really needed, this prescribing behaviour carries considerable medical costs (side effects, increased resistance) and economic costs (several hundreds of millions of dollars to insurance schemes or individual patients). In primary care in developing countries a similar picture is seen, with between 30% and 60% of all outpatients receiving one or more antibiotics. In Australia a medicine that is reimbursed for one indication for which it is cost-effective is often promoted and used in other indications for which it is not. One example is the cyclo-oxygenase (COX)-2 inhibitors, which may be cost-effective when used in high risk patients but are not cost-effective when used for analgesia in low risk patients. In Australia a term was coined for this phenomenon – "leakage". Irrational use of cost-effective medicines reduces their effectiveness and their cost-effectiveness.

Programmes of quality use are therefore needed to ensure that the maximum benefit of the medicines is gained, to reduce unnecessary risks to the patient, and to reduce unnecessary expenditure. In doing this, efforts should focus on those types of interventions that are proven to be effective.

There is a good body of evidence on the effectiveness of the various interventions to promote the quality use of medicines.[2,3] The following interventions are probably effective:

- locally adapted clinical guidelines (if accompanied by targeted face to face education)
- medicines (drugs) and therapeutics committees
- supervision, audit, and feedback
- undergraduate training in good prescribing skills
- continuing medical education (CME).

Simultaneous interventions reinforce each other. Negative influences such as perverse financial incentives and unregulated drug promotion should also be prevented or corrected. An environment that encourages more rational prescribing can be created through appropriate and enforced regulation, for example limiting availability of certain medicines by level of prescriber. An example of a national programme is provided in Box 11.1.

Box 11.1 Promoting quality use of medicines in Australia

In the late 1980s concern began to be expressed about the quality of use of medicines in Australia. Despite a long history of strong drug regulation, a universal access scheme that guaranteed the provision of medicines of high quality to the whole community, and the existence of an established pharmaceutical industry support scheme, there was good evidence that the use of medicines was less than ideal. Several national meetings engaged consumer groups, government, the pharmaceutical industry, and health professionals in debating the evidence for irrational use of medicines. The local and national partnerships developed then have persisted as a central aspect of all subsequent work.

This groundswell led to the adoption of a Policy on the Quality Use of Medicines (1992) as the fourth arm of the Australian National Medicines Policy,[4] and to the creation of two major national committees – one a representative body and the other more research

(Continued)

Box 11.1 (Continued)

orientated – to work through the issues and carry out strategic research. In a short period much local evidence was collected about the nature and extent of the problems and about interventions that had been shown to be effective both in Australia and elsewhere.

The National Prescribing Service (NPS)[5] was created in 1997 as a not-for-profit company, funded entirely by the federal government to implement proven interventions. It was directed by a board representing all of the partners. Its intervention programmes now include the following:

- training, placement, and support of pharmaceutical education visitors in 110 of the 121 divisions of general practice nationwide
- provision of objective information on therapeutic topics with the option for doctors to conduct and obtain external scrutiny of a practice based prescribing audit related to that topic
- confidential feedback to doctors of personal prescribing information coupled with relevant educational material
- free telephone medicine information services for both health professionals and consumers
- development of curricula on quality prescribing of medicines for undergraduate medical students,[6] interns, registrars, nurses, and pharmacists (see Box 11.4).

Most recently the NPS has been awarded a government contract to embark on comprehensive consumer education about medicines.

Evaluative evidence supports the view that significant changes in prescribing have resulted from some of these activities – especially in the area of the unnecessary and irrational use of antibiotics.

Anthony Smith and Lynn Weekes

Local practice guidelines

Evidence-based clinical guidelines should, and often do, constitute the basis for essential medicines lists and local formularies. They serve as the basis for prescribing, training, medicine supply and reimbursement, and as a standard for audit and feedback. In the future they may increasingly serve as a standard for litigation and malpractice. Guidelines can be highly effective for promoting rational prescribing,[7] especially when combined with the development of local ownership, an official launch, training in their use, and prescribing feedback.[2,8]

The right balance must be found between national guidelines based on best evidence and local guidelines adapted to local preferences (which usually gain in local ownership but may lose in terms of evidence base). For example, in Scotland the first guidelines of the Scottish Intercollegiate Guideline Network[9] were intended and used for local adaptation, but it was soon found that local adaptation had led to, or maintained, the variation in treatment practices that the guidelines were intended to correct. Local adaptation has now been replaced by local involvement in national guideline development.[10] The fact that the Scottish Intercollegiate Guideline Network guidelines have established a reputation of solid evidence and wide consultation has of course helped, but their acceptance is still incomplete.

The same applies to Australian guidelines, such as the Antibiotic Guidelines,[11] which were originally developed for one hospital, then for one province/state, and now, through extensive involvement and wide consultation, for the country as a whole. In both cases more emphasis is now put on efforts to promote the full acceptance and use of the guidelines. A long-term solution may be to ensure that the guidelines are actively promoted to medical students and widely used in teaching hospitals.

Some methodological guidelines and sources of independent information that can support national or institutional committees in the development of clinical guidelines and national formularies are presented in Box 11.2.

Medicines and therapeutics committees

Medicines and therapeutics committees (MTCs) are active and known to be effective in industrialised countries such as Australia.[12] Several countries have made such committees mandatory at the hospital and/or district level. It is assumed that MTCs are also effective in developing countries but there is no real proof of this; early experience in Zimbabwe showed that such committees were difficult to maintain because of the large workload of most clinicians.

Governments may encourage hospitals to have MTCs by making it an accreditation requirement of various professional societies. MTC members should represent all of the major

Box 11.2 Selected sources of independent information

- WHO Essential Medicines Library, WHO Model List of Essential Medicines and WHO Model Formulary. http://www.who.int/medicines
- British National Formulary, Royal Pharmaceutical Society of Great Britain, 1 Lambeth High Street, London SE1 7JN, UK. http://www.bnf.org/
- Cochrane Collaboration (systematic reviews). http://www.cochrane.org/
- Guidelines International Network (database on guidelines, guidelines methodology, exchange of evidence tables). http://www.g-i-n.net

Examples of high quality national guidelines:

- Australia (Victoria): Therapeutic Guidelines Limited. http://www.tg.com.au
- Scotland: Scottish Intercollegiate Guidelines Network (SIGN). http://www.sign.ac.uk/
- Essential Drugs List for Zimbabwe (EDLIZ), including guidelines for treatment of medical conditions common in Zimbabwe. Harare: Ministry of Health and Child Welfare, 1994
- Standard Treatment Guidelines and Essential Drugs List for South Africa (Paediatrics, Adults, and Primary Care). Pretoria: Department of Health, 1998
- Sharma S, Sethi GR, Gulati RJ (editors). Standard treatment guidelines for Delhi. Delhi: Ministry of Health and the Delhi Society for the Promotion of Rational Use of Drugs. http://www.dsprud.org

Methodological guidance on the development of clinical guidelines

- Managing drug supply. The selection, procurement, distribution and use of pharmaceuticals, 2nd edition. Management Sciences for Health in collaboration with the World Health Organization. West Hartfort, Connecticut: Kumarian Press, 1997 (Chapters 10 and 11)
- Scottish Intercollegiate Guidelines Network (SIGN). A guideline developers' handbook SIGN Publication No. 50. Published February 2001, last updated October 2002. http://www.sign.ac.uk/guidelines/fulltext/50/html
- Slovene Guidelines Group, Ministry of Health, Štefanova 5, 3rd Floor, Ljubljana, Slovenia. http://www2.gov.si/index.nsf
- WHO Declaration of Interest Forms: http://www.who.int/medicines/organization/par/edl/expcom14/expertcomm14/shtml

Hans Hogerzeil and Kathleen Holloway

specialities and the administration; they should also be independent and declare any conflict of interest. A senior doctor would usually be the chairperson, and chief pharmacist the secretary.

Important tasks of MTCs include the following: local adaptation of national guidelines and development of institutional guidelines and formularies; review of requests for introduction of new medicines; provision of ongoing staff education through training and printed materials; provision of prescribing audit and feedback; evaluation of drug use; control of pharmaceutical industry access to staff with its promotional activities; monitoring and taking action to prevent adverse drug reactions and medication errors; and liaising with antibiotic and infection control committees. They may also include the approval of individual requests for very expensive treatments. Managing the medicines budget and the supply system are not primary tasks of MTCs, although they play an advisory role. However, too much involvement can easily degrade into a monthly complaint session to the pharmacist, which usually heralds the end of the committee.

Factors critical to success of MTCs include a firm mandate, senior administrative support, transparent decision making, a multidisciplinary approach, wide representation, technical competence, and sufficient resources to implement decisions.[13]

Supervision, audit, and feedback

Supervision is essential to ensuring good quality of care. Supervision that is supportive, educational, and face to face will be more effective and better accepted by prescribers than simple inspection and punishment. Effective forms of supervision include prescription audit and feedback, peer review, and group processes. Academic detailing is a form of support to prescribers that may involve supervision, prescription audit and feedback, and peer review. It probably started in the USA,[14,15] was taken up in Northern Ireland,[16] and is now generally available in Australia and the UK (Box 11.3). Academic detailing programmes provide support to prescribing physicians, mainly general practitioners, which includes encouragement to develop practice guidelines, free access to independent medicine information, advice on prescribing, and voluntary review of their (often computerised) prescribing records. There is often a component of counteracting commercial detailing. These efforts could perhaps best be focused on opinion leaders – this is what the industry does.

Box 11.3 Prescribing support in the UK

In England, general or family practices are organised into administrative divisions known as primary care trusts (PCTs) covering around 100,000 patients and 50 general practitioners (GPs). Each PCT has responsibility for about 70% of all health budgets for its population, which includes prescribing. Each PCT has one or more prescribing advisers (PAs), usually pharmacists, whose role is to advise both the PCT administrators and the individual GPs on all matters related to prescribing. This includes the following:

- encouraging development of formularies at practice level (PCT level formularies are rare)
- implementation of government policies that may affect prescribing (for instance, guidance issued by the National Institute of Clinical Excellence)
- setting and managing drug budgets for the PCT
- advising GPs on good prescribing
- negotiating with hospitals on prescribing issues (for example, regarding continued medication to patients discharged from hospitals).

PAs have informal networks for support and training in therapeutics and other skills, both locally and nationally through the National Prescribing Centre.

PAs also advise on managing PCT prescribing budgets. Any overspend on drugs must come out of the PCT budget, which is cash limited. Each general practice is set an indicative or hypothetical budget for its prescribing spending, and is encouraged to stay within it. There are cash incentives for the practice (to be spent on patient benefit, not a payment to the doctor) to achieve this, and other more quality driven and locally determined prescribing targets. There are no penalties for failing to meet these but the performance of each doctor is often shared with their peers and peer pressure encourages conformity.

(Continued)

Box 11.3 (Continued)

PAs undertake practice visits, where they meet with GPs and other practice staff, and target specific aspects of a GP's prescribing for change (for example, changing the choice of a medicine to a less expensive and equally effective alternative, or encouraging greater prescribing of statins to meet government targets on reduction of ischaemic heart disease). These aspects are therefore a mixture of cost related and quality related issues. To assist them in this task, PAs have access to excellent data about which medicines each practice has prescribed, but not on the indication or the type of patient who received the prescription. There is often an implicit element of counter-detailing against pharmaceutical industry activities in this.

It is difficult to say which if any elements of this mix of activities are most effective. A randomised controlled trial[17] showed a definite but relatively small effect of academic detailing in the UK, but this was an artificial scenario that does not really reflect the day to day activities of the PA. The role of incentive schemes has not been well studied, although GP fund holding – a former form of incentive – had a short lived but powerful effect in cost minimisation.[18]

The key lessons may be the importance of good information systems on what is prescribed, the personal credibility of the PA to the doctor (which depends on their pharmaceutical and clinical knowledge), the credibility of the sources they can quote, their interpersonal skills, and the degree to which PAs are seen to promote quality and not just cost saving. The two main motivators for prescribing change appear to be peer pressure and incentive schemes.

Tom Walley

Undergraduate training in prescribing skills

Irrational prescribing is a disease that may be easier to prevent than to cure. It is therefore important that a national programme on quality use of medicines also includes a programme to promote better teaching of prescribing to medical students. This often implies that teaching of pharmacology and pharmacotherapy must move away from transferring drug centred knowledge toward developing a critical attitude and the right prescribing skills. Problem based teaching is an approach to this that has proven effective[19] and is increasingly being used, even within otherwise traditional curricula. Skill based learning also implies skill based examinations, such as Observed Standardised Clinical Examinations.

The World Health Organization's (WHO) *Guide to Good Prescribing*[20] is a practical student manual on the principles of rational prescribing, and has been translated into 21 languages. A teacher's manual is also available.[21] The method is increasingly being used all over the world, for example in the Netherlands where it originated, in Argentina and other countries of Latin America, and more recently in Australia, where it is now used in most medical schools (Box 11.4).

Box 11.4 Problem based pharmacotherapy teaching in Australia

The National Prescribing Service (NPS) of Australia was created in 1997, and is funded by government but is autonomous in its activities (see Box 11.1). The work of the NPS includes a programme to improve teaching of prescribing skills to medical students.

In close collaboration with all 11 medical schools in the country, the Curriculum and Training Working Group of the NPS has developed a modular course based on the WHO guide to good prescribing.[20] It is a problem based course covering 12 topics relevant to senior medical students, and it is delivered as a web based self-learning programme. In 2002, its year of introduction, nine of the medical schools made use of it – some very extensively. Each module teaches the student a specific prescribing problem. While going through the process of solving the problem, the students are continuously referred to (and expected to use) the materials they will later encounter in real life prescribing, such as the Australian prescribing guidelines, the price list of the national Pharmaceutical Benefits Scheme, and the standard prescription form. In 2003 the programme was expanded to include six patient problems for registrars; cases for general practitioners are in preparation.

The programme is being evaluated, but it looks sufficiently promising that negotiations are ongoing with a number of groups around the world to modify the curriculum for medical students elsewhere. One of the modules can be freely accessed through the NPS website[6].

Anthony Smith

Continuing medical education

CME is critical in the world of therapeutics and medicine, which is changing rapidly. In the past, keeping up to date has been left to the individual professional. However, with the huge increase in information and greater demand for quality of care and accountability to patients, CME programmes are becoming more structured. Many industrialised countries are now making attendance in a CME programme compulsory by making it a requirement for licensure. CME is likely to be more effective if it is problem based, targeted, involves professional societies, universities and the ministry of health, and is face to face. Printed materials, including clinical guidelines, that are not accompanied by face to face interventions have been found to be ineffective in changing prescribing behaviour.[7-9] Often, CME activities are heavily dependent on the support of pharmaceutical companies because public funds are insufficient. Such education may be biased, and every effort should be made by government and national professional associations to provide independent CME.

Ethical promotion

Much increase in medicine expenditure is due to introduction of new medicines. For example, 55% of the 93% cumulative increase in the average cost of prescriptions in Canada between 1987 and 1993 was due to the introduction of new medicines; price increases of existing medicines and increased mean quantities per prescription contributed much less to the increase. New medicines are often very expensive; annual costs of over $10,000 per patient are no longer exceptional. Also, irrespective of whether they offer a real or a minor advantage over existing treatments, they are heavily promoted. On average, 25–35% of the revenue of the research based industries in the *Fortune* 500 list is spent on promotion, which is about twice as much as is spent on research and development. Promotion is often effective in changing prescriber attitudes, in changing prescribing patterns, in getting medicines included in hospital formularies, and in steering research. However, most doctors do not realise how much they are being influenced, and they often deny that they are.[22]

There are very few effective answers to this huge marketing effort. A recent systematic review of the evidence found that strict regulation of promotion is probably the only effective measure;[22] other approaches such as voluntary self regulatory codes and training of prescribers in dealing with promotion are not. A counterbalance to industry sponsored information may also be found in a systematic evaluation of the evidence on efficacy, safety, and cost-effectiveness of new medicines, leading to the development of evidence-based clinical guidelines (see above) and probably the most effective reimbursement decisions.

Generic policies

The second cornerstone of the essential medicines concept (apart from evidence-based selection of medicines for priority condition) is the promotion of generic policies. The first implies that active ingredients within therapeutic classes are compared in a systematic way and that clinical guidelines are established to assist the prescriber in selecting the most safe and cost-effective treatments. The second implies that the choice of the actual product containing the prescribed active ingredient is left to the pharmacist, who will base the choice on a review of the quality and price of the various products. Of course, this applies only when the prescribed medicine is not on patent anymore.

In their efforts to influence the choice of the actual product among generic or therapeutic competitors, companies expend much effort on creating brand loyalty among prescribers. Generic policies aim to reduce medicine prices by creating conditions for fair competition on the basis of quality and price. They should be introduced in stages, starting with the introduction of legal possibilities for optional and later obligatory generic substitution by pharmacists, and moving toward promotion of generic prescribing, especially in teaching hospitals. The generic policy should consist of advocacy of the concept, information and training of prescibers and dispensers, quality assurance of generic products (which is sometimes lacking in developing and middle income countries), and financial incentives for prescribing, dispensing, and using generics.[23]

Financial incentives

There are several perverse incentives that may lead to irrational prescribing. For example, a percentage mark up for the pharmacist, which remains the most common way of defining retail prices, encourages the sale of expensive brands and goes against a generic policy. This is especially the case when prescription medicines can be purchased without prescription and the pharmacist becomes a *de facto* prescriber with a conflict of interest. The solution to this dilemma is a fixed dispensing fee, which increases the price of cheaper medicines but reduces overall costs.

The opposite, a dispensing doctor, creates the same conflict of interest and is also well documented as leading to the prescription of more and more expensive medicines, often for a shorter duration.[24] This situation may be worse when companies offer the dispensing doctor special price deals for certain medicines, and even more so when the doctors can still charge the full retail price to reimbursement schemes. The same conflict of interest could arise if financial kick backs from companies to prescribers of their medicines are allowed. In all these cases, legal or regulatory provisions are needed. Separation of the prescriber and dispenser functions avoids such conflicts of interest.

Finally, governmental patient co-payment schemes may create an unintended perverse incentive. For example, a flat fee for consultation plus medicines leads to over-prescribing, because patients who need little or no treatment may exert pressure on the consultant to prescribe their "money's worth".[25,26] Here, the solution is an itemised medicine bill (which most patients would find reasonable anyway), or at least the use of price bands depending on the type of medication received.

Financial incentives to patients can also be used to support rational prescribing. For example, if only essential medicines are provided free of charge by the government or reimbursed through health insurance, and if the list of essential medicines closely follows evidence-based clinical guidelines, then patient pressure to prescribe the free medicines almost certainly leads to better adherence to the guidelines. Similarly, reference pricing (see Chapter 13) may discourage the use of less cost-effective medicines.

Appropriate regulation

Regulation of the activities of the pharmaceutical sector is critical to promoting rational use of medicines. If regulations are to have any effect, then they must be enforced and the regulatory authority must be sufficiently funded and backed up by the judiciary. Regulatory measures include the following:[3]

- registration of medicines to ensure that only safe and efficacious medicines of good quality are available in the market, and that unsafe and non-efficacious medicines are banned
- limiting prescription of medicines by level of prescriber; this includes limiting certain medicines to being available only with prescription and not available over the counter
- setting educational standards for health professionals and developing and enforcing codes of conduct; this requires the cooperation of the professional societies and universities
- licensing of health professionals – doctors, nurses, and paramedics – in order to ensure that all practitioners have the necessary competence with regard to diagnosis, prescribing, and dispensing
- licensing of medicine outlets – retail shops and wholesalers – in order to ensure that all supply outlets maintain the necessary stocking and dispensing standards
- monitoring and regulating medicine promotion to ensure that it is ethical and unbiased. All promotional claims should be reliable, accurate, truthful, informative, balanced, up to date, capable of substantiation, and in good taste. The WHO ethical guidelines[27] may be used as a basis for developing control measures.

Conclusion

Evidence-based selection of cost-effective medicines alone is not enough to ensure their quality use and to prevent unnecessary expenditure. Recommended interventions to promote quality use include the local development and use of evidence-based clinical guidelines, MTCs, prescriber supervision, audit and feedback, prescribing training in the basic medical curricula, and CME. Ethical drug promotion must be ensured through regulation, and commercial information needs to be counterbalanced by clinical guidelines and generic policies. Perverse financial incentives, such as the combination of prescribing and dispensing, percentage based pharmacist's mark ups, and flat consultation plus medicines co-payments by patients should be avoided; reimbursement should be limited to essential medicines. A national programme is needed to plan, coordinate, execute, and monitor all of these activities.

Acknowledgement

We thank Anthony Smith (University of Newcastle, Australia), Lynn Weekes (National Prescribing Service, Australia), and Tom Walley (National Prescribing Centre, Liverpool) for writing boxes included in this chapter.

Summary

- The careful selection of cost-effective medicines does not guarantee rational prescribing. Irrational use of essential medicines is widespread.
- Recommended strategies to promote the quality use of medicines include clinical guidelines; medicines and therapeutic committees; supervision, audit, and feedback; problem based pharmacotherapy training in undergraduate curricula; CME; independent drug information; public education about medicines; avoidance of perverse financial incentives; and appropriate enforced regulation.
- A national programme is needed to plan, coordinate, implement, and monitor all of these activities.

References

1 Gonzales R, Steiner JF, Sande MA. Antibiotic prescribing for adults with colds, upper respiratory tract infections, and bronchitis by ambulatory care physicians. *JAMA* 1997;278:901–4.

2   Laing R, Hogerzeil H, Ross-Degnan D. Ten recommendations to promote improved use of medicines in developing countries. *Health Policy Plan* 2001;**16**:13–20.
3   WHO. Promoting rational use of medicines: core components. WHO Policy Perspectives on Medicines, nr 5. Geneva: WHO, 2002. http://www.who.int/medicines/library/edm_general/6pagers/ppm05en.pdf (accessed 5 February 2004).
4   http://www.health.gov.au/nmp/objectives/index.htm (accessed 2 April 2004).
5   National Prescribing Service Limited homepage. http://www.nps.org.au (accessed 5 February 2004).
6   National Prescribing Service. National Prescribing Curriculum. http://nps.unisa.edu.au (accessed 2 April 2004)
7   Grimshaw J. Russell IT. Effect of clinical guidelines on medical practice: a systematic review of rigorous evaluations. *Lancet* 1993;**ii**:1317–22.
8   Kafuko J, Zirabamuzaale C, Bagenda D. *Impact of national standard treatment guidelines on rational drug use in Uganda health facilities*. Kampala: UNICEF/Uganda, 1994.
9   Scottish Intercollegiate Guidelines Network homepage. http://sign.ac.uk (accessed 5 February 2004).
10 Petrie JC. Clinical guidelines in Scotland: a SIGN of the times. *Essential Drugs Monitor* 1996;**22**:13–14.
11 Therapeutic Guidelines Ltd. *Therapeutic guidelines: antibiotics*. North Melbourne, Therapeutic Guidelines Ltd, annual. (see also www.tg.com.au) (accessed 2 April 2004).
12 Weekes LM, Brooks C. Drug and therapeutic committees in Australia: expected and actual performance. *Br J Clin Pharmacol* 1996;**42**:551–7.
13 Pedersen CA, Schneider PJ, Santell JP. ASHP national survey of pharmacy practice in hospital settings: prescribing and transcribing. *Am J Health Syst Pharm* 2001;**58**:2251–6.
14 Avorn J, Soumerai SB. Improving drug therapy decision through educational outreach. *N Engl J Med* 1983;**308**:1457–63.
15 Soumerai S, Avorn J. Economic and policy analysis of university-based drug "detailing". *Med Care* 1986;**24**:313–31.
16 McGavock H. Improving the rationality and economy of family doctor drug prescribing by means of feed-back interviews: the 13-year N-Ireland experience. Geneva, Switzerland: WHO, 1989. DAP/89.
17 Freemantle N, Nazareth I, Eccles M, Wood J, Haines A, and the Evidence-based OutReach (EBOR) trialists. A randomised controlled trial of the effect of educational outreach by community pharmacists on prescribing in UK general practice. *Br J Gen Pract* 2002;**52**:290–5.
18 Walley T, Mrazek M, Mossialos E. Regulating pharmaceutical markets: improving efficiency and controlling costs in the UK. *Int J Health Plan Man* 2004; in press.
19 De Vries TPGM, Henning RH, Hogerzeil HV, *et al*. Impact of a short course in pharmacotherapy for undergraduate medical students. *Lancet* 1995;**346**:1454–7.
20 De Vries TPGM, Henning RH, Hogerzeil HV, Fresle DA. *Guide to good prescribing: a practical manual*. Geneva, Switzerland: WHO, 1994. WHO/DAP/94.11.
    http://www.who.int/medicines/library/par/ggprescribing/who-dap-94-11en.pdf (accessed 13 February 2004).
21 Hogerzeil HV (editor). Teachers guide to good prescribing. Geneva, Switzerland: WHO, 2001. WHO/EDM/PAR/2001.2. http://www.who.int/medicines/library/par/teachers_guide.pdf (accessed 13 February 2004).

22 Department of Essential Drugs & Medicines Policy. Major outcomes from the reviews. http://www.drugpromo.info/read-reviews.asp?id=8 (accessed 5 February 2004).

23 WHO. *How to develop and implement a national drug policy.* Geneva, Switzerland: WHO, 2001:34–5.

24 Trap B, Hansen EH, Hogerzeil HV. Prescription habits of dispensing and non-dispensing doctors in Zimbabwe. *Health Policy Plan* 2002;**17**:288–95.

25 Holloway KA, Gautam BR, Reeves BC. The effects of different kinds of user fees on prescriber costs in rural Nepal. *Health Policy Plan* 2001;**16**:421–7.

26 Holloway KA, Gautam BR, Reeves BC. The effects of different kinds of user fees on prescribing quality in rural Nepal. *J Clin Epidemiol* 2001;**54**:1065–71.

27 WHO. Ethical criteria for medicinal drug promotion. Geneva, Switzerland: WHO, 1988.

12: Using economic evaluation to inform health policy and reimbursement: making it happen and making it sustainable

ANDREW MITCHELL

Introduction

In 1987 Australia passed legislation that substantially affected the process of deciding which pharmaceutical products should be eligible for its national subsidy programme. The legislation requires consideration of both costs and effectiveness, including comparing the new pharmaceutical product with currently available therapies, regardless of whether the current therapies are pharmaceutical products or other treatments.

This chapter primarily draws on insights gained from and experiences with implementing this legislation to derive three key messages.

- There needs to be a consolidation phase after the tremendous effort that is required to introduce the requirements that enable cost-effectiveness considerations to help achieve health policy aims.
- The main benefit of the legislation is to establish more explicitly the suite of factors that are involved in evaluating the worth of pharmaceutical products.
- The main challenges in the implementation are to maintain a constructive collaboration across the many interconnected elements and to identify and address the pressure points as they arise.

Making it happen

There are many contexts in which a consideration of the cost-effectiveness of pharmaceutical products can contribute to achieving health policy aims, ranging from the decisions taken by individuals to prescribe and consume pharmaceutical products to decision at the national level. Each nation's approach to pharmaceutical policy is different – let alone that of each prescriber and consumer. This section analyses those common features that must be met if consideration of cost-effectiveness is to be useful across this range. In particular, this section demonstrates that a successful link is necessary between the high level steps required to establish a workable system and the technical level initiatives to sustain it.

High level steps

High level steps are those taken to initiate consideration of cost-effectiveness. In practice, these steps are usually taken by those outside the decision making process who wish to ensure that the process has a firm basis, although it can also involve those within decision making processes.

High level step 1: link to policy

The first high level step is to nest cost-effectiveness considerations into an appropriate policy setting. A consideration of the comparative cost-effectiveness of pharmaceutical products is most directly pertinent to those who pay for them. This anchors the cost-effectiveness consideration to where it is most useful, by providing the clearest connection between pharmaceutical purchasing policy and the broader health policy of the payer. Comparative cost-effectiveness is most powerful when it is used to inform the most difficult decisions (i.e. those that involve a judgement of value for money represented by a new product that both costs more overall and delivers more health outcomes). As an "outcomes based reward system",[1] it promises the greatest price reward to those products that provide the greatest quality-adjusted survival gains (and taking into account attributable changes in the provision of other health care resources and, if deemed relevant, other attributable indirect economic impacts). As such, this promise forms the basis of a "win–win" approach between providers and payers, each seeking to achieve a common goal in partnership. Furthermore, the quantitative and evidence-based nature of contemporary cost-effectiveness considerations is a source of increasing support to this promise (Box 12.1).

Box 12.1 Controversy 1: is consideration of cost-effectiveness detrimental to the pharmaceutical industry?

A particular limitation of the consideration of cost-effectiveness as described in this chapter is that, although it can form an informative basis for judging health policy (promotion of health) against fiscal policy (constraint of expenditure), it does not directly inform industry policy. Industry policy is primarily concerned with maintaining viability of industry, but extends to positive industry contributions such as research and development activities, employing a highly skilled workforce and contributing to the balance of payments. The pharmaceutical industry strongly argues that a linchpin to its viability is the ability to generate monopolies based on long-term patents for "new and innovative" products. This tends to clash with cost-effectiveness considerations, which define innovation in terms of the extra health that a new product brings. At best, cost-effectiveness considerations may be industry friendly through the outcomes based reward system, helping to identify those innovations that would be most valuable to payers. At worst, they could be industry neutral by being indifferent to industry policy. However, they may be perceived as being detrimental to the industry because they give no basis for rewarding new patented products, that do not offer any extra health gain, with a higher price.

For the individual, a consideration of cost-effectiveness is most relevant to policy when it is directly applicable to the circumstances of that individual. At the national level, systematically considering cost-effectiveness quickly makes apparent the need to link this consideration to mechanisms that account for varying cost-effectiveness of each new product across individuals in the population. This is because cost-effectiveness decisions are largely driven by the incremental effectiveness manifested by each new product, which forms the denominator of each cost-effectiveness consideration, and incremental effectiveness varies across each population of individuals. Two particularly important levers of control therefore are as follows: the ability to control unit costs (prices); and the ability to control volumes of use by identifying those individuals for whom the product is acceptably cost-effective and satisfactorily restricting use to those individuals only. So, at its most simple, if costs are completely fixed then there is a single dividing line separating use of or payment for a new product according to whether it is or is not acceptably cost-effective. Conceptually, however, by matching this varying incremental effectiveness with appropriate variations in incremental costs, this single line can be varied in an almost infinite number of ways. Some of these ways have been identified in response to evidence that there is use beyond predefined restrictions, resulting in negotiated risk sharing or price volume agreements to minimise the impact of such use on reducing efficiency. In practice, linking considerations of cost-effectiveness to price controls and subsidy restrictions has tended to tarnish its role as a basis of a win–win outcome between providers and payers.

High level step 2: establish authority and infrastructure

The second high level step is to authorise the system of considering cost-effectiveness and to establish the basic infrastructure of this system. The first of these related components involves enacting the authority (whether legislative, regulatory, and/or administrative) to ensure that consideration of cost-effectiveness becomes an integral part of the decision making process. At the individual level, this may merely mean accessing the relevant information, however possible, whenever there is an important level of doubt about whether use of a new product would be worthwhile. At the national level the level of authority should be sufficient to support a much more rigorous process. For example, the inevitable linking of consideration of cost-effectiveness to the important and controversial policy levers of controlling price and restricting (and thus denying) subsidised access discussed above at the national level gives this criterion of cost-effectiveness particular importance. In the event of a substantial disagreement with a subsidy decision based on cost-effectiveness considerations, it should be expected that the authority of the decision would be tested, including by judicial examination.

The second of these related components is the infrastructure necessary to obtain relevant information in relation to cost-effectiveness, to appraise the rigour and applicability of this information, and then to incorporate this information appropriately into the decision making process. Given that, at its heart, consideration of cost-effectiveness involves value judgements, and that there is inevitable uncertainty in each consideration of cost-effectiveness, it is important that such infrastructure is clear in how it handles issues relating to the burden of proof. The simplest approach is for the payer to request that the sponsor of a new product submit the evidentiary basis for the cost-effectiveness consideration in order to inform the payer's decision as to whether to accept the product. This approach shares many elements with the more universally applied processes of requesting tenders for the procurement of goods or services. However, the approaches to handling issues of burden of proof become more complicated if a third party payer either makes recourse (in the interests of independence and avoiding conflicts of interest) to sources of cost-effectiveness information other than the sponsor of a product or seeks to review the current arrangements for subsidising a product (Box 12.2).

Box 12.2 Controversy 2: could a strict interpretation of conflicts of interest weaken a partnership approach to pharmaceutical policy?

Placing the burden of proof on sponsors to demonstrate cost-effectiveness tends to promote an adversarial approach between sponsors and third party payers rather than a partnership approach, which would seek to identify health gains that could be rewarded with higher prices. One manifestation of this is judging how to handle conflicts of interest. For example, the appointment of someone employed by a pharmaceutical industry organisation or a pharmaceutical company to an advisory committee inevitably raises questions about these judgements that may be resolved differently in different jurisdictions. One possible implication of strictly eliminating any such conflicts of interest is that this may result in two mutually exclusive "worlds", with an innate tendency to be distrustful of each other. One world comprises those who prepare cost-effectiveness information for sponsors to help promote new products; the other world comprises those who evaluate and use this information to help decide whether the new products are justified at the prices requested.

High level step 3: define framework and scope and issue guidelines

The third high level step involves establishing the scope and framework of how cost-effectiveness is to be considered. The discipline of health economics tends to play a dominant role here in identifying and addressing the key issues. For example, this discipline has sought to ensure that complete economic evaluations[2] are provided. These evaluations compare each new intervention with current practice in terms of both the costs of the provision of resources for the therapy involving the new intervention and current practice and the outcomes of these therapies. The most widely recommended variable with which to summarise this information is the incremental cost-effectiveness ratio. This ratio divides the change in overall costs by the change in overall outcomes resulting from the introduction of the intervention under consideration. Other important matters here include the time horizons of these evaluations, defining the perspective(s) to be taken (for example, society as a whole, the overall health sector, a particular third party payer), and the use of discounting in recognition of time preference. Having established the scope and framework of these considerations, it is also essential for influential decision makers (for example, at the national level) to promulgate them, and typically each decision making process has achieved this by publishing a set of guidelines requesting the provision of information in preferred ways.

The technical level

The technical level is primarily concerned with ensuring that the process can be defended as being consistent across individual decisions. Defending a process tends to be an increasingly important concern as more people are affected by the outcomes of the process, and so is more important to national systems than to individual decisions. As discussed below, the technical level has also become concerned with making it clear that a set of relevant factors beyond comparative cost-effectiveness is necessary to explain apparent inconsistencies when decisions are compared solely in terms of incremental cost-effectiveness ratios. Another theme that has emerged at the technical level has been the pre-eminence of the clinical evaluation as a basis for the economic evaluation.[3] Those working within the decision making processes are mainly responsible for maintaining the technical level, although they usually refer extensively to and integrate with external expertise, particularly those that interact regularly with the processes.

Technical issue 1: maximising scientific credibility and grappling with uncertainty

A technical issue that became apparent early in the implementation phase of the Australian experience was the imperative of establishing and maintaining scientific credibility. Comparative cost-effectiveness requires a systematic appraisal of best available clinical evidence as encompassed by the rigour of what has become known as evidence-based medicine. In practice, this involves understanding and applying the best tools of clinical epidemiology and optimally linking these with sound biostatistical analyses. Frequently, even the best available evidence is not ideal evidence, and decision makers are often required to grapple with substantial uncertainty. It thus becomes necessary in preparing guidelines for submitting cost-effectiveness information to decide whether to set a minimum standard when seeking to encourage provision of the best available evidence. Not setting a minimum standard allows the decision maker to consider cost-effectiveness on a case by case basis. In this way, each decision can rely on the conclusions based on the clinical and economic evidence provided, an understanding of the limitations of these conclusions, and an ability to take the accompanying uncertainties into account, together with the other relevant factors applicable to the circumstances of each decision.

Two particularly important and occasionally related issues that arise in the context of appraising clinical evidence and that support cost-effectiveness considerations are as follows.

- The appropriate comparator for a new product can be different across different health care systems and countries.
- Rather than head to head trials comparing the new product with its main comparator, the best evidence available may be an indirect comparison involving a common reference.

(Such a comparison can be constructed from one set of trials comparing the new product with this common reference, and another set of trials comparing the main comparator with this common reference.) Relevant issues are discussed in Chapter 3.

Technical issue 2: applying the evidence

Rarely does the clinical trial evidence exactly match the circumstances and needs of each decision maker. The international acceptance of high quality randomised trial evidence by drug regulatory agencies, irrespective of the country of origin, has established some principles upon which judgements can be made as to the applicability of this evidence. However, more important (as discussed above) is that the extent of incremental effectiveness for a new product over its comparator frequently varies across individuals in a population. If the ensuing incremental cost-effectiveness ratios at the price requested for the new product encompass results that are both acceptable and unacceptable, then the cost-effectiveness approach provides a strong incentive to restrict the use to only those patients in whom the cost-effectiveness justifies the price requested. However, in practice this incentive has also meant that more careful consideration has had to be given to whether the evidence available is sufficient to demonstrate the extent to which there is predictable variation in the incremental effectiveness, and thus in the incremental cost-effectiveness. New approaches to considering this question may prove to be more accepted as the basis of informing such considerations,[4] but this remains an important area for more active research.

Technical issue 3: extrapolating the evidence

A related set of issues arises because of the frequent need to extrapolate the available trial evidence. This is because the primary research question addressed in a randomised trial is usually sufficient to demonstrate that an incremental treatment effect does exist, but the trial still leaves substantial uncertainty around the estimated extent of overall incremental effectiveness. In some instances the available trials measure an outcome that is most relevant to the patient and adequately establish an incremental treatment effect on this outcome, but the trials have not been continued for long enough to establish the overall extent of this incremental effect in the longer term. In many other instances the trial measures a surrogate outcome, which is claimed to be predictive of a final outcome that is more relevant to the patient. Predicting a quantitative change in this final outcome based on the measured extent of change in the surrogate outcome continues to be a particularly difficult matter, and remains an important area for more active research.

Technical issue 4: internal consistency across claims and supporting information

As discussed above in this section on technical issues, the comparative economic evaluation of a pharmaceutical product is usually a composite of clinical and economic evidence, which frequently also involves adjustments beyond the direct evidence. Preparing and appraising these evaluations requires the intelligent cooperation of individuals across multidisciplinary teams. Although other disciplines may be important to these tasks on occasion, the composition of the multidisciplinary team that has proven to work in the Australian appraisal context comprises clinical epidemiologists, biostatisticians, and health economists. A team approach is important because an analysis or adjustment that is not controversial for one discipline can raise important doubts for another. In such a situation it is unhelpful if one discipline inappropriately dominates over the other. Rather, the evaluation should be presented with and without the adjustment, together with the reasons for the doubts. This may not resolve the issue if the adjustment reverses the acceptability of the resulting incremental cost-effectiveness ratio, but it does provide both a quantified estimate of the direction and impact of the uncertainty and an assessment of its nature. Depending on the other relevant factors, this can assist in providing a sufficient basis on which to make a decision.

Technical issue 5: "scaling up" to the overall impact on costs and outcomes across the population

This has proven particularly important when growth in overall expenditure is increasing at a rate that is considered by the decision maker to be unsustainable. Budget impact analyses focus less on a ratio of the incremental costs and outcomes for the average person who would qualify for subsidy, and more on the financial implications of the extent and duration of use across the eligible population, together with any unintended usage beyond any subsidy restriction. This usually has a different evidence base than that used to determine the incremental cost-effectiveness ratio, but it is also possible to scale up all costs and outcomes as a potentially more informative approach. However, in practice, combining these two sources of uncertainty may outweigh the apparent advantage in summarising the overall clinical and economic implications.

Making it sustainable

Following any successful implementation of a new approach, particularly for a large organisation or country, there comes a time of consolidation. This is largely characterised by reactions to the approach and second phase developments that require a sufficient basis in the initial implementation if they are to be established. Other organisations or jurisdictions seeking to introduce a similar approach can take heed of the lessons learnt by a trailblazer to enable a faster and more comprehensive initial implementation elsewhere. The following sections review the key consolidation steps taken in the Australian approach to considering the cost-effectiveness of pharmaceutical products.

Consolidation step 1: making defensible efficiency decisions

In Australia, decisions about which pharmaceutical products to subsidise had been made for at least four decades by a highly respected committee process. The main implications of the new approach were that these decisions were to be based formally on the evidence available and that explicit consideration of comparative effectiveness and comparative costs was required. The expectation was that more comprehensively informed decisions could be more rigorously defended. The new approach also led inevitably to a desire for a common outcome measure across all pharmaceutical interventions to improve the comparability of decision making. However, extensive review of the potential role of quality-adjusted life years (QALYs) has suggested that, although it may be the best approach developed to date for this purpose, it remains limited by difficulties in its elicitation and thus its interpretation (Box 12.3). Limitations in the interpretation of QALYs have weakened the basis for developing an incremental cost-effectiveness threshold to distinguish between those interventions that are acceptably cost-effective and those that are not, as a way of demonstrating the consistency of decision making across interventions.

Box 12.3 Controversy 3: is the QALY concept a Holy Grail?

The application of QALYs to decision making has provoked extensive debate, including debate across disciplines that are involved in conducting economic evaluations. It is possible to argue from sound theory that a common outcome is desirable and can be validly elicited. Many clinicians and decision makers seek to summarise cost-effectiveness complexities into a number they can "trust". However, there are practical considerations such that residual uncertainties associated with eliciting and applying utilities to generate QALYs must be considered in order to avoid QALYs becoming an unhelpful form of reductionism. There is often a range of "utilities" (across accepted techniques such as standard gamble and time trade-off and across various well validated multi-attribute utility instruments) for the same health state or across the same health state transitions. This questions whether the apparent increased comparability via QALYs justifies the increased uncertainty arising from "forcing" clinical outcomes measured in trials into QALY outcomes. In particular, there are doubts about the usual methods used to define the health states and associated utilities being prone to the very selection and observer biases that the randomised blinded trial methodology was designed to minimise. These methods generally require that scenarios describing health states be generated as the indirect basis of eliciting utilities. The direct elicitation of utilities in trial subjects using multi-attribute utility instruments may have advantages over these methods because the trial methodology is capable of minimising such biases. However, an increasing impression is that, when used longitudinally to detect treatment effects, these instruments are "lumpy" (i.e. they appear be relatively insensitive until the change in quality of life is sufficient to show a difference, which then is reflected in a disproportionately large change in utility). Also, another possible explanation for the variation in utilities measured using different instruments for the same health state may be that different instruments detect different aspects of what contributes to perceived health. If so, then it is unlikely that these instruments are each measuring the same thing – the true strength of preference for changes in health status.

Consolidation step 2: identifying the influence of other relevant factors

As the previously established decision making process in Australia grappled with the new challenges of systematically reviewing evidence-based comparisons of interventions on the basis of both costs and effectiveness, the decision maker increasingly realised that other influences on its considerations were both relevant and important. Reviews of apparently inconsistent decisions arising from numerically similar incremental cost-effectiveness ratios indicated that these differences could be accounted for by the presence of these multiple factors weighing on the decision maker. These reviews reassured the decision maker of both the centrality of the cost-effectiveness criterion and the validity of allowing other relevant factors to influence its decisions.[5]

There are three important implications of this realisation. First, it allows for a balancing of the strict efficiency criterion (with its ethical roots in utilitarianism) with other factors, such as "the rule of rescue" (with its deontological ethical roots). Even if the ideal common outcome measure could be created, incremental cost-effectiveness ratios with such an outcome in the denominator would not completely predict the subsidy decision. Second, it means that different decision makers, including those at different stages in the same decision making process, may be influenced differently by the same set of factors. For example, a technical advisory committee may be more influenced by the health impacts of the cost-effectiveness considerations, whereas a final funding decision may be more influenced by the bottom line financial implications. Third, this means that it not easy to predict how the play of these factors will influence each decision maker, because each tends to build up its own framework of decisions based on the cumulative effect of the precedents it sets and the environment within which it operates. This can be frustrating to those outside the decision making process, who seek predictability of outcomes from the process. It also has implications for those who may be called upon to review the merits of individual decisions as they seek to reconstruct the framework of previous decisions in order to ensure that any such review is both consistent and fair.

Consolidation step 3: promoting accountability and transparency

This third implication of the influence of other relevant factors is most readily addressed by nesting the decision making process into a legal and administrative framework that promotes natural justice enforced by access to procedural review by the judiciary. This has the salutary effect of ensuring that the highest levels of procedural fairness are attained and maintained by the decision maker and its supporting processes.

This third implication can also be addressed by promoting the accountability of decisions by putting them into the public domain, together with a detailed breakdown of the influence of the clinical and economic evidence available for each decision and of the interplay of the other relevant factors (Box 12.4). This can be further assisted by maintenance of the guidelines to reflect current decision making requirements and the current technical state of play. However, this introduces an inevitable tendency to move from broad flexible guidelines to becoming more prescriptive in order to reflect the impact of the building framework of precedents set by previous decisions. Then all stakeholders can independently construct the decision making framework and seek to ensure adherence of the decision maker to its own framework of precedents.

There are other issues. The confidentiality and hence sensitivity of some sources of information for a decision maker may mainly be a matter of timing (for example, to allow an agreed peer reviewed publication to take its course). However, it is difficult to justify slowing a decision making process that may facilitate access to a drug simply to allow publication of all information (even if this were possible). A decision maker may also have to relate to many potentially affected stakeholders, and allowing all of them to understand each decision may increase the need to allow for satisfactory interactions between this array of stakeholders and the decision maker, particularly on controversial decisions. Greater transparency may therefore come at the cost of greater delays in access.

Box 12.4 Controversy 4: should all information used to justify positions taken by jurisdiction in relation to cost-effectiveness be put into the public domain?

It is easier to support the principle of putting decisions, with their supporting facts and reasons, into the public domain than to carry this out in practice. This is not due to a lack of commitment to the principle but to a need to prepare for the practicalities and flow-on implications of doing so. One implication is the conflict of intellectual property over the information provided to the decision making process. A decision maker operates best with access to all of the relevant information and, if information is to be denied because it can only be provided in confidence, then an inevitable tension arises between basing a decision on the best information available and making the decision publicly accountable. Such a tension may be resolved, but it takes time. Another implication is the potential conflict of differing interpretations of the information provided to decision makers. Conflicting interpretations can affect the extent and speed of uptake of a new pharmaceutical intervention by prescribers and patients, and this can be critical to the contribution of the intervention to the continuing viability of the sponsor. Combined with any sense of unpredictability from the decision making process, it should not be surprising that a sponsor would seek to protect its perception of the reputation of its products. This could include challenging the right of a decision maker to put the sponsor's information and the decision maker's interpretation into the public domain, especially if the latter is disputed. A third implication is that this increases the range and interest of stakeholders empowered to seek more engagement in and influence over the process. From a practical perspective, such a process may need more resources to handle this without slowing the process down.

Consolidation step 4: establishing a culture of continuous improvement

A vital element of sustaining any new approach is to establish and nurture a culture of always looking for ways to improve what has already been achieved. For cost-effectiveness, it is particularly important to manage a scarce set of skills. This involves establishing, developing, maintaining, and then improving individuals with the necessary skill elements, and integrating them into a cohesive and collaborative multidisciplinary team. The work at all levels can be intensive, and so planning for turnover of individuals through training and succession management has proven to be an essential feature of all technical steps of the process in Australia.

As well as considering the people who operate the process, this culture of continuous improvement should be applied to the output of each step in the process:

- in the collation, evaluation, and appraisal of the available information
- in the use of this information across decisions
- in keeping up with relevant technical developments to enable their assimilation into the process as appropriate.

Consolidation step 5: collaborating internationally with similar decision makers

It should be expected that there would be two stages in the international collaboration across decision makers. In the early stages, there has tended to be some agreement across the application of the theory to an actual process. The various national guidelines in preparing and using economic evaluations published over the past decade or so have a general consistency in their main features. However, each national decision maker has a sovereign right to apply this general methodology in a way that is consistent with its context and expectations. Furthermore, all jurisdictional processes considering cost-effectiveness are constrained to keep at least some information confidential, which limits the practical exchange of useful insights and lessons. Thus, a recognition of the common difficulties and limitations of the evidence available are therefore likely to be the stimulus for any second wave of more determined international collaboration, this time in applying economic evaluations to defensible decision making across different contexts.

Such collaboration would need to be able to tolerate differences in the scope of what is to be identified for inclusion into the economic evaluations. An example here includes whether the primary perspective is the full societal perspective or that of the health care system. More importantly, flexibility will need to be retained in the determination of such contextual matters as defining any restriction of a new product to a particularly eligible population and in identifying any one or more main comparators for the introduction of the new product. In addition, such international collaboration would also need to tolerate a range of other relevant factors with ranging influence on decision makers.

However, a focus for useful collaboration could be in agreeing the fundamental methodology for determining how best to transport and to apply the most rigorous evidence available.

Currently, there are two widely used alternatives. The first alternative is to take the explanatory phase III trials designed for the regulatory criteria of efficacy and safety as a basis of determining whether marketing approval should be granted. These often measure surrogate outcomes over the short term in homogeneous populations. On this basis, an extensive modelling framework is required and this often indicates that the residual uncertainty is large enough to cover a wide range of decisions. The second alternative is to rely on long-term observational designs, which may detect numerical differences, but few differences are large enough to be confidently attributed to the change in a particular therapy as the only explanatory cause.

Thus, a possible foothold for this collaborative focus could be the detection and quantification of an incremental treatment effect for a new product over current therapy. This usually requires the optimal design and conduct of a randomised and fully blinded trial to minimise selection and observer bias as the most likely alternative explanations for a treatment effect. On this foundation, a collaboration could seek to build a more rigorous methodology for determining how such a treatment effect would vary in quantified terms across different contexts and settings and across different population characteristics. A second layer upon this foundation would be a more rigorous methodology for determining how such a treatment effect would predict quantified changes in longer term and more patient-relevant outcomes, including changes in the subsequent provision of health care resources, and thus linking the clinical data into an economic evaluation framework.

On the basis of such a methodological concurrence, an approach could be developed that would resemble the current harmonisation of the international regulatory agencies in determining marketing approval. The core clinical dataset developed would still be derived from randomised, blinded trials, but would probably be more pragmatic in design, be of longer duration, measure more patient relevant outcomes (both clinical and economic), and recruit more heterogeneous trial populations. Robust methods of applying the results of this core clinical dataset to the context of each jurisdiction would be more efficient than, say, replicating a series of jurisdiction specific studies, and it would be a worthy product of international collaboration on methodology.

Conclusion

The systematic use of economic evaluation techniques to help promote efficient allocation of pharmaceutical resources is still relatively new. Although the early promise has been realised, with decision makers now adopting a much stronger and more informative evidence base, much more is expected of these techniques and the decision makers who use them. This descriptive overview has sought to identify some of the more important aspects to the implementation of this approach, and some of the more important challenges, both now and in the future.

Summary

What is required to ensure that cost-effectiveness considerations can be usefully furnished to help achieve health policy aims? This chapter derives three key messages from the insights and experiences of the implementation of Australian legislation requiring the consideration of cost-effectiveness when deciding which pharmaceutical products should be eligible for the Australian national pharmaceutical subsidy programme.

- There needs to be a consolidation phase after the tremendous effort that is required to introduce the requirements that enable cost-effectiveness considerations to help achieve health policy aims.
- The main benefit of the legislation is to establish more explicitly the suite of factors involved in valuing the worth of pharmaceutical products.
- The main challenges of the implementation are to maintain a constructive collaboration across the many interconnected elements and to identify and address the pressure points as they arise.

References

1 Mitchell AS. Antipodean assessment: activities, actions, and achievements. *Int J Technol Assess Health Care* 2002;**18**:203–12.
2 Drummond MF, O'Brien BJ, Stoddart GL, Torrance GW. Basic types of economic evaluation. In: *Methods for the economic evaluation of health care programmes, 2nd ed.* Oxford: Oxford University Press, 1997:8–11.
3 Hill SR, Mitchell AS, Henry DA. Problems with the interpretation of pharmacoeconomic analyses: a review of submissions to the Australian Pharmaceutical Benefits Scheme. *JAMA* 2000;**283**:2116–21.
4 National Health and Medical Research Council. *How to use the evidence: assessment and application of scientific evidence.* Canberra: Biotext, 2000.
5 George G, Harris A, Mitchell A. Cost-effectiveness analysis and the consistency of decision making: evidence from pharmaceutical reimbursement in Australia (1991 to 1996). *Pharmacoeconomics* 2001;**20**: 104–14.

13: Pricing of pharmaceuticals

DAVID NEWBY, ANDREW CREESE, ALAN
STEVENS

Introduction

The price of a pharmaceutical has impacts on affordability and
therefore access to essential medicines. The spiralling costs of
medicines to insurers and third party payers are a consequence
not only of the increasing consumption of medicines but also
of the rising price of new medicines. In response to the
escalating drug costs governments around the world are
looking for ways to control drug prices, but why control
prices? Why not let the market determine the price of a
pharmaceutical?

In perfect free markets prices result from the balance
between supply and demand of a commodity.[1] In this
"perfect" environment, as the equilibrium is reached, the price
of a product will approach the marginal cost of production.
The production costs include a number of factors such as the
cost of raw materials, labour costs, and economies of scale. For
a free market to operate effectively a number of important
elements must be present. These include the following:[1,2]

- effective competition between suppliers
- homogeneity of the products
- comprehensive and accurate information for consumers
- multiple suppliers and few barriers to entry into the market
- adequate supply of the product
- suppliers acting as profit maximisers.

Although perfect free markets rarely exist, several good
examples of market driven pricing can be found. These
include the automobile, computer, and home electronic

Table 13.1 Comparison of HMG-CoA reductase inhibitor (statin) prices in the USA

Drug	Strength and pack size	US$*
Atorvastatin	10 mg × 30	61·99
Pravastatin	20 mg × 30	79·99
Simvastatin	20 mg × 30	116·99

*Based on prices from www.drugstore.com (July 2003).

industries. For example, in most developed countries the costs of technologies such as computers have continued to decline while the features have improved. Furthermore, for similarly optioned computers the price is reasonably similar. Market driven pricing also characterises the commodity (i.e. unbranded) generics market and, to a lesser extent, the branded generics market.

However, a comparison with drug prices in the market for newer drugs reveals a different picture. In the USA, which is considered to be the best example of a free market for medicines, prices of pharmaceuticals vary enormously, even when therapeutically equivalent. Table 13.1 presents the price of three commonly prescribed lipid lowering agents in the USA.

It can be seen that, at comparable therapeutic doses,[3] the price of statins can vary by nearly twofold. So why do pharmaceuticals not act like other commodities in a free market?

Market failure in the pharmaceutical sector

As noted above, a number of elements must be present for effective free markets to exist; the multinational, research based pharmaceutical industry and the production of medicines generally fail to meet any of these criteria. First, new medicine development and production is concentrated in a small number of manufacturers.[4] Ten companies accounted for almost half ($175 out of $364 billion) of world pharmaceutical sales in 2001. This situation is likely to worsen as mergers continue in the pharmaceutical sector. In 1987 the top 10 manufacturers accounted for 27·5% of world sales; in 2000 this share had risen to 45·7%. Second, pharmaceutical companies are granted patents on new medical entities, which provide protection from competition for a period of time.[5] Third, there is often informational imbalance when a new medicine in launched.[6] Trials used to support marketing of medicines are often unpublished when a new medicine reaches the public.

The pharmaceutical companies' defence of the high price of new medicines rests on claims of the risks involved with drug discovery and the increasing cost of developing new medicines. The pharmaceutical manufacturers claim that it costs $500 million to bring a new medicine to market;[7] recently this figure was updated to over $800 million.[8] However, there are a number of uncertainties about the basis of these calculations, and other analysts have estimated the after tax, out of pocket cost of developing new medicines to be closer to $100 million.[9] Many manufacturers would recoup this kind of cost in the first few months after a product is launched. Furthermore, there is little evidence that drug development is a "risky" business. Pharmaceutical companies consistently outperform all other industries in terms of their returns on revenue, with average annual profits nearing 20%, as compared with under 3% for most other businesses.[10]

Given the imperfections in the pharmaceutical market, and the public "good" that the knowledge embodied in medicines represents, a number of strategies have been employed to control drug prices. The next section describes some of the methods used to manage the price of new drugs entering the market. The third section discusses elements that can influence the price of medicines once they are marketed.

Approaches to pricing new medicines

Reference based pricing

Reference based pricing (RBP) means that the purchase or reimbursement price for a particular medicine is determined by reference to a benchmark (reference) from medicines that are considered therapeutically similar. RBP is one of the most popular methods employed to control new drug prices, with

Australia, Canada, Germany, Italy, New Zealand, Norway, Sweden, and the Netherlands all adopting some degree of RBP.[11-13] It is important to note that RBP does not directly control the price of a medicine. In some cases a manufacturer (or drug sponsor) is free to set whatever price it wishes under RBP, with the difference between the reimbursed price and the manufacturer's price being paid by the consumer through a co-payment. In other cases the manufacturer's price is determined by the price of the alternative and there is no ability to charge a higher price. For example, in the case of Medicaid in the USA, if a consumer chooses a higher priced product then the person must pay the entire price of the product, not just the difference above the reference price.[11,13] However, in most settings in which RBP has been introduced and price differentials exist, there are ways for clinicians to apply for exemptions for certain patients on clinical grounds to avoid the additional payment.[12] In all cases a RBP system will determine the maximum level of reimbursement for a group of drugs considered to be therapeutically interchangeable.[12] The reference price may be the average price in a group, the lowest price in a group, or the lowest priced generic plus some amount.[12,14]

There are three levels at which the RBP can be set.[12] Level I involves grouping drugs with identical active ingredients (i.e. all brands of the same drug). Level II groups drugs that are related pharmacologically but may have different indications (for example, angiotensin converting enzyme [ACE] inhibitors, proton pump inhibitors). Level III considers all drugs in all classes used for a particular indication (for example, hypertension, lipid lowering). Different countries have adopted different levels of RBP (Table 13.2).

Most countries adopting RBP have done so at level I. This is the simplest and least controversial level at which to group drugs. At levels II and III difficulties arise in attributing therapeutic equivalence, which is further complicated by drugs being used for multiple indications with different comparative efficacies.

Germany has had the longest experience with RBP, first introducing it in 1989 (at level I).[15,16] Level II RBP was implemented in 1992, followed by level III in 1993. By late 1997 Germany had 186 groups of drugs in level I, 23 in level II, and 29 in level III,[16] representing nearly 60% of the German drug market.[11] Most other European countries using RBP

Table 13.2 Levels of reference based pricing

Country	Level I	Level II	Level III
Germany	+	+	+
Australia	+	+	
The Netherlands			+
New Zealand		+	
Sweden	+		
Denmark	+		
Norway	+		
Canada*		+	

Adapted from Ioannides-Demos et al.[12] *British Columbia.

started in the early 1990s, with Australia and British Columbia (Canada) introducing RBP in the mid to late 1990s.

In Australia, there is a combination of approaches. For level I RBP, the government sets the subsidy price equal to that of the lowest priced brand, and manufacturers of other brands are free to charge a higher price (the difference being payable by the patient). For level II RBP the subsidy price is set at the level of the lowest priced product, as with level I. However, the manufacturer's freedom to set higher prices only applies to four groups of products (ACE inhibitors, calcium channel blockers, H_2 receptor antagonists, and the statins). For other groups manufacturers are compelled to supply at the subsidy price if their product is to remain on the subsidy scheme.

A number of policy objectives have been proposed for RBP.[11] First, it sends a price signal to consumers. The result of this is that doctors will be pressured to prescribe the less expensive options so that patients will avoid any co-payment. In turn this compels manufacturers who charge above the reference price to consider dropping their price or face losing their market share. The savings to third party payers come from lower pharmaceutical costs because they no longer pay higher prices for therapeutically similar products. All of this is presumed to occur without adverse outcomes such as increased health resource utilisation as patients are changed from one medicine to another, or adverse health outcomes due to patients receiving drugs that are not truly equivalent.[12]

Data on the effects of RBP on drug expenditure are limited and provide mixed messages. A review of drug expenditure in

Germany found that while the average cost per defined daily dose of drugs under RBP generally declined, total expenditure continued to increase.[15] However, a number of factors unique to the German health system, such as the reunification of Germany, may have contributed to this observation.[16] Other reasons for the apparent increases included the possibility that doctors switched from drugs covered by RBP to those that were not subject to RBP and whose prices rose more steeply than those under RBP.[15] Despite these limitations, the authors of the review concluded that RBP had been an effective tool for price control. Data from Australia also indicate that total spending has continued to increase despite the introduction of RBP; however, there is evidence of decreased spending on those drugs covered by RBP.[12] Similarly, data from Canada have shown RBP can modify the prescribing habits of doctors and reduce the costs of H_2 receptor antagonists and proton pump inhibitors.[17]

Also, there are few data on the adverse effects, if any, of introducing RPB. An analysis of the effects of RBP of ACE inhibitors found that, although there was a small and transient increase in physician visits and hospital admissions for patients switched from higher priced ACE inhibitors to the lower priced ones, there were no long-term effects on health resource utilisation or mortality.[18]

In summary, RBP appears to influence drug expenditure, particularly in the short term. However, the long-term effects, both economically and in terms of health outcomes, are poorly understood. For a detailed review of RBP the reader is referred to two reviews of the topic by Ioannides-Demos et al.[12] and Lopez-Casasnovas and Puig-Junoy.[13]

Performance based pricing: pharmacoeconomics

The concept of performance based pricing should be familiar to most readers. Decisions such as "Am I prepared to pay more for one washing powder over another?" or "How much more would I pay for a computer with twice the RAM?" include performance-based decisions. Within these examples can be seen the elements of performance based pricing. First, there is some sort of comparison, usually old with new (for example, existing washing powder with new powder). Second, there must be a decision regarding whether there is some difference between the products in outcomes that are important to the user (for example, "Does one computer do things faster, and will I notice it?"). If the new product does nothing more meaningful than the old product, then common sense dictates that one would pay no more for the new product. If the new product does have some advantage over the comparator, then one must "value" that extra advantage to decide how much one is prepared to pay for the gain in some outcome (for example, "How much will I pay for a computer that opens programs 10% faster?"). Also, some of the difficulties that arise in performance based decision making are clear from these examples. These include questions such as the following.

- Am I comparing the right two products? (Should I compare a new computer with not having one at all, or compare the new computer with the one I have?)
- Do I have enough information about the performance of the two products?
- What outcomes are important to me?
- How do I "value" those outcomes? (How much faster must it open programs before I will pay $100 more for one computer over another?)
- Are there things other than performance that are important to me? (Is one computer made locally and the other imported from overseas?)

Within these examples are also the implications that spending is constrained. If we had an unlimited budget then we would just buy the faster but more expensive computer. However, funds are never limitless, and decisions about how best to spend funds must be made. Economics is the study of choice among alternative ways of using limited resources, and pharmacoeconomics is the application of economic theories to pharmacotherapy.[19]

Australia and some provinces in Canada have been the leaders in the use of performance based pricing for pharmaceuticals. However, RBP described above can be seen as a form of performance based pricing. In the case of RBP the assumption is that there is no meaningful difference in performance between drugs that are grouped together, and thus they are all given the same reimbursed price. One advantage of performance based pricing is that it can be used even when no other drug exists as a comparator (i.e. it is possible to compare the first drug treatment for a condition with standard management, which may be to "do nothing"); RBP requires two or more drugs to allow grouping and cannot be applied to new therapeutic breakthroughs.

Australia began formally using economic data in reimbursement decisions in 1993.[20] It is important to note that the recommendation for the reimbursement and the pricing of drugs are made by two separate committees, namely the Pharmaceutical Benefits Advisory Committee (PBAC) and Pharmaceutical Benefits Pricing Authority (PBPA), respectively. An evidence-based approach has been adopted for the listing and pricing of drugs, and in this respect the PBAC's advice on both the clinical aspects and the cost-effectiveness of new drugs forms an essential basis for the pricing approach adopted by the PBPA. Other factors that the PBPA take into account include the cost of manufacture, the probable total cost to the government, and prices in other countries. The price that is included in the economic data considered by the PBAC is often viewed as the maximum price, and in most cases a price lower than that included by the manufacturer in its application is achieved; this improves the cost-effectiveness ratio.[20]

Differential pricing

The need to consider differential pricing has arisen from the growing inability of developing countries to afford essential medicines because of the high cost of patented medicines.[21,22] The difficulties in affordability were highlighted in the recent debate over the pricing of products to treat HIV/AIDS in Africa.[22,23] Differential pricing, also referred to as "equity pricing" or "preferential pricing", involves creating a segmented market by charging different prices in different countries or groups of countries according to the ability of each country's ability to pay.[23-25] The principles of differential pricing are based on "Ramsey pricing", which implies that prices are inversely related to price sensitivity or demand elasticity.[21] Danzon notes that, "although price elasticity is not directly observable, per capita income is an important determinant and can serve as a good approximation".[21] Thus, lower prices should be charged in low income countries, and higher prices in high income countries.

For differential pricing to be effective, markets in low income and high income countries must be kept separate. This means preventing the sales of products from lower priced markets in higher priced markets (i.e. parallel importing).[26] Related to this, prices in low income countries should not be included in comparative pricing (see below) strategies in high income countries.[27] Manufacturers themselves can take important steps to prevent products from flowing from low to high income markets (for example, by registering them under different names in the different market segments, and by changing the appearance and packaging of the products so that they do not look identical). Governments, regulatory bodies, and agencies such as customs can also assist in minimising backflow. Consultants for the pharmaceutical industry have pointed to the latter problem – international comparative pricing – as a greater threat to companies' willingness to implement more widespread market segmentation to the benefit of low income countries.

Differential pricing is currently implemented on a relatively modest scale in a number of low income (mainly African) countries by several major manufacturers on selected medicines, most notably on antiretroviral drugs for the treatment of HIV/AIDS. Generic competitors for many of these drugs are also on sale in these markets. The more widespread and systematic segmentation of the global market necessary for dependable preferential pricing of medicines for low income countries requires both better guarantees of sustained financing and the active support of companies, governments, and international bodies.

Average/comparative pricing

Several countries take into account the cost of medicine in other countries before making a pricing decision.[28–32] This is particularly the case in the European Union, where there are close international borders and concerns about parallel importing.[33] In Italy pharmaceuticals have been priced since 1994 according the "average European price".[31] The average European price is calculated in reference to four countries – France, Germany, the UK, and Spain.[34] A similar approach is adopted by Slovenia and Croatia.

Reliable data on international drug prices are difficult to find, and where available they must be carefully interpreted in spite of growing e-pharmacy over the internet. The difficulties in locating reliable cross-country data has led the World Health Organization and Health Action International to develop a standard methodology for measuring medicine prices in low and middle income countries.[35] Data for 30 "core list" medicines collected according to this methodology can be consulted on the website of Health Action International (http://www.haiweb.org/medicineprices). Sometimes referred to as "international reference pricing", formal international comparisons have been illustrated as involving countries on all continents.[27]

Profit control

The UK and Spain rely on controls on the profitability of pharmaceutical companies, rather than regulating the price of individual drugs, to manage the cost of medicines.[36] In the UK the Pharmaceutical Price Regulation Scheme (PPRS) is the main mechanism for controlling drug prices in the National Health Service (NHS).[37] The aims of the PPRS are to secure the provision of safe and effective medicines for the NHS at reasonable prices, while promoting a strong and profitable pharmaceutical industry that is capable of sustained research and development.[38] Under the PPRS profits made by pharmaceutical companies are monitored to ensure that they are reasonable, with the permitted rate of return on capital being between 17% and 21%.[38] However, some would argue that this still permits a level of profitability well above "reasonable" compared with other industries.

Although the aim of the PPRS is to control the price of medicines, data suggest that it has had little effect on cost containment.[37] One of the major limitations of the PPRS is that the relationship between cost and performance is broken.[39] The result of this is that drugs with similar actions may have widely divergent prices, and considerable effort and expense must be expended diverting prescribing away from one member in a drug class to an almost identical, less costly drug in the class, in order to save money.[39]

Tendering

The Pharmaceutical Management Agency Ltd of New Zealand has used a system of sole supplier, and preferred brand tendering for drugs subsidised under their national pharmaceutical schedule since 1996.[40] The number of drugs covered by tenders has progressively increased; in 2001–2002, 160 sole supplier tenders were awarded, with estimated savings of more than NZ$20 million over three years.[41] In addition to savings being made directly by tendering, price reductions have also occurred in exchange for deferring tenders.[40] In 1997 pharmaceutical manufacturers offered reductions in price of between 20% and 60% if the Agency deferred tendering for 23 chemical entities. This resulted in NZ$18 million in savings in the first year.

One of the major impacts of the tendering system has been a shift in the generic market. Over a five year period the market share of generics in New Zealand increased to 20–25%.[40] Tendering is seen as the major tool for delivering savings to the pharmaceutical budget in New Zealand, and as a result the growth in drug expenditure in 2001–2002 was only 3%.[41] However, some authors have criticised the New Zealand system, claiming that the effect has been to "create a generic industry which is perceived as hostile to innovative companies."[42] Richardson et al. argue that a number of multinational pharmaceutical companies have left New Zealand as a result of the pricing policy.[42] Consequently, investment in pharmaceutical research and development in New Zealand has also decreased. However, others have noted that there was no substantial pharmaceutical industry in New Zealand before the implementation of tendering.[40]

Other pricing methods for new drugs

Some countries use a cost-plus approach to pricing medicines.[43] Cost-plus pricing takes into account all relevant costs related to producing a medicine. In Spain this includes the price of the imported active ingredient, basic costs, promotion, research and development, and a fixed profit margin.[43] In Australia costs considered include landed costs, packaging, drug content, quality assurance, plant and equipment, manufacturing overheads, and costs for obtaining regulatory approval. Distribution costs, promotional and marketing activity, or general administration costs are not included.[28] The main problem with the cost-plus approach is that it is difficult to assess the true cost of production from data supplied by manufacturers because several products from one company may share the same costs (for example, capital equipment, research and development staff).[43]

Another method of controlling drug prices is the use of price–volume agreements. These involve agreements by manufacturers to reduce the unit price once a specified volume limit is reached. There are three basic types of price–volume arrangements.

- Once an agreed volume has been reached, the unit price reduces across the board.
- Once an agreed volume has been reached, the additional usage beyond that level is priced lower. The lower price could be the price of alternative therapy for the wider indication or simply an agreed price. Once the agreed volume level has been triggered a weighted price is calculated using the respective volumes and prices.
- A similar arrangement to the second type of agreement exists for products that are listed for more than one indication and where the indications have different cost-effectiveness levels or comparators, for example a drug that is listed for both cancer and endometriosis. The price agreed for the cancer indication may be of the order of $430 whereas the price for the endometriosis indication may be about $90. A weighting on volume for each indication could result in a list price of around $340.

Price–volume agreements have advantages when there is uncertainty about the demand for a product, or where there is potential for use outside indications that have been determined to be cost-effective ("leakage"). Under a price–volume arrangement manufacturers are discouraged from promoting drugs outside indications for which reimbursement was agreed. However, enforcing price–volume agreements can be difficult, and agencies may be faced with having either to continue paying for the drug even once the limits have been reached or to remove the product from the list and deny access to those for whom the drug was deemed cost-effective.

Other methods to control pharmaceutical prices

The manufacturer's price of a pharmaceutical represent only part of the final price of a medicine. On top of the ex-manufacturer's price are often transport and storage costs, import duties, taxes, and wholesaler and dispensing margins.[25,44,45] Combined, these additional costs may increase the ex-manufacturer price by over 100%.[46] For example, in Peru the total mark up of medicines incorporating custom fees, insurance, import tax, VAT, and wholesale and retail mark ups has been estimated to increase the price of a medicine by as much as 140%[47] over and above the manufacturer's price. These "hidden" costs are important not only because they must be considered in any international price comparison (see above) but also because they are often directly influenced by government policies.[44]

Taxes and duties

Although most developed countries levy no tariffs or duties on pharmaceuticals, many developing countries have significant import duties and tariffs.[48] This is despite most developing countries having little or no pharmaceutical manufacturing and being reliant on importing medicines.[48] These tariffs can be as high as 30% in some countries (Tables 13.3 and 13.4).

Taxes such as VAT may also be as high as 20% in some developing countries, and together with import tariffs they can inflate the manufacturer's prices by as much as 60%, as seen in India.[49] The effect of these taxes and duties can be significant. A study examining the effect of taxes and tariffs on the cost of drugs to treat communicable disease in 57 developing countries estimated that the total amount of duties collected in 2001 amounted to over €2·75 billion (over $3 billion).[49] These taxes and duties represented 17% of the public health expenditure of the least developed countries in the study.

Table 13.3 Top five developing countries with highest tariffs on active ingredients

Country	Year	Active ingredients
Burkina Faso	1993	31%
Pakistan	1998	30·9%
United Republic of Tanzania	1998	30%
India	1999	29·9%
Kenya	1994	26·8%

Data from Bale.[48]

Table 13.4 Top five developing countries with highest tariffs on final manufactured drugs

Country	Year	Final manufactured product
Tunisia	1998	20·6%
Nigeria	1995	17·1%
Mauritius	1998	16%
Congo	1997	12·5%
Peru	1999	12%

Data from Bale.[48]

Wholesaler and dispensing margins

Like tariffs and taxes, the margins added at the wholesaler and dispensing level can significantly increase the final cost of a medicine. Some of the mechanisms proposed to control margins are summarised in Table 13.5.[50,51]

Combinations of the above strategies have also been used. For example, in Australia pharmacists are paid a fixed percentage (currently 10%) of the wholesale cost plus a fixed dispensing fee (currently AU$4·62) for most drugs they dispense.[28] However, expensive drugs are reimbursed with a flat mark up (currently AU$18 for drugs with wholesale prices greater than AU$180 but less than AU$450) or a reduced percentage mark up (currently 4% for drugs wholesaling for AU$450 or more) plus the dispensing fee. Denmark and Finland also use a similar system; however, as the wholesale price increases, the percentage mark up decreases but the dispensing fee increases.[52,53]

Table 13.5 Options for wholesaler and dispensing mark ups*

Mechanism	Description	Comments	Examples where used[†]
Cost + fixed percentage	Wholesalers and retailers add a fixed percentage to price	May encourage the sale of more expensive items	Belgium[†] Portugal
Cost + declining percentage	The more costly the drug, the lower the percentage mark up	Provides incentives to sell less expensive items	Italy France
Cost + fixed dispensing fee	A fixed fee is paid per prescription	Reduces the incentive to prescribe higher priced drugs	Canada*
Cost + differential dispensing fee	Fee paid per prescription is higher for generic products	Encourages generic prescribing	

Data from the World Health Organization.[50] [†]Data from the London School of Economics.[51] [†]Upper limit of BFr 300 applied. *Set within each province; may vary across different provinces and across different drugs.

Role of generics

Encouraging the use of generic medicines is seen as one of the most important ways to reduce the price of medicines.[25,44,50] Most of the drugs currently listed on the World Health Organization Essential Medicines List are available as generics, often at prices that are 50–70% less than branded alternative.[50] However, choosing generics for reimbursement alone does not guarantee their use. Physicians and the public may need to be educated about the availability of generic drugs and be provided with reassurance about their quality.

Generic policies are particularly effective as part of an RBP system (see above). Many countries use the price of a generic in a class or group of drugs to set the benchmark price.

Furthermore, many counties also allow generic substitution to occur by the pharmacist during dispensing. However, rules governing substitution vary. For example, in Australia the pharmacist is allowed to substitute a generic equivalent (if available) for a branded product without reference to the prescriber unless the prescriber has indicated on the prescription that brand substitution is not permitted.[28] In some provinces of Canada substitution is mandatory and cannot be prevented by the physician.[29] However, in Germany – one of Europe's largest generic markets – pharmacists are only allowed to substitute generic products where the physician indicates on the prescription that generic substitution is permitted, or if they prescribe generically.[43]

Conclusion

Spiralling health care costs continue to place pressures on governments to find ways to control the costs of medicines in order to ensure they are affordable and available. Market failure in the pharmaceutical market has led governments to implement a number of different methods to control the price of medicines. It is important to note that a single strategy is unlikely to be successful, and most countries use a combination of approaches to control prices. For example, Australia uses both performance based pricing and RBP, while also controlling wholesaler and retail mark ups.

The challenge for countries with significant pharmaceutical manufacturing is balancing health policy (paying the lowest price possible for medicines to increase availability) with industrial policy (to have a viable pharmaceutical industry that contributes to the economy). However, there are ways of rewarding pharmaceutical manufacturers for innovation without awarding higher prices on individual drugs. For example, in Australia pharmaceutical companies can be awarded payments to compensate for the monopsony purchasing power of the government, and to increase the level of research and activity undertaken in Australia, under the Pharmaceutical Industry Investment Program.[54]

Summary

- Market failure in the pharmaceutical sector means that strategies must be in place to control the price of new medicines.
- RBP is a popular method of controlling price in the short term; however, the longer term impacts are poorly understood.
- Differential pricing can be an effective mechanism for controlling prices in developing countries, but it requires market segmentation and sustained financing to be successful.
- Governments can make significant impacts on the final price of a medicine by reviewing taxes and duties on imported drugs, and controlling the profit margins of those responsible for distribution and selling of medicines.
- Generic medicines play an important role in controlling prices, particularly where RBP is used.

References

1 Anonymous. Economics A–Z. http://www.economist.com (accessed 23 July 2003).
2 Bannock G, Baxter R, Davis E. *Dictionary of economics*. London: Penguin Books, 1998.
3 Anonymous. Therapeutic Relativity Sheets. Pharmaceutical Benefits Pricing Authority. Australian Federal Government. http://www.health. gov.au/pbs/pricing/therelativity.pdf (accessed 20 July 2003).
4 Sager A. Seven myths impeding prescription drug reform in the United States. http:www.dcc2.bumc.bu.edu/hs/sager/seven myths final.pdf (accessed 9 July 2003).
5 Vogel R. Pharmaceutical patents and price control. *Clin Ther* 2002;**24**:1204–22.
6 Henry D, Lexchin J. The pharmaceutical industry as a medicines provider. *Lancet* 2002;**360**:1590–5.
7 Pharmaceutical Research and Manufacturers of America. Why do prescription drugs cost so much? http://www.phrma.org/publications/ publications/brochure/questions/questions.pdf (accessed 20 July 2003).
8 DiMasi JA, Hansen RW, Grabowski HG. The price of innovation: new estimates of drug development costs. *Health Econ* 2003;**22**:151–85.
9 Young B, Surrusco M. Rx R&D myths: the case against the drug industry's "R&D scare card". Public Citizen. http://www.publiccitizen.org/ documents/rdmyths.pdf (accessed 09 July 2003).
10 Anonymous. Pharmaceuticals rank as most profitable industry, again. Public Citizen. http://www.citizen.org/documents/fortune500_2002erport. pdf (accessed 11 July 2003).
11 Dickson M, Redwood H. Pharmaceutical reference prices: how do they work in practice? *Pharmacoeconomics* 1998;**14**:471–9.
12 Ioannides-Demos L, Ibrahim J, McNeil J. Reference-based pricing schemes: effect on pharmaceutical expenditure, resource utilisation and health outcomes. *Pharmacoeconomics* 2002;**20**:577–91.
13 Lopez-Casasnovas G, Puig-Junoy J. Review of the literature on reference pricing. *Health Policy* 2000;**54**:87–123.

14 Bloor K, Maynard A, Freemantle N. Lessons from the international experience in controlling pharmaceutical expenditure: regulating industry. *BMJ* 2003;**313**:33–5.
15 Giuliani G, Selke G, Garattini L. The German experience in reference pricing. *Health Policy* 1998;**44**:73–85.
16 Schneeweiss S, Schoffski O, Selke G. What is Germany's experience on reference based drug pricing and the etiology of adverse health outcomes or substiution? *Health Policy* 1998;**44**:253–60.
17 Marshall J, Grootendorst P, O'Brien B, Dolovich L, Holbrook A, Levy A. Impact of reference-based pricing for histamine-2 receptor antagonists and restricted access for proton pump inhibitors in British Columbia. *CMAJ* 2002;**166**:1655–62.
18 Schneeweiss S, Walker A, Glynn R, Maclure M, Dormuth C, Soumerai S. Outcomes of reference pricing for angiotensin-converting-enzyme inhibitors. *N Engl J Med* 2002;**346**:822–9.
19 Eisenberg J. Why a journal of pharmacoeconomics? *Pharmacoeconomics* 1992;**1**:2–4.
20 Drummond M, Jonsson B, Rutten F. The role of economic evaluation in the pricing and reimbursment of medicines. *Health Policy* 1997;**40**:199–215.
21 Danzon PM. Differential pricing for pharmaceuticals: reconciling access, R&D and patents. http://hc.wharton.upenn.edu/danzon/PDF%20Files/commissionfinal12.15.01.pdf (accessed 21 March 2003).
22 Lopert R, Lang D, Hill S, Henry D. Differential pricing of drugs: a role for cost-effectiveness analysis? *Lancet* 2002;**359**:2105–7.
23 Anonymous. Differential pricing of essential drugs. *Pan Am J Public Health* 2003;**9**:275–9.
24 Grace C. Equitable pricing of newer essential medicines for developing countries: evidence for the potential of different mechanisms. http://www.who.int/medicines/library/par/equitable_pricing.doc (accessed 20 July 2003).
25 Perez-Casas C, Herranz E, Ford N. Pricing of drugs and donations: options for sustainable equity pricing. *Trop Med Int Health* 2001;**6**:960–4.
26 Barton, J. Differentiated pricing of patented products. http://www.icrier.res.in/pdf/WP-JOHN%20BARTON.pdf (accessed 20 July 2003).
27 World Health Organization. Report of the workshop on differential pricing and financing of essential drugs. http://www.who.int/medicines/library/edm_general/who-wto-hosbjor/wholereporthosbjorworkshop-fin-eng.pdf (accessed 19 February 2003).
28 Stevens A. Pharmaceutical pricing and reimbursement policies in Australia. http://pharmacos.eudra.org/F3/g10/docs/tse/Australia.pdf (accessed 20 July 2003).
29 Corvari R, King D, Sanidas M. Canada: pharmaceutical pricing and reimbursment. http://pharmacos.eudra.org/F3/g10/docs/tse/Canada.pdf (accessed 24 July 2003).
30 Le Pen C. Drug budget silo mentality: the French case. *Value Health* 2003;**6**:S10-S19.
31 Mapelli V, Lucioni C. Spending on pharmaceuticals in Italy: macro constraints with local autonomy. *Value Health* 2003;**6**:S31-S45.
32 Antonazas F. Challenges to achieving value in drug spending in a decentralized country: the Spanish case. *Value Health* 2003;**6**:S52-S62.
33 Watson R. EU attempts to tackle parallel pricing of drugs. *BMJ* 1998;**316**:1769.
34 Jommi C. Italy: pharmaceutical pricing and reimbursement. http://pharmacos.eudra.org/F3/g10/docs/tse/Italy.pdf (accessed 20 July 2003).
35 World Health Organization and Health Action International. Medicine prices: a new approach to measurement. 2003. http://www.haiweb.org/

medicineprices/articles/Synthesis_paper_20031100.pdf (accessed 5 February 2004).

36 Ess S, Schneeweiss S, Szucs T. European healthcare policies for controlling drug expenditure. *Pharmacoeconomics* 2003;21:89–103.

37 Borrell J. Pharmaceutical price regulation: a study on the impact of the rate-of-return regulation in the UK. *Pharmacoeconomics* 1999;15:291–303.

38 Anonymous. The Pharmaceutical Price Regulation Scheme. www.doh.gov.uk/pprs.htm (accessed 19 July 2003).

39 Freemantle N. Does the UK National Health Service need a fourth hurdle for pharmaceutical reimbursment to encourage the more efficient prescribing of pharmaceuticals? *Health Policy* 1999;46:255–65.

40 OXERA Consulting Ltd. Fundamental review of the generic drug market. http://www.doh.gov.uk/generics/oxera_report.doc (accessed 20 July 2003).

41 PHARMAC. Annual review. http://www.pharmac.govt.nz/pdf/AR02.pdf (accessed 20 July 2003).

42 Richardson R, Shaw I, Nolan S. A perspective on New Zealand's medicines regulatory environment. *Int J Pharm Med* 2003;17:17–22.

43 Kanavos P. Financing pharmaceuticals in transition economies. *Croat Med J* 1999;40:244–59.

44 Levison L. Policy and programming options for reducing the procurement costs of essential medicines in developing countries. http://dcc2.bumc.bu. edu/richardl/IH820/Resource_materials/Web_Resources/Levison-hiddencosts.doc (accessed 20 July 2003).

45 Watal J. Workshop on differential pricing and financing of essential drugs: background note. http://www.wto.org/english/tratop_e/trips_e/wto_background_e.pdf (accessed 23 July 2003).

46 Woodward D. Trade barriers and prices of essential health-sector inputs. http://www.cmhealth.org/docs/wg4_paper9.pdf (accessed 23 July 2003).

47 Madden J. Medicine prices: a new approach to measurement: Illustrative examples of results from pilot studies, 2001–2002. http://www.haiweb. org/medicineprices/articles/Synthesis_paper_final.pdf (accessed 20 July 2003).

48 Bale H. Consumption and trade in off-patented medicines. http://www.cmhealth.org/docs/wg4_paper3.pdf (accessed 23 July 2003).

49 Director-General for Trade–European Commission. Working document on developing countries' duties and taxes on essential medicines used in the treatment of the major communicable diseases. http://europa.eu.int/comm/trade/issues/global/medecine/docs/wtosub_100303.pdf (accessed 20 July 2003).

50 World Health Organization. Selected topics in health reform and drug financing. http://www.who.int/medicines/library/dap/who-dap-98-3/who-dap-98-3.pdf (accessed 22 July 2003).

51 London School of Economics. LSE study on healthcare in individual countries: worldwide survey on pharmaceutical pricing and reimbursement structures. http://pharmacos.eudra.org/F3/g10/p6.htm (accessed 13 February 2004).

52 Heinsen B. Denmark: pharmaceutical pricing and reimbursement policies. http://pharmacos.eudra.org/F3/g10/docs/tse/Denmark.pdf (accessed 23 July 2003).

53 Sirkia T, Rajaniemi S. Finland: pharmaceutical pricing and reimbursement policies. http://pharmacos.eudra.org/F3/g10/docs/tse/Finland.pdf (accessed 23 July 2003).

54 Pharmaceutical Benefits Pricing Authority. Pharmaceutical Benefits Pricing Authority annual report. Canberra: Australian Government Publishing Service, 2002.

14: Evaluating pharmaceuticals for health policy in low and middle income country settings

ANDREW CREESE, ANITA KOTWANI, JOSEPH
KUTZIN, ANBAN PILLAY

Introduction

Some key characteristics of the experiences of high income countries with pharmaceutical evaluation (USA, Australia, Canada, UK) discussed in Chapters 4 and 5 can readily be identified. Each of these countries has high levels of prepayment in its health financing mix, through insurance or taxation, or both, resulting in large pools of financial power. Also, each country has organised these pooled funds into large blocks of purchasing power.

Large financial pools – such as the revenue of a public or private health insurance scheme, or a health ministry's share of general tax revenue – mean that the sharing of financial risks between sick and healthy, and between richer and poorer people, is feasible. In addition, most but not all high income countries have very high levels of access to care for all segments of the population.

When pooled, finance is converted into actual health care by the purchase of clinical services and other inputs such as drugs, and the purchasing bodies are able to negotiate or to impose (depending on their relative strength) the ground rules for such transactions. In sharp contrast to individual, fee paying patients, purchasing bodies can shift the basis of payment and incentives from open ended subsidies to hard budgets for drugs, and from fee for service to capitation systems for the payment of providers, as the example from Kyrgyzstan illustrates (see below).

As previous chapters in this book show, it is this concentration of purchasing responsibility on the one hand and the promotional pressure for expensive new drugs from manufacturers on the other that has pushed public bodies and competing private health insurers to evaluate drugs systematically. Drug evaluation processes and institutions have thus resulted from both competitive market pressure (as in the USA with managed care organisations) and public stewardship, as in Canada and Australia.

The short accounts of approaches to evaluation of pharmaceuticals that follow in this chapter relate to four countries (two low income and two middle income) with very different characteristics. First, their health financing generally, and drugs financing in particular, is organised into pools to a much lesser degree. At the opposite end of the financing spectrum to the national pool is the individual and household, which are responsible for their own health care costs. Most commonly, and particularly in the low income countries, households meet their drug and other health care costs "out of pocket". This means from income, domestic savings, borrowing, or the sale of assets. Over 80% of India's health financing is in this form; in China it was over 60% and in Georgia almost 90% in 2000.

Lebanon has the highest per capita income of the four countries whose experience is examined below. It also has the least managed pharmaceuticals marketplace. South Africa has the great advantage of having a high level of prepayment, albeit through a large number of "pools". However, the government budget for health is the largest of these pools, and so South Africa has the potential to exert considerable leverage in setting the rules for evaluation of medicines. Kyrgyzstan is the poorest of the countries examined here, but it is implementing a major set of reforms in health that, among other goals, are raising the level of spending on drugs and refocusing incentives in favour of generic drugs. Kyrgyzstan's experience illustrates very clearly how these components of medicines policy must be seen within the perspective of integrated health system development. India is India; it is representative of nothing else, but is of importance because of the magnitude of events. India's huge domestic pharmaceutical industry is highly competitive, and drug prices reflect this. Nevertheless, a major problem with access remains. The dominance of the under-organised private sector in India poses a major regulatory challenge for public stewardship. Good practice by the public sector, as illustrated below, may serve to set standards for private hospitals and physicians.

A health system that is dependent on out of pocket payment at the time of illness is basically an unorganised health system, responding to demand on a purely market basis and not on the basis of medically defined need, public health priorities, or social equity. Without organised purchasing power, service suppliers of all types will tend to charge what the market will bear. On the other hand, accountable health purchasers, both public and private, must ensure that their budgets achieve maximum health gains, and will take a close interest in the value for money of major budget items such as drugs.

Table 14.1[1,2] clearly illustrates one of the major differences between industrialised and "developing" country health systems – that the majority of finance for pharmaceuticals comes from private, out of pocket sources in the latter. It shows that the range in per capita spending goes from about $4·83 in the lowest income country illustrated, namely Kyrgyzstan, to over $500 in the USA, with Lebanon (middle income) being notably high relative to other middle income countries. Table 14.2[3] summarises average pharmaceutical spending by income level for 192 countries. Drugs spending as a share of total health spending is generally higher in the poorer countries with the exception of Kyrgystan, where it has clearly been at too low a level for many years, but is now increasing. Contrasting with this are levels of "pooled" spending. These are lowest in India (where 82% of spending is out of pocket) and highest in the UK; South Africa's combination of government budget and "medical aid" insurance schemes allows effective pooling of more health spending than in some high income countries.

Chapter 11 has identified a number of steps that any country can take to promote good use of cost-effective medicines, including careful selection, measures to promote rational use by prescribers and patients, generic promotion strategies, and public health-appropriate financial incentives at all stages in the distribution chain. As Chapter 13 illustrates, policies on price

Table 14.1 Differing country contexts: income and drug spending levels and sources of health financing in selected countries (2000)

Country (income group)	Income per capita in US$ (2000)	Per capita spending on drugs in US$ (2000)	Drugs spending as a percentage of all health spending (2000)	Non-pooled spending for health: out of pocket payment as a percentage of total health spending (2000)
USA (H)	34,370	537	12	15·3
UK (H)	25,200	252	14·1	10·6
Canada (H)	21,720	313	15·2	15·5
Australia (H)	20,120	200	11·8	16·8
Lebanon (M)	4,010	128	21·2	58·6
South Africa (M)	3,060	60	16·4	12·6
Kyrgystan (L)	280	4·83	41·0	51·7
India (L)	450	3	14·7	82·2

Data from the World Health Organization[1] and the World Bank.[2] H, high income; L, low income; M, middle income.

Table 14.2   Average and ranges of per capita pharmaceutical spending in countries by level of income (1995 and 2000)

	Year	
Country income group	1995	2000 (range)
High income	387	407 (84–549)
Middle income	24	31 (4–198)
Low income	4	4 (0·6–26)
All countries (n = 192)	70	74

Values are given in US$. Data from WHO National Health Accounts database (2003).

also have a role to play in promoting good selection practice. Numerous strategies and combinations of strategies for regulating drug prices have been described for countries in the Organisation for Economic Cooperation and Development.[4] They range from drug by drug appraisals of cost-effectiveness to set reimbursement levels or measure a new drug against an existing benchmark, to blanket measures such as the control of retail margins, which affect large groups of drugs or all. Clearly, blanket approaches to price control are an extremely crude form of evaluation – they represent the judgement that, without such a control, prices will be too high. Nevertheless, not all countries attempt to influence price.

A survey undertaken in 1999 by the World Health Organization (WHO)[5] suggests that policies on medicine prices are less frequently found in low and middle income countries than in high income ones. Of the 135 countries responding, four out of 18 high income countries (less than a quarter) reported having no policy to regulate price, 30 out of 65 middle income countries and 20 out of 39 (just over half) of low income countries also reported no policy to regulate price. In view of the market peculiarities discussed in Chapter 13 and the high burden of medicine costs falling directly on poor people, such widespread *laissez faire* is hard to explain.

One possible explanation lies in capacity limitations in management and regulation. These also illustrate the degree of differences among and within "developing" countries – heterogeneity means that different approaches to pharmaceutical evaluation are needed, not a "one size fits all" approach. Nevertheless, some approaches to pharmaceuticals evaluation require little or no developmental capacity, and may best be regulated by ensuring consumer awareness of what people should pay for essential medicines.

Conclusion: given the more limited resources of low income countries, avoiding waste by careful selection is of even greater urgency than in more affluent settings. However, critical selection can be skill and information-intensive and thus expensive. So low income countries need to be able to adapt and simplify other countries' approach.

Provided below are examples of current practice in pharmaceutical evaluation from two middle income and two low income countries. They are not in any sense "representative"; rather their purpose is to illustrate some of the variety in contexts, possibilities, and approaches to evaluation of medicines.

South Africa: a dualistic health system faces different challenges

The first democratically elected post-apartheid government (in 1994) in South Africa faced many challenges, including the delivery of essential health care services to communities that had previously been disadvantaged by apartheid. There was a dual system of health care financing (public and private sector), with 20% of the population consuming 80% of the health care resources. The public sector was fragmented, inefficient, and focused on curative care. The pharmaceutical sector reflected many of these deficiencies, most notably lack of equity in access to essential drugs, irrational use of drugs, losses through malpractice and poor security, and cost-ineffective procurement and logistic practices.

In an attempt to address some of these deficiencies the National Department of Health developed a national drug policy. The policy identified the need for an essential drugs list, standard treatment guidelines, selection of cost-effective drugs, and the rational use of drugs. The development of an essential drugs list has certainly streamlined procurement of pharmaceuticals, but the more difficult task of changing irrational prescribing remains a challenge. It is worthwhile noting that the introduction of an essential drugs list can actually produce increases in drug prices, especially where there is a single supplier. Pharmaceuticals in the public sector are procured centrally using a tender system that achieves significantly lower prices (approximately 70% lower) compared with the private sector.

In the private sector medical insurance schemes provide essential and non-essential health care services (including pharmaceuticals) that cater for the needs of approximately 20% of the South Africa population. Members of medical schemes pay a monthly subscription for a defined list of benefits. Medicine prices in the private sector are considered to be unaffordable by most South Africans. The high prices of medicines account for a substantial portion of the health care budget in the private sector. Consequently, most schemes have introduced cost cutting measures such as co-payments, promotion of generics through reference pricing, capped medicines budgets, and a negative list of pharmaceuticals.

The challenges facing the South African pharmaceutical market are thus different in the public and private sectors. The challenges in the public sector include irrational use of drugs, losses through poor security, and cost-ineffective selection and procurement. Geographical equity in the distribution of overall health resources is now being addressed. The challenges in the private sector relate to the high price of medicines, the effect of the supply chain on medicines prices, irrational use of medicines, and the adoption of the essential drugs list for the private sector.

The Government of South Africa has attempted to address these problems through a number of legislative changes. These include the following:

- development of a transparent pricing system so that prices can be tracked from ex-manufacturer through to the purchase price in a pharmacy
- regulation of wholesaler and retail pharmacist margins
- establishment of a pharmaceutical expenditure directorate and a pricing committee to determine whether current prices represent value for money
- regulation of dispensing doctors
- pharmacist initiated generic substitution.

The legislative changes relating to the private sector are based largely on international experiences. It is anticipated that the proposed interventions will improve medicine access, affordability, and use.

Conclusion: South Africa is borrowing critically from experiences elsewhere. And by establishing good practices in public purchasing, it should ensure downward pressure on prices in other sectors.

Lebanon: weak public stewardship

Lebanon is a middle income market economy with a medicines market dominated by drugs imported from high income countries (96% of total sales; main sources: France, Switzerland, USA, UK, and Germany). Lebanon shares the first two of the characteristics of Kyrgyzstan at independence, namely fragmented financing and provision of services, and high dependence on out of pocket payments, but Lebanon has no problem with informal charging because it has a highly market based economy. The country's delicate political balance since the end of the civil war has meant that major reforms, inevitably challenging some established interests, have been impossible.

Decisions regarding which drugs should be available are made primarily by hospital physicians, whose funding comes via a high level of out of pocket payment, backed by open ended public subsidies for the poor, with a network of for-profit and not-for-profit insurers covering about 40% of the population. At an estimated 5% of the market, generic penetration is very low. The Ministry of Public Health currently practises no "active" purchasing of drugs, such as by bulk purchasing or price negotiation (although the Lebanese armed forces and security services both buy in bulk and negotiate prices for drugs purchased for their beneficiaries). Instead, drug prices are regulated by a requirement that the import price should be lower in Lebanon than in the country of origin (as authenticated by the manufacturer). Mark ups add over 50% to this price to yield the "public price".

Data provided in Table 14.1 show that Lebanon has relatively high per capita spending on drugs for a country at its income level, and a high share of drugs in total health spending. The incentives facing importers and health professionals militate against cost-effective behaviour in their use of health care in general and drugs in particular. Importers add a percentage to the FOB (free on board) price and thus benefit from high prices; the same applies in wholesale and retail activities.

Because the countries of origin of most drugs sold in Lebanon are relatively high priced countries (data provided by Ministry of Health, Beirut, 2002),[5] it is likely that people in Lebanon pay higher prices for many of their drugs than "lower" price but higher income European countries such as Spain and Italy.

Clearly, medicines policy in Lebanon cannot be made to operate on a "value for money" basis without systemic changes. Principal among these would be a toughening of public stewardship with the use of public purchasing (which at present is used mainly to reimburse fees for services provided to indigent patients by private hospitals). Substantial savings on medicine prices are already being made by more organised purchasing in other parts of the public sector. A generics friendly policy from government is also needed.

Much simpler measures could also be introduced to save Lebanese patients some of the $128 they each paid for medicine in the year 2000. One would be to revise downward the international basis for price comparison, and to use something like the Italian "average European price" (discussed in Chapter 13). Even this would be accepting prices from countries with per capita incomes of four or five times those of Lebanon. A set of prices from selected neighbouring countries, where income differences are smaller, would lower the benchmarks further. Perhaps above all, the support of the Lebanese public needs to be engaged through public information and advocacy by the Ministry of Health.

Kyrgyzstan: drugs stewardship proves central to improved health system performance

A recently established national health insurance fund in Kyrgyzstan now uses strategic purchasing and reimbursement for pharmaceuticals as key to a more productive national health care system.

At independence in 1991 the post-Soviet health system was characterised by low productivity and inequitable access to care resulting from three factors:[6] fragmented finance (local and central government sources as well as growing out of pocket payments) and service provision (over-specialised); over-emphasis on physical infrastructure (hospital beds) and medical specialists; and widespread informal payments for drugs, particularly in hospitals.

A reform phase from 1997 created an additional, national pool of funds – the Mandatory Health Insurance Fund (MHIF). Central and local government shares in total health spending fell during the period from 1998 to 2000, whereas the MHIF share rose steadily to become biggest single source of funds for drugs (42% of total) by 2000. Coverage under this scheme increased from 23% of the population in 1997 to 84% in 2001, by which time the MHIF had become the largest public source of drug spending, and was funding over 40% of the total drugs bill.

MHIF payments to hospitals are targeted to relieve two major constraints: adequate supplies of drugs (70% of total) and performance related staff pay (30%). Only 2% of drugs purchases may be for non-essential drugs. Concurrent with development of the MHIF, a new approach to bulk procurement of pharmaceuticals was implemented (reducing purchase costs overall by 12%) and an essential drugs list was introduced for hospitals. Pharmacies were privatised in 1997, and drugs benefits were subsequently introduced into the primary health care system. However, growth in MHIF funding for drugs has not led to an overall increase in drugs expenditure, which has remained constant in nominal terms (and thus has fallen in real terms) since 1999.

Following introduction of a formal system of co-payments by inpatients (a single fee per admission) in 2001 and improvement in the supply of drugs to hospitals, a survey of hospital patients in one of the two pilot regions for this reform showed that expenditures by patients for drugs and medical supplies fell by 92%.

In 2000 a new drug benefits programme for outpatients was introduced, with partial drugs reimbursement for insured persons. Items covered include 49 generics and 154 brand-name medicines based on the essential drugs list, with the average reimbursement level at about 60% of a calculated "basis price". (The "basis price" is calculated from wholesale prices on the basis of defined daily dosages for each medicine covered; reimbursement rates ranged from a low of 35% to a high of 100%, with a mean of 61% in August 2001.) The policy requires generic prescribing, gives a limited (capitation based) budget to each family group practice, and gives patients the incentive to shop around for the cheapest price for any prescribed drug while allowing them to pay for brand name items should they wish to pay the extra for them. During the first eight months of operation, generic prescribing rose from 60% to 96% of all prescriptions. Hospital referrals for the four leading causes of admission fell from sites introducing the new benefit package, and a large share of patients' medicine costs are now met by reimbursement.

Excess capacity of the former Soviet-style system was put to better use through funding mechanisms, which relieved the bottlenecks of drugs and staff funds. "By targeting its resources to drugs and personnel, the MHIF payment system ... enabled substantial improvements in the quality and quantity of output as well as diminishing the need for out-of-pocket payment for drugs."[6]

In summary, improving access to drugs played a major role in transforming the performance of the country's health system. This was achieved by better public financing for essential drugs, better purchasing linked to evidence-based clinical guidelines, and budget limited prescribing.

India: the public sector shows the way but private provision of drugs dominates

India has a very substantial and competitive drug manufacturing and exporting industry. A total of about 20,000 individual companies, including some 250 large units, among which five national firms are under public ownership, are engaged in (mainly generic) pharmaceutical manufacturing. About 70% of Indian demand for bulk drugs and the entire demand for formulations are met from local sources.[7] India is the world's 10th largest net exporter (value of exports minus value of imports) of pharmaceuticals. Two-thirds of India's exports go to other low and middle income countries.

Industrial and trade considerations, not surprisingly, play major roles in Indian policy on drugs. An important policy aim is to create an environment that is conducive to channelling new investment into the pharmaceutical industry and new drugs, and strengthening the local capability for production of drugs. People's access to drugs also features as a policy concern, with some direct price controls, and this objective is aided by the intensely competitive nature of the domestic market. Imported life saving drugs are exempted from customs duties.

As Table 14.1 shows, the Indian health care system is highly dependent on out of pocket payments, reflecting the importance of the private sector in delivery of health care in general. In order to ensure drug availability at reasonable prices, the Government of India (Ministry of Chemicals) has established an independent body of experts – the National Pharmaceutical Pricing Authority (NPPA).[8] The NPPA's primary functions include price determination, revision, and related activities such as updating the list of drugs under price control by inclusion and exclusion on the basis of the established criteria/guidelines. In recent years the number of price controlled drugs has fallen progressively. NPPA currently fixes prices (using a standard formula) of 74 scheduled drugs, which are available throughout the country at the same fixed price. For other medicines not under price control (non-schedule) there are no guidelines for fixation of price, but the NPPA monitors the prices of these uncontrolled drugs and formulations.

In the public sector, medicines prescribed in hospitals and dispensaries are usually supplied free of cost to poor patients. As recently as 1994, the availability and use of medicines in Delhi hospitals and health centres were described by the Minister of Health as "chaotic". Many prescribed drugs were not available, or were of poor quality and irregularly supplied. There was no essential drug list.[9]

Delhi State formulated a drug policy with technical assistance from the WHO in 1996.[9] The Delhi State Minister of Health and ministry officials, the WHO, and a non-government organisation (the Delhi Society for Promotion of Rational Use of Drugs [DSPRUD]) collaborated to ensure implementation of the essential drugs list, and provided the administrative framework for pooled procurement. The policy's main emphasis was on the development and rigorous use of the essential drugs list in public hospitals and dispensaries. The "Delhi model" proved to be so successful that it was adopted (comprehensively or partly) in Rajasthan, Haryana, Himachal Pradesh, Madhya Pradesh, Punjab, West Bengal, Municipal Corporation of Greater Mumbai, Andhra Pradesh, Assam, Orissa, Kerala, and Tamil Nadu.

Table 14.3   Cost of same drug in different years of Delhi government hospitals

	Procurement rate by year (rupees)	
Drug (formulation)	1993	2002
Amoxycillin (capsules; 500 mg)	21·50 per 10	13·83 per 10
Ciprofloxacin (capsules; 500 mg)	24·30 per 10	9·48 per 10
Ceftazidime (injectable; 1 gm)	214 per vial	62·15 per vial
Streptokinase (injectable; 15 MU)	1770·00 per injection	885·00 per injection

Table 14.4   Cost advantage in supply of essential drugs by pooled procurement

Drug (formulation)	Open tender (rupees)	Pooled procurement (rupees)	Cost reduction
Amoxycillin (syringe)	14·65	7·50	50%
Erythromycin (tablets; 250 mg)	3·24	1·54	50%
Atenolol (tablets; 50 mg)	0·42	0·17	60%
Ranitidine (injectable)	1·87	1·63	12·50%
Diazepam (injectable)	5·53	0·93	80%

In January 1998 the WHO–India Essential Drugs Programme, based on the guidelines of the Geneva Essential Drugs and Medicines Policy Department and Drug Action Programme, was spearheaded by the DSPRUD. This initiative was mainly aimed at increasing the availability and access to essential medicines at public facilities, and rational prescription and use. In the public facilities of Delhi, 90% of drugs prescribed are now found in the essential drugs list, and 80–90% of drugs on the list are actually available in the facility itself. The essential drugs list is updated every two years and new drugs are only included in the list on the basis of better efficacy, fewer side effects, or lower cost (with comparable efficacy). The pooled procurement system for public facilities for Delhi State (namely Rational Use of Drugs, a programme of the DSPRUD) has led to less duplication of work and better prices (about 30–40% cheaper), better quality, and increased availability of essential drugs (Tables 14.3 and 14.4).

WHO–India Essential Drugs Programme and DSPRUD in Delhi; the World Bank in Karnataka, Andhra Pradesh and Punjab; and DANIDA (a Danish development assistance agency) in Tamil Nadu and Madhya Pradesh have helped in recent evaluations of pharmaceuticals, leading to greater availability of drugs at lower prices. The system of pooled procurement provides the distinct advantage of purchasing medicines centrally and in bulk, encouraging drug manufacturers to price their products competitively.

The safety and effectiveness of medicines matters greatly, and are usually central concerns of regulatory bodies. But prices also matter, as they have a major impact on people's access to needed medicines. On prices, public policy in low income countries should concentrate on (i) getting the best possible prices by efficient public procurement, and (ii) keeping prices down by prescribing and dispensing incentives, and by public information.

Strategies for evaluation of pharmaceuticals in low income country contexts

Existing evidence suggests that many low income countries do not have anything like sufficient mechanisms in place to encourage value for money assessments, allowing critical selection, purchasing, prescribing, and use. Pharmaceutical evaluation, like other forms of highly skilled activity, can be costly. In settings with highly constrained resources, it could prove wasteful to imitate the institutions and practices of countries such Australia or of organisations such as Kaiser-Permanente.

What are the low cost, low capacity approaches to managing the pharmaceuticals market? The key stewardship function is to raise and promote consumers' awareness of value for money in medicines. Governments lack the resources to manage this market, and so their role is to inform and empower consumers, and to try to shape incentives for manufacturers, importers, prescribers, and dispensers to support equitable and cost-effective use of medicines.

Experience from high income countries provides useful information on the drugs available for reimbursement, indications for listing, and the reimbursement price (for example, prices paid by the Australian Pharmaceutical Benefits Scheme and by the UK for generics). The benefits associated with an essential drugs list and generic policy are addressed elsewhere in this book.

The evidence on price regulation suggests that a multifaceted approach is required in this dynamic market. A useful first step is the establishment of transparency in the market place. Often the contribution of each component of the pharmaceutical supply chain to the final price is not clearly defined. Promoting transparency in the supply chain through price catalogues and internet based price lists raises public awareness of drug prices. Consumer price sensitivity is useful in driving down the overall cost of medicines in markets that lack transparency.

Many European countries use international price comparisons as the basis for reference based pricing. International benchmarking is a useful tool when there is parity in purchasing power, but comparisons across countries become unreliable when there are differences in purchasing power. A number of surveys continue to employ this flawed price comparison methodology. The WHO pricing methodology uses a civil servant's salary as the basis for comparing prices, which is a more reasonable approach.

Approaches to price regulation could be dealt with, in a broad sense, using two approaches: informed purchasing and domestic cost control. Informed purchasing involves a careful assessment of the benefits and adverse effects of new drug therapy over currently available therapies. The determination of the incremental benefit of a new therapy requires a rigorous process using the principles of evidence-based medicine. These incremental benefits are the related to the costs of a drug using the basic principles of economic analysis. The methodology is not an attractive option for developing countries because it is both resource intensive and time consuming. Domestic control involves regulation of each component of the pharmaceutical supply chain; this includes controlling manufacturer profit margins, wholesaler margins, retailer margins, dispensing fees, taxes on medicines, price freezes, and promotion of generic medicines.

Experiences gained in South Africa, India, and Kyrgyzstan all illustrate some of the actions that can be taken to regulate medicine prices. Transparency and consumer awareness of medicine prices is a powerful tool for reducing prices. Promoting price transparency and consumer awareness does not demand significant resources, making this an attractive option in settings with limited resources. Furthermore, the focus should largely be on essential medicines because these are the drugs that provide the most benefit to the most disadvantaged sectors of the community. Surveillance of medicine prices using the WHO methodology is a useful basis for international price comparisons. Prices could be benchmarked against countries with similar levels of wealth. Other interventions such as the removal of VAT and general sales taxes on essential medicines could reduce medicine costs by 10–15%. Price transparency would also serve to identify those domestic components that contribute significantly to the overall cost of medicines.

Other reforms – reference based pricing and economic analyses of pharmaceuticals – are detailed in the Chapter 13. These interventions are resource intensive and best implemented after all of the above interventions.

A brief summary of global resources to support better practice in pharmaceutical selection is provided in Box 14.1.

Box 14.1 Where to get support: better practice in pharmaceutical selection

- WHO EML process (http://www.who.int/medicines/organization/par/edl/procedures.shtml)
- Pharmacoeconomics skill building (http://www.who.int/medicines/organization/par/edmcourses2003.shtml)
- WHO website – various government sources of drug price information (http://www.who.int/medicines/organization/par/ipc/drugpriceinfo.shtml)
- "Medicine prices" manual – a standardized approach to measuring the prices people pay for a defined list of 30 widely used medicines and analysing the components that make up the final price to the patient. (http://www.who.int/medicines/library/prices.shtml)

Conclusion

Prices and costs of pharmaceuticals are a legitimate object of policy concern, although not in isolation of their effectiveness, which is missing from the agenda in many poorer countries. Different approaches to pharmaceutical policy are appropriate in different countries. Policy makers should concentrate on (i) getting the best possible prices and thus ensuring efficient public procurement; and (ii) ensuring cost control prescribing and dispensing initiatives and public information campaigns to put downward pressure on private sector prices.

Summary

- A balanced policy on pharmaceutical choice involves trade-offs between several factors such as safety, quality, efficacy and price.
- Cost-effectiveness analysis allows these to be considered simultaneously, but its routine use requires levels of resources that may not be available in many low income countries.
- Low income countries can use information on prices, and decisions based on cost-effectiveness, in other countries, making allowances for differing contexts and circumstances.
- The growing public availability of such information is an important international public resource.

References

1 WHO. *World health report 2002: reducing risks, promoting healthy life.* Geneva, Switzerland: WHO, 2002.
2 World Bank. *World development indicators 2000.* Washington, DC: The World Bank Group, 2000.
3 WHO. *National Health Accounts database.* Geneva, Switzerland: WHO, 2003.
4 Jacobzone S. Pharmaceutical policies in OECD countries: reconciling social and industrial goals. Labour market and social policy occasional papers no. 40. April 2000. DEELSA/ELSA/WD(2000)1.
5 EDM/WHO. World Drugs Situation Survey, 1999.
6 Kutzin J, Ibraimova A, Kadyrova N. *Innovations in resource allocation, pooling and purchasing in the Kyrgyz health system. Manas health policy analysis project, research paper, 21 August 2002.* WHO, Ministry of Health, Department of Reform Coordination and Implementation, Bishkek, Kyrgyztan, 2002.
7 Government of India, National Pharmaceutical Pricing Authority. Modifications in Drug Policy, 1986. http://www.nppaindia.nic.in/drug_pol86/modif86/mod1.html (accessed 6 February 2004).
8 Government of India, National Pharmaceutical Pricing Authority homepage. http://www.nppaindia.nic.in/index1.html (accessed 6 February 2004).
9 WHO–India Essential Drugs Programme, Activity Report, January 1998–December 1999. World Health Organization, New Delhi and Delhi Society for Promotion of Rational Use of Drugs.

Glossary

Absolute risk (AR)

The probability that an individual will experience the specified outcome during a specified period of time. Its value lies in the range 0–1, or 0–100%. In contrast to common usage, the word "risk" may refer to adverse events (such as myocardial infarction) or beneficial/positive ones (such as cure).

Absolute risk difference

The difference between treatment and control groups in the proportions with the outcome and is calculated as $AR_{treatment} - AR_{control}$.

If the outcome is an adverse event (such as death or myocardial infarction) and the risk difference is negative (below zero), then this suggests there are more adverse outcomes in the control group and that the treatment reduces the risk of the outcome. In this situation the risk difference (without the negative sign) may be called the "absolute risk reduction".

If the risk difference has a positive sign (the risk in the treatment group is higher than in the control group) then the risk difference may be called the "absolute risk increase".

Acquisition cost

The purchase price of a drug (or item) to an institution, agency, or person.

Average cost

The cost per unit of an activity or output, calculated by dividing the total costs of an activity (treatment) by the number of units of outcome it produces.

Bias

Deviation of study results from the "true" results, perhaps due to the way(s) in which the study was conducted.

Case–control study

Patients with a certain outcome or disease and an appropriate group of controls without the outcome or disease are selected (usually with careful consideration of appropriate choice or controls, matching, etc.), and then information is obtained on whether the subjects have been exposed to the treatment/intervention or other factor being studied.

Clinically significant

A finding that is clinically important. Here, "significant" takes its everyday meaning of "important" (compare with "statistically significant", below).

Cohort study

Outcomes for a group receiving the treatment or intervention being studied (exposed group) are compared with the outcomes for a control group that is not receiving the treatment or intervention (non-exposed group). Note that this is different from a randomised controlled trial, in which subjects are randomly assigned to treatment or no treatment.

Concurrent controls undergo assessment at the same time as the group exposed to the intervention of interest. Sometimes, a prospectively collected group of patients exposed to the new technology is compared with either a previously published series or previously treated patients in the same institution. These controls are described as historical controls.

Completer analysis

Analysis of data from only those participants who completed the study protocol. This is different from an intention to treat analysis (see below), which uses data from all participants who enrolled in the study regardless of the treatment that they received.

Confidence interval (CI)

The 95% confidence interval is taken to indicate the likely range of values in which the true population value of the effect of treatment lies 95 times out of 100. All values within the confidence interval are not equally plausible estimates of the true population effect. The best estimate of the true effect from a single study or meta-analysis comes from the point estimate. As you move away from the point estimate it becomes increasingly unlikely that a point actually represents the true population value of the treatment effect. To confuse matters further, there is nothing magical about the choice of the confidence interval (for example, 95% or 99% confidence intervals), but the choice is guided by convention. A value just outside the 95% confidence interval is only marginally less plausible an estimate of the true population effect than one just inside it.

Consequences

The health outcomes associated with a health care option.

Continuous

Continuous outcomes can take on any value on a numerical scale – as far as the precision of measurement allows – within a certain range. Examples are weight, height, or symptom scores. Also, see "dichotomous" below.

Controls

Subjects with whom comparison is made in a case–control study, a randomised controlled trial, or other varieties of epidemiological study. Selection of appropriate controls is crucial to the validity of epidemiological studies.

Cost

"To be obtainable for a sum of money." (*Oxford English Dictionary*)

Opportunity cost is a definition of cost used by economists. At the heart of opportunity cost is the notion of scarcity. The opportunity cost is what must be given up in order to obtain something. If you choose to spend money on a particular treatment programme, the money is then not available to spend on other programmes. Opportunity cost is sometimes described as the benefits forgone because the next best use was not selected.

Cost analysis

Cost analysis deals only with costs, and it is therefore considered only a partial form of economic evaluation.

Cost-benefit analysis (CBA)

A type of economic evaluation that measures the costs and benefits of options in monetary amounts. This allows direct comparison of programmes both in and out of the health sector and is potentially the broadest form of economic evaluation.

Cost-consequence analysis (CCA)

Various outcome measures associated with alternative courses of action are presented alongside the costs, and it is left to the decision maker to assess their relative importance.

Cost-effectiveness analysis (CEA)

A type of economic evaluation that compares options that have a common health outcome. The output is generally displayed as a cost per unit of effect. Unlike a cost-benefit analysis, it does not require that health consequences (benefits) be translated into dollar amounts.

Cost-minimisation analysis (CMA)

A type of economic analysis that compares programmes to find the least costly option. It is used when two or more programmes are assumed to have the same outcomes.

Cost-utility analysis (CUA)

A type of economic evaluation where the health outcomes are rated by strength of preference for the outcome, for example quality-adjusted life years (QALYs) or disability-adjusted life years (DALYs). These measures comprise both duration of life and subjective levels of well being. In this type of analysis, competing interventions are compared in terms of cost per utility (for example, cost per QALY or cost per DALY).

Cross-sectional study

A study design that involves surveying a population about an exposure or condition, or both, at one point in time. It can be used for assessing prevalence of a condition in the population.

Decision analysis

A systematic quantitative approach for assessing the relative value of one or more different decision options.

Decision tree

A graphical representation of a decision, including options, uncertain events, and their outcomes. This gives a framework for representing alternatives for use in a decision analysis.

Dichotomous

Dichotomous outcomes can take on isolated values corresponding to predefined categories. Examples are death or no death, myocardial infarction or no myocardial infarction. Also, see "continuous", above.

Direct costs

Usually defined as those costs that are directly related to the resource use associated with a service or commodity in dealing with the health care intervention.

Disability-adjusted life year (DALY)

Concept developed by the World Bank and World Health Organization to measure the burden of disease, in terms of both premature death and disability. With adequate data, it can be used to compare potential health gains from different disease control programmes and thus to prioritise resource allocation according to cost-effectiveness principles.

Discounting

A technique that allows the calculation of present values of inputs and benefits accruing in the future. It is based on a time preference, which assumes that individuals prefer to forgo a part of the benefits if they accrue them now, rather than fully in the uncertain future. This strength of preference is expressed by a discount rate that is inserted in economic evaluations. The discount rate is the rate used to convert the value of future costs and consequences into equivalent present values. The choice of discount rate and which items it should be applied to is a matter of intense debate.

Dominance

When one strategy or option is always superior to another because it is more effective and less costly.

Economic evaluation

The application of analytical methods to define cost and consequences of interventions and aid explicit choice making in resource allocation.

Effect size

The size of the benefit/disbenefit of an intervention. Many methods are used to quantify the size of an effect. Relative risk and odds ratio are examples of effect size metrics for dichotomous or binary (yes/no) outcomes. The standardised mean difference or weighted mean difference (see below) are commonly used effect size metrics for continuous variables (such as pain scores or height).

Efficiency

Making the best use of available resources. There are two types: allocative efficiency, which assesses competing programmes and judges the extent to which they meet objectives; and technical efficiency, which assess the best way of achieving a given objective.

Equivalence studies

Equivalence studies attempt to establish that a treatment is approximately similar in effectiveness and safety to an alternative treatment. For licensing purposes arbitrary boundaries are set up in advance, and if the results are within these bounds then the intervention is considered equivalent. There is no reason why we should share the same arbitrary boundaries as the licensing body, and studies we use as equivalence studies may have been originally conceived as superiority studies. However, the point estimate and 95% confidence intervals provide the most likely range of the true effect, and if we consider these on a suitable metric we can decide for ourselves whether the treatments are shown to be sufficiently similar for our purposes. Non-inferiority studies are similar to equivalence studies but are interested only in the one sided case – that a new treatment is not worse than an existing one.

Event

The occurrence of an outcome that is being sought in the study (such as myocardial infarction, death, or a four-point improvement in pain score).

Extrapolation

- The application of results to a wider area or population than that studied.
- To infer values of a variable in an unobserved interval from values within an already observed interval.

Gross national product (GNP)/gross domestic product (GDP)

GNP is the current value of all final goods and services produced by a country during a year. GDP is a closely related measure that includes the value associated only with domestic factors of production.

Hazard ratio (HR)

The hazard ratio is the risk of an event over time in one group divided by the risk of an event over time derived from a comparison group. It is analogous to the relative risk, although it accounts not just for whether an event occurred but also for when it occurred.

Heterogeneity

Heterogeneity in meta-analysis means systematic differences between the results of studies included. We expect the results from studies to differ simply due to the play of chance. Heterogeneity denotes the circumstances when the degree of differences in the results from different studies is greater than that which we would expect to see from chance alone. Confusingly, the term heterogeneity is increasingly used more loosely (for example, so-called "clinical heterogeneity", where it seems to mean simply "differences").

Homogeneity

The absence of heterogeneity.

Human capital approach

Method of valuing outcomes in terms of the productive capacity of the patients treated. For example, the death of a patient may be quantified in terms of lost productivity (the production capacity he would have had if he had lived).

Incidence

The number of new cases of a condition occurring in a population over a specified period of time.

Incremental cost

Difference between the cost of a programme (treatment) and the cost of the comparison programme.

Incremental cost-effectiveness ratio (ICER)

A comparison of the net costs and benefits of alternative courses of action (for example, intervention A and intervention B), as summarised in the following equation.

$$\text{ICER} = \text{net costs/net effects} = (\text{cost A} - \text{cost B})/(\text{effect A} - \text{effect B})$$

Indirect costs

These are the costs that are not directly related to the provision of a service or commodity. Often they refer to production losses. For example, in prevention of stroke from atrial fibrillation, an indirect cost might be decreased production due to leave from work in attending appointments.

Input

Those resources that are required for the production of an output (goods or services). For example, some of the inputs required for the production of a hip replacement are a surgeon, theatre staff, anaesthetists, and a prosthesis (artificial hip).

Intention to treat analysis

The analysis of patients on the basis of their initially allocated treatment group (intended treatment) regardless of whether they subsequently received that treatment or indeed a treatment intended for patients in a different group. Although occasionally providing challenges for interpretation (particularly in equivalence studies), intention to treat analysis has the advantage over all other approaches in that it is unbiased.

Margin

Refers to the extra or incremental costs or consequences of each option when compared with the other.

Marginal analysis

The process that examines the effect of small changes in the existing pattern of health care expenditure in any setting.

Marginal benefit

The extra benefit received for the consumption of an extra unit of a commodity or service.

Markov model

Used to represent more accurately complex processes that involve transitions into and out of various health states. Markov models are particularly useful when a decision problem involves a risk that is ongoing over time. There are two consequences of events that have ongoing risk: the times at which events occur are uncertain and a given event may occur more than once. Events that are repetitive or occur at uncertain times are difficult to represent in a decision tree model. Markov models are used to attempt to capture the complexity of these transitions and incorporate this complexity into the decision analysis.

Meta-analysis

A statistical technique that summarises the results of several studies in a single weighted average, in which weights are derived from the statistical information available in each trail (fixed effects). In random effects meta-analysis, an additional weight is added that is derived from the observed variability between trials (heterogeneity).

Number needed to harm (NNH)

One measure of treatment harm. It is the number of people you would need to treat with a specific intervention for a given period of time to produce one additional adverse outcome. NNH can be calculated as 1/ARD (absolute risk difference).

Number needed to treat (NNT)

One measure of treatment effectiveness. It is the number of people you would need to treat with a specific intervention for a given period of time to prevent one additional adverse outcome or achieve one additional beneficial outcome. NNT is calculated as 1/ARD (absolute risk difference).

Odds

The odds of an event happening is the ratio of the probability that an event will occur to the probability that the event will not occur. For example, if in a group of 100 smokers 60 develop a chronic cough and 40 do not, the odds of developing a cough are 60/40 or 1·5. Note that this is different from the probability that these smokers will develop a cough, which is 60/100 or 0·6.

Odds ratio (OR)

One measure of treatment effectiveness. It is the ratio of the odds of an event happening in the treatment group to the corresponding odds of the event happening in the control group. When the OR is 1, there is no difference in effect between the treatment intervention and the control intervention. If the OR is greater (or less) than 1, then the effects of the treatment are more (or less) than those of the control treatment. Note that the effects being measured may be adverse (for example, death or disability) or desirable (for example, survival). The OR is analogous to the relative risk (RR). In some studies (for example, population based case–control studies) the OR is a reasonable estimate of the relative risk. It is not a good estimate when the outcome is common or is measured as a prevalence.

Opportunity cost

Opportunity cost is a definition of cost used by economists. At the heart of opportunity cost is the notion of scarcity. The opportunity cost is what must be given up in order to obtain something. If you choose to spend money on a particular treatment programme, then the money is then not available to spend on other programmes. Opportunity cost is sometimes described as the benefits forgone because the next best use was not selected.

p value

The probability that an observed difference, or a bigger one, occurred by chance alone. If this probability is less than 1 in 20 (which is when the p value is less than 0·05), than the result is conventionally regarded as being "statistically significant".

Placebo

A biologically inert treatment given to the control participants in trials.

Power

The ability of a study to demonstrate an association if one exists. The power of a study is determined by several factors, including the frequency of the condition under study, the size (magnitude) of the effect, the study design, and the sample size.

Prevalence

The proportion of people with a finding or disease in a given population at a given time.

Price

Price is what the customer is asked to pay for the goods or service and reflects the value of resources for which there are markets.

Publication bias

This occurs where studies with positive results are more likely to be published than studies with negative results, so making it appear from surveys of the published literature that treatments are more effective than is truly the case.

Quality-adjusted life year (QALY)

A common measure of health improvement used in an economic analysis that combines mortality and quality of life gains (or losses).

Randomised controlled trial (RCT)

A trial in which participants are randomly assigned to two groups: one (the experimental group) receiving the intervention that is being tested, and the other (the comparison or control group) receiving an alternative treatment or placebo. Randomisation ensures that the treatment and control groups differ only by the intended treatment and the play of chance.

Relative risk (RR)

The ratio of the proportions in the treatment and control groups with the outcome. This expresses the risk of the outcome in the treatment group relative to that in the control group (i.e. the number of times more likely [RR >1] or less likely [RR <1] that an event is to happen in one group compared with another). It is similar in concept to an odds ratio (OR; see above).

Relative risk reduction (RRR)

The proportional reduction in risk between experimental and control participants in a trial. It is the complement of the relative risk (1 – RR).

Resources

Classically, the term "resources" refers to land, labour, and capital. Specifically, any input into health service production (time, goods, equipment, etc.).

Sensitivity analysis (economic)

A technique that is used to quantify the uncertainty in an economic evaluation. This involves testing how a result might change if key variables are altered. Relevant variables to test are those for which there is uncertainty about their expected range of values. A range of realistic values is then drawn up, and the end result recalculated to see whether the conclusions of the evaluation would be altered if those values were in fact the correct values to use in the analysis.

Standard gamble

A method of estimating health preferences using a choice between two options. One option has a certain outcome that is the health state to be rated, and the other option is a gamble with a chance of full health and a chance of death. The chance of death is varied until the person choosing finds the options to be of equal value.

Standardised mean difference (SMD)

A measure of effect used when outcomes are continuous (such as height, weight, or symptom scores) rather than dichotomous (such as death and myocardial infarction). The mean differences in outcome between the groups being studied are standardised by an estimate of the standard deviation of the measurements in the study to account for differences in scoring methods.

Statistically significant

This means (rather unhelpfully) that the findings of a study are unlikely to be due to chance. Significance at the commonly cited 5% level (p = 0·05) means that the observed result, or a larger one, would occur by chance in only 1 in 20 similar studies. Estimation and confidence intervals are much more useful.

Systematic review

A review in which all of the trials on a topic have been systematically sought, appraised, and summarised according to predetermined criteria. It can, but need not, involve meta-analysis as a statistical method of adding together and numerically summarising the results of the trials that meet minimum quality criteria.

Time trade-off

A method of estimating health preferences using a choice between two options. Each option has a certain outcome. One option is the amount of time in the health state being rated and the other is perfect health for a lesser amount of time. The amount of time in the perfect health state is varied until the person choosing finds the options to be of equal value.

Utility

A technical term used by economists to denote satisfaction or well being. In health economics it is generally used to show the preferences that an individual, group, or society has for a health state.

Validity

The degree to which the inferences drawn from a study are warranted when account is taken of the study methods, how representative the study sample is, and the nature of the population from which it is drawn. There are two types of study validity: internal validity and external validity. Internal validity relates to the study itself; the two groups are selected and compared in such a manner that observed differences are likely to be due to the effect under investigation. External validity relates to how generalisable the results of the study are to other subjects who were not in the study.

Weighted mean difference (WMD)

A measure of effect size used when outcomes are continuous (such as symptom scores or height) rather than dichotomous (such as death or myocardial infarction). The mean differences in outcome between the groups being studied are weighted to account for different sample sizes and differing precision between studies. The WMD is an absolute figure and so takes the units of the original outcome measure.

Willingness to pay (WTP)

A technique that relies on direct explicit eliciting of individual preferences in the views of samples of the general public, who are asked how much they would be prepared to pay to accrue a benefit or to avoid certain events.

Index

The following abbreviations have been used in this index:

AMCP   – Academy of Managed Care Pharmacy
ASCOT-LLA – Anglo-Scandinavian Cardiac Outcomes Trial – Lipid Lowering Arm
CCOHTA   – Canadian Coordinating Office for Health Technology Assessment
DSPRUD   – Delhi Society for Promotion of Rational Use of Drugs
ICH   – International Conference on Harmonisation of Technical Requirements for the Registration of Pharmaceuticals for Human Use
NICE   – National Institute for Clinical Excellence
PBS   – Pharmaceutical Benefits Scheme

absolute risk (AR) 40, 244
academic detailing 179–80, 180
Academy of Managed Care Pharmacy (AMCP) 74
access 49, 51, 193, 202
  fourth hurdle policy 77–8
  stakeholder interests *see* stakeholder interests
accountability 202, 203
  see also transparency
acquisition cost 244
"Action for Access" 146
advertising
  direct to consumer (DTC) 53–4, 145–6
  see also media coverage
affiliations 144
  see also stakeholder interests
Agreement on Trade Related Aspects of Intellectual Property Rights (TRIPS) 149
alendronate 162, 163, 164, 165, 166
alteplase 32–4
amoxycillin 239
amyotrophic lateral sclerosis 121–38
  riluzole *see* riluzole
angiotensin converting enzyme (ACE) inhibitors 211, 212, 213
angiotensin II receptor blockers 150
Anglo–Scandinavian Cardiac Outcomes Trial – Lipid Lowering Arm (ASCOT-LLA) 30, 31, 40
Antibiotic Guidelines, Australia 177

antibiotics 139–40, 174, 177, 239
antidepressants 69, 145, 239
antifungal drugs 37
antihypertensives 140, 150, 160, 212
antipsychotics 37, 140
antiretrovirals 35, 216
ASCOT-LLA 30, 31, 40
aspirin 160, 162, 165
assessors, mutual recognition procedure 11
Association of the British Pharmaceutical Industry 151–2
atenolol 239
atorvastatin 30, 162, 163, 209
Australia
  Antibiotic Guidelines 177
  economic evaluation guidelines 72
  income and drug spending levels 230
  Medicines Australia 152
  National Medicines Policy 175–6
  National Prescribing Service 176, 182
  Pharmaceutical Benefits Scheme *see* Pharmaceutical Benefits Scheme (PBS), Australia
  Policy on the Quality Use of Medicines (1992) 175–6
  Therapeutic Guidelines 178
autologous bone marrow transplant 170
average pricing 216–17, 244
awareness raising campaigns 146

base case analysis 129–30, 131
baseline risk 41
Bayesian reasoning 90
bias 244
   clinical trials 24–6, 37–8, 200
   pharmacoeconomic studies 76–7
   publication 28, 38, 144–5, 255
   systematic reviews 28
biotechnological products 5
blocking (RCT design) 25–6
bone marrow transplant, breast
   cancer 170
brand-leaders 11
"break-out session" 11
breast cancer
   autologous bone marrow
      transplant 170
   media coverage 160
British National Formulary 178
bupropion 69
Bureau of Industry Economics 78

calcium channel blockers 160, 212
Canada 68–9
   economic evaluation
      guidelines 72
   income and drug spending
      levels 230
Canadian Coordinating Office for
   Health Technology Assessment
   (CCOHTA), prescribing
   guidelines 68–9, 71, 72
capping (reimbursement) 51, 56
case-control studies 245
celecoxib (Celebrex) 98–9
   media coverage 157–8, 162,
      164, 165, 166
Celecoxib Long-term Arthritis Safety
   Study (CLASS) 98–9
centralised procedure, marketing
   authorisation 5, 6–7, 9, 12
China 228
cholesterol-lowering drugs see statins
cimetidine 51
clinical evidence
   cost-effectiveness considerations
      196–9
   fourth hurdle policy see
      fourth hurdle policy
   interpretation, clinical trials
      see randomised controlled
      trials (RCTs)
   pharmacoeconomic studies 76–7
   priority setting see priority
      setting (in health care)
   see also evidence-based medicine

clinical heterogeneity
   (in meta-analysis) 251
clinical significance 245
clinical trials, randomised controlled
   see randomised controlled trials
   (RCTs)
Cochrane Collaboration 27,
   159, 178
cohort studies 245
Committee for Proprietary
   Medicinal Products (CPMP) 5
   rapporteur appointment 7
   riluzole licensing 122–3
community pharmacists 146–7
comparative cost-effectiveness
   191, 196
comparative pricing 216–17
comparators 72
completer analysis 245
composite outcomes,
   meta-analysis 29–31
concerned member states 7
condition specific health
   measures 100
"conference tourism" 59
confidence intervals 26, 245–6
confidentiality 83–4, 202
conflicts of interest 144
   cost-effectiveness and 194, 194
   media coverage 162, 165–6, 168
   prescribing, financial incentives
      59–61, 175, 185–6
confounding factors 24–6
Consolidated Standards of Reporting
   Trials (CONSORT) 31
consumer awareness 241–2
continuing medical education
   programmes 183
Continuous Infusion versus
   Double-Bolus Administration
   of Alteplase (COBOLT) 32–4
continuous outcomes 246
controls 246
co-payment schemes 185
coronary heart disease (CHD) 30
corticosteroids 38, 40
cost analysis 247
cost-benefit analysis (CBA) 247
cost-consequence analysis
   (CCA) 247
cost-effectiveness see economic
   evaluation
cost-effectiveness analysis (CEA)
   170, 247
   see also economic modelling
      (in drug reimbursement)

cost-minimisation analysis
(CMA) 247
cost per life year gained (LYG)
77–8
cost per quality-adjusted life year
(QALY) 77–8
cost-plus pricing 218–19
costs (of drugs)
fourth hurdle policy impact
78–82
media coverage 162, 165, 167–8
see also economic evaluation
cost sharing policies 53
cost-utility analysis (CUA) 247
Council Regulation 2309/93/EEC 6
critical appraisal 27–8
cross-sectional studies 248
cyclo-oxygenase (COX)-2
inhibitors 174

Danish Development Assistance
Agency 240
data incorporation (and
modelling) 94
decision analysis 248
decision analytic modelling see
economic modelling (in drug
reimbursement)
decision trees 91, 91, 92,
95–6, 248
"decision validity" 101
Declaration of Helsinki 19
Delhi Society for Promotion of
Rational Use of Drugs (DSPRUD)
238–9, 240
demand (patient) 50, 50–8
see also expenditure,
pharmaceutical policy
developing countries 174, 231–2
see also individual countries
diazepam 239
dichotomous outcomes 248
differential pricing 215–16
direct costs 248
Directive 2001/83/EC 7, 11
direct to consumer (DTC)
advertising 53–4, 145–6
disability-adjusted life years
(DALYs) 247, 248
discounting 72, 248–9
"disease mongering" 146, 169
dispensing margins 221, 222
dissemination, information 57–8
doctors
expenditure, pharmaceutical
policy 54–8

media coverage, health service
utilisation effects see
media coverage
pharmaceutical companies,
interactions 142–3, 149–52
donepezil 92, 92–4, 162, 163
drug reimbursement
economic modelling see
economic modelling (in
drug reimbursement)
riluzole 123–32
drugs
cost-effective, promotion see
promotion (of prescription
medicines)
costs see costs (of drugs)
prescribing see prescribing
pricing see pricing
DSPRUD 238–9, 240

economic evaluation 249
cost-effectiveness 49,
190–207, 192
access based on see fourth
hurdle policy
accountability and
transparency 202, 203
clinical evidence and 196–9
comparative 191, 196
conflicts of interest
194, 194
efficiency decisions
199–200
generic products 56–7,
59, 143, 184–5
health service utilisation
167–8, 170
high level steps 191–5
international collaboration
72, 204–6
prescribing see prescribing
technical level 195–9
evidence quality 76–7
fourth hurdle policy see fourth
hurdle policy
economic modelling (in drug
reimbursement) 88–104, 89
advantages 90
data incorporation 94
preference elicitation 100–1
sensitivity analysis 94–7,
96, 256
structure 91–4
decision trees 91, 91, 92,
95–6, 248
guidelines 93

trial based evidence use
97–100, 98
validation 97
effect size 249
efficacy 4, 17, 49
economic modelling and *see*
economic modelling (in
drug reimbursement)
fourth hurdle *see* fourth hurdle
policy
indirect comparisons 29
riluzole 122
efficiency 201, 249
decisions 199–200
prescribing 57
see also expenditure,
pharmaceutical policy;
prescribing
priority setting *see* priority setting
(in health care)
equity (of access) 49, 51, 72
priority setting *see* priority
setting (in health care)
"equity pricing" 215–16
equivalence 18, 31–4, 33, 249–50
erythromycin 239
esomeprazole 51
Essential Drugs List for Zimbabwe
(EDLIZ) 178
etanercept 69
ethics
clinical trial design 19
financial incentives 175, 185–6
prescribing 183–4
priority setting (in health
care) 106–7
ethylene glycol disaster 3
Europe
fourth hurdle policy
development 70–3
see also individual countries
European Agency for the Evaluation
of Medicinal Products 122–3
European licensing procedures *see*
marketing authorisation
procedures
European Medicines Evaluation
Agency (EMEA) 4–6, 12, 83
legislation and subordination
perspective 13–14
riluzole, effectiveness evidence
124–6, 125
European Pharmaceutical Directive
(65/65/EEC) 5
European Public Assessment
Report 15

evaluation models, economic *see*
economic evaluation
evidence-based medicine 89–90
evidence, clinical *see* clinical
evidence
expenditure, pharmaceutical policy
46–66, 48
financial incentives 59–61,
175, 185–6
objectives 47–9
regulation, international 49–59,
50, 54–8
patient demand 50–4
extrapolation 250

"fair innings argument" 108–10,
114–17
"fast-track" procedure 15–16
"Feminine Forever" 54
Fieller's Theorem 96–7
financial incentives
ethics 175, 185–6
pharmaceutical expenditure
59–61, 175, 185–6
prescribing 59–61, 175, 185–6
fluconazole 37
Food and Drug Administration,
USA 74
Fosamax 162, 163, 164, 165, 166
fourth hurdle policy 67–87
emergence 67–9
future 82–4
global development 69–75
Europe 70–3
USA 73–4
impact 75–82
access 77–8
drugs pricing 78–82, 80, 81
pharmacoeconomic evidence,
quality 76–7
methodological issues 72
requirements 70–3, 71
France 60
Freedom of Information Act
(USA) 14

G10 Medicines Group 16–17
generic health measures 100
generic products 11, 51, 79,
140, 218
prescribing 56–7, 59, 143, 184–5
pricing 79–82, 81, 222–3
Germany 73
gifts 143, 152
glatiramer acetate 84
GlaxoSmithKline 140

"Global Competitiveness in
Pharmaceuticals" 60, 142
gross domestic product (GDP) 250
gross national product (GNP) 250
Guidelines for Good Clinical
Practice 144
Guidelines International
Network 178

H₂ receptor antagonists 51, 212, 213
harmonisation (of regulatory
requirements) 72, 82–3,
205–6
ICH 8–9, 32
harms, drug (media coverage of
medicine) 162, 163–4, 167
hazard ratio (HR) 250
health care priorities *see* priority
setting (in health care)
health economics *see* economic
evaluation
health inequalities, priority setting
see priority setting (in health
care)
health measures, condition
specific 100
health policy
evaluation for low income
countries *see* low income
countries
pharmaceutical evaluation *see*
economic evaluation
priority setting *see* priority setting
(in health care)
see also pharmaceutical policy
health service utilisation, media and
see media coverage
hernia (inguinal) repair 55, 56
heterogeneity
(in meta-analysis) 251
high income countries
income and drug spending levels
230, 231
see also individual countries
HIV 160, 216
HMG-CoA reductase inhibitors
209, 209
homogeneity
(in meta-analysis) 251
hormone replacement therapy
(HRT) 54
human capital approach 251
Hungary 70
hypertension treatment 140, 150,
160, 212
hysterectomies 160

incentives
financial *see* financial incentives
gifts 143, 152
incidence 251
incremental cost 251
incremental cost-effectiveness ratio
(ICER) 132, 195, 201, 251
independent information sources,
prescribing 178
India 228–9, 237–40, 239
income and drug spending
levels 230
"indication leakage" 84
indirect comparisons 28–9
indirect costs 251–2
infliximab 69
information dissemination 57–8
information sources, prescribing 178
inguinal hernia repair 55, 56
input 252
insurance plans 51
intention to treat analysis 252
β-interferon 84, 146
internal consistency 198
international benchmarking 241
international collaboration 72,
204–6
International Conference on
Harmonisation of Technical
Requirements for the
Registration of Pharmaceuticals
for Human Use (ICH) 8–9, 32
see also harmonisation (of
regulatory requirements)
International Federation
of Pharmaceutical
Manufacturers 145
International Joint Efficacy
Comparison of Thrombolysis
(INJECT) 32–4
"international reference
pricing" 217
International Society for
Pharmacoeconomic and
Outcomes Research (ISPOR),
Task Force on Good Research
Practice – Modelling Studies 91
Internet 54

Japan 60, 74–5

Kyrgyzstan 228, 229, 230, 235–7

law suits 147
"leakage" phenomenon 174, 219
Lebanon 228, 230, 234–5

legislation 147
  marketing authorisation
    procedures *see* marketing
    authorisation procedures
  licensing decisions 121–38
life expectancy 108–10, 114–17
"lifestyle diseases" 141
lipid lowering agents *see* statins
Lipitor 30, 162, 163, 209
lobbying 147
low income countries 51–2, 227–43
  income and drug spending
    levels 230, 231
  pricing 217
  see also individual countries

Maine prescription programme 52
managed care companies 54–5
Mandatory Health Insurance Fund
    (MHIF) 236
manufacturing companies 209–10
marginal analysis 252
marginal benefit 252
marketing authorisation procedures
    3–23
  centralised procedure 5,
    6–7, 9, 12
  criteria 4
  licensing data limitations
    17–20, 18
  mutual recognition procedure
    5, 7–8, 10–11
  strengths 9
  weaknesses 9–11, 12–17, 13
  see also European Medicines
    Evaluation Agency (EMEA)
market orientated health systems
  economic evaluation *see* economic
    evaluation
  expenditure control 47
  media coverage *see* media
    coverage
  pharmaceuticals, pricing *see*
    pricing
Markov Cohort simulation
    method 91
Markov models 91–3, 92, 127,
    127–8, 252–3
Markov State Transition models
    91–3, 92
mastectomies 160
media coverage 157–73, 167–8
  breast cancer 160
  celecoxib 157–8, 162, 164,
    165, 166
  donepezil 162, 163

health service utilisation effects
    158–70, 160, 161
  benefits 161–3, 162, 164
  conflicts of interest 162,
    165–6, 168
  cost-effectiveness 170
  costs 162, 165, 167–8
  harms 162, 163–4, 167
  medicalisation 168–9
  HIV 160
  hysterectomies 160
  mastectomies 160
  oseltamivir 162, 164
  osteoporosis therapy 162,
    163, 164
  pravastatin 162, 165
  raloxifene 162, 164
  Reye's syndrome 160
  statins 162, 165
  tamoxifen 162, 163
  zanamivir 164
  see also advertising
Medicaid 51–2, 211
medicalisation 168–9
Medicare 52, 60, 61
"Medicine prices" manual 242
medicines and therapeutics
    committees 177–9
Medicines Australia 152
member states, concerned 7
meta-analysis 26–31, 246, 253
  composite outcomes 29–31
  heterogeneity and
    homogeneity 251
  indirect comparisons 28–9
meta-regression 27, 37
"me-too" drugs 99–100
  pricing 79–82, 80
middle income countries 227–43
  income and drug spending levels
    230, 231
  pricing 217
  see also individual countries
models
  economic *see* economic modelling
    (in drug reimbursement)
  partnership 149–51
  risk sharing 84
  stochastic compartment 91–3, 92
  Tavakoli 127, 127–8
multinationals 140
multiway sensitivity analysis 95
Mutual Recognition Facilitation
    Group (MRFG) 8
mutual recognition procedure (MRP)
    5, 7–8, 10–11

National Institute for Clinical
  Excellence (NICE)
  confidentiality 83
  fourth hurdle requirements
    70–3, 71
  legal challenge, Relenza 148
  prescribing guidelines 55–6,
    70–3, 71, 72
  riluzole reimbursement decision
    123–32, 134–5
National Medicines Policy, Australia
  175–6
National Pharmaceutical Pricing
  Authority (NPPA), India 238
National Prescribing Service,
  Australia 176, 182
National Service Frameworks 55
Netherlands 70, 73
network meta-analysis 29
new products 57–8, 141
  pricing *see* pricing
  promotion 183–4
non-inferiority 31–4, 33
non-product advertising 146
non-steroidal anti-inflammatory
  drugs 36, 37, 98–9
number needed to harm (NNH) 253
number needed to treat (NNT) 253

observational studies 205
Observed Standardised Clinical
  Examinations 182
odds 253
odds ratio (OR) 38–41, 254
one-way sensitivity analysis 94–5
Ontario, Canada 68–9
opportunity costs 246, 254
Organisation for Economic Co-
  operation and Development
  (OECD) countries 47, 48, 231
"orphan" drugs 6, 12, 69
oseltamivir 95–6, 96, 162, 164
osteoporosis therapy 35, 162,
  163, 164
outcomes 72
  composite 29–31
  continuous 246
  dichotomous 248
"outcomes based reward system"
  191–2
over the counter (OTC) products
  53–4

papaverine-phentolamine 100–1
parallel importing 216
partnership models 149–51

patent protection 149
patient co-payment schemes 185
patient demand 50, 50–8
patient information/support
  54, 146
penicillin 139–40
performance based pricing 213–15
Pfizer 46, 54, 140
Pharmaceutical Benefits Advisory
  Committee 148
Pharmaceutical Benefits Scheme
  (PBS), Australia 24, 59, 182
  confidentiality 83
  drug costs 78
  efficacy 97–8, 98
  fourth hurdle requirements
    70–3, 71
  legal challenge, sildenafil 148
  prescribing guidelines 70–3,
    71, 72
  "rule of rescue" 115–17, 116
pharmaceutical companies
  doctors, interactions with
    142–3, 149–52
  media coverage *see* media
    coverage
  stakeholder interests *see*
    stakeholder interests
pharmaceutical industry-funded
  trials *see* sponsorship (of
  research)
Pharmaceutical Management
  Agency Ltd, New Zealand 218
pharmaceutical policy
  health creation vs wealth
    creation 46–66
  international regulations
    49–59
  objectives 47–9
  see also expenditure,
    pharmaceutical policy;
    prescribing
Pharmaceutical Price Regulation
  Scheme, UK 60, 217
Pharmacia 140
pharmacists 146–7, 180–1
pharmacoeconomic evidence,
  quality 76–7
pharmacoeconomic studies 76–7,
  213–15
pharmacotherapy teaching
  181–2, 182
physicians *see* doctors
placebo 254
placebo controlled studies 18
"Poggolini affair" 147

Policy on the Quality Use of
    Medicines (1992), Australia
    175–6
pooling results, clinical trials *see*
    meta-analysis
power (clinical studies) 254–5
pravastatin 162, 165, 209
"preferential pricing" 215–16
"premature death" 115
    see also priority setting (in
        health care)
prescribing
    cost-effectiveness interventions
        174–89, 175–6
    continuing medical education
        programmes 183
    ethical issues 183–4
    generic policies 56–7, 59,
        143, 184–5
    guidelines, local practice
        176–7, 178
    medicines and therapeutics
        committees 177–9
    supervision, audit and feedback
        179–81, 180–1
    undergraduate training
        181–2, 182
    ethical issues 183–4
    financial incentives 59–61, 175,
        185–6
    guidelines and protocols 54–8
        AMCP 74
        CCOHTA 68–9, 71, 72
        NICE 55–6, 70–3, 71, 72
        PBS 70–3, 71, 72
    inappropriate 53, 174–5
    independent information
        sources 178
    support 179–80, 180–1
prescribing advisors (PAs) 180–1
prescribing analysis and cost scheme
    (PACT) 55
prevalence 255
price-volume agreements 219–20
pricing 208–26, 255
    average/comparative pricing
        216–17
    controls 58–9, 149, 193, 231
    cost-plus 218–19
    differential 215–16
    duties 220, 221
    generic policies 79–82, 81, 222–3
    international comparison 78–82,
        80, 81, 217
    performance based 213–15

profit control 217
reference based 58, 210–13, 212,
    222–3
taxes and duties 220, 221
tendering 218
wholesaler and dispensing
    margins 221, 222
primary care 57, 174
priority setting (in health care)
    105–20
    efficiency and equity
        trade-offs 113
    empirical basis identification 111
    "fair innings argument"
        108–10, 114–17
    "rule of rescue" 114–17
probabilistic sensitivity analysis
    95, 96
probability 26, 91, 92
Productivity Commission 78–9,
    80, 81
profit control 217
promotion (of prescription
    medicines) 142–7
    media and *see* media coverage
    self-regulation 151
    see also advertising
proton pump inhibitors 51, 211, 213
publication bias 28, 38, 144–5, 255
Public Health Directorate 14
P value 254

quality 4, 49
    fourth hurdle *see* fourth hurdle
        policy
    pharmacoeconomic evidence
        76–7
quality-adjusted life years (QALYs)
    91, 96, 247, 255
    cost 77–8
    efficiency decisions, role in
        199–200, 200
    "fair innings argument" 108
quality of life (QoL) 100
Quality Use of Medicines
    programme 150–1

raloxifene 162, 164
"Ramsey pricing" 215–16
RAND Health Insurance
    Experiment 51
randomised controlled trials
    (RCTs) 255
    bias 24–6, 37–8, 200
    confounding 24–6

design 18–20
evidence interpretation 24–45
equivalence issues 18, 31–4, 33,
249–50
meta-analysis *see* meta-analysis
non-inferiority 31–4, 33
reporting and metrics 38–41, 39
surrogate outcomes 34–6, 205
problems 88–90, 89
results, reporting 38–41, 39
ranitidine 239
rapporteurs 7
Rational Use of Drugs programme
239, 239
rationing *see* priority setting (in
health care)
reference based pricing 58, 210–13,
212, 222–3
regulatory systems (drugs),
marketing authorisation *see*
marketing authorisation
procedures
reimbursement *see* drug
reimbursement
relative risk (RR) 38–41, 255–6
relative risk reduction (RRR)
38–41, 256
Relenza 148
research sponsorship 143–4
resources 242, 256
results, pooling *see* meta-analysis
Review 2001 16, 16–17
Reye's syndrome 160
riluzole 82
cost-effectiveness evidence
126–8, 127
base case and sensitivity
analyses 129–30, 130, 131
effectiveness evidence 124–6, 125
survival curves 129
licensing 122–3
reimbursement 123–32
trial results 125
risk sharing models 84
"rule of rescue" 78, 82, 114–17,
116, 201

safety 4, 49
economic modelling and *see*
economic modelling (in drug
reimbursement)
fourth hurdle *see* fourth hurdle
policy
Scottish Intercollegiate Guidelines
Network (SIGN) 177, 178

secrecy 14–15
selective serotonin reuptake
inhibitors 69, 145
sensitivity analysis (economic)
94–7, 96, 256
riluzole 130–2, 131
sertindole 148
sildenafil 69, 78, 100–1, 148
simvastatin 209
Slovene Guidelines Group 178
smoking cessation 69
Society for Women's Health
Research 54
sodium fluoride 35
South Africa 147, 228, 229,
232–4, 234
income and drug spending
levels 230
Spain 73
sponsorship (of research) 36–8,
143–4
conflicts of interest, media
coverage 165–6
stakeholder interests 139–56
affiliations 143–4
doctor/industry interactions
142–3
management strategies 149–52
standard gamble 256
standardised mean difference (SMD)
256–7
Standard Treatment Guidelines and
Essential Drugs List for South
Africa 178
statins 30, 163
ASCOT-LLA study 30, 31, 40
media coverage 162, 165
price comparison, USA 209,
209, 212
statistical significance 257
stochastic compartment models
91–3, 92
stratification (RCT design) 25–6, 27
submissions, reimbursement 67–8
summaries of product characteristics
(SPCs) 11
supervision (prescribing support)
179–81, 180–1
supply 50
see also expenditure,
pharmaceutical policy
surrogate outcomes 34–6, 205
of clinical trials 20
systematic reviews 257
bias 28

Cochrane Collaboration 27
see also meta-analysis

tamoxifen 52, 162, 163
tariffs 220, 221
Tavakoli model, riluzole economic
  evaluation 127, 127–8
taxanes 69
taxes 220, 221
tendering 218
thalidomide 3–4, 141
Therapeutic Guidelines
  (Australia) 178
thrombolytics 32–4, 140
time trade-off technique
  100–1, 257
transparency 14–15, 202, 203,
  241–2
see also accountability
tricyclic antidepressants 69
tropical diseases 140, 149
tuberculosis 149

UK 229
  guidelines
    economic evaluation 72
    prescribing 55–6, 70–3, 71, 72
  income and drug spending
    levels 230
undergraduate training 181–2, 182
Upjohn 140

USA
  fourth hurdle policy
    development 73–4
  income and drug spending
    levels 230
utility 257

validity 29, 257–8
Viagra 69, 78, 100–1, 148

weighted mean difference
  (WMD) 258
WHO-India Essential Drugs
  Programme 240
wholesaler margins 221, 222
willingness to pay (WTP) 258
World Health Organization
  Conference of Drug Regulatory
  Authorities 8
World Health Organization
  Declaration of Interest
  Forms 178
World Health Organization Essential
  Medicines List 75, 178
World Health Organization Guide to
  Good Prescribing 182, 182
World Medical Association,
  Declaration of Helsinki 19
Wyeth 54

zanamivir 56, 69, 82, 164